Enterprise Architecture for Strategic Management of Modern IT Solutions

Enterprise Architecture for Strategic Management of Modern IT Solutions

Tiko Iyamu

CRC Press
Taylor & Francis Group
Boca Raton London New York

CRC Press is an imprint of the
Taylor & Francis Group, an **informa** business
AN AUERBACH BOOK

First edition published [2022]
by CRC Press
6000 Broken Sound Parkway NW, Suite 300, Boca Raton, FL 33487-2742

and by CRC Press
4 Park Square, Milton Park, Abingdon, Oxon, OX14 4RN

Library of Congress Cataloging-in-Publication Data
A catalog record for this title has been requested

ISBN: 978-1-032-14529-7 (hbk)
ISBN: 978-1-032-21435-1 (pbk)
ISBN: 978-1-003-26842-0 (ebk)

DOI: 10.1201/9781003268420

Typeset in Garamond
by KnowledgeWorks Global Ltd.

Contents

Preface

More than ever before, organisations rely on information technology (IT) solutions for growth, business enhancement, sustainability and competitiveness. Also, the evolution of IT solutions is fast paced making its selections, deployments and practices increasingly challenging. Some of the challenges lead to constraining instead of enabling organisations in their reliance on IT solutions. Some of the ramifications are continued duplications, redundancies, incompatibilities and lack of coexistence of IT solutions in organisations. These constraints negatively affect efficiency and effectiveness in enabling goals and objectives. Also, the complexities are prohibitive and have consequence on return on investment (ROI).

In addition, there are governance implications for both IT solutions and business processes, which contribute to vulnerability of an environment. This book presents detailed insights of how some of the challenges came to be in environments. Thereafter, it comprehensively examines how the challenges manifest themselves to derail and obstruct the enablement and support of business' goals and objectives. On the backdrop of these intricacies, many business and IT managers begun to have concerns about some IT solutions and the ways in which they are deployed including whether the solutions are as useful as claimed by the specialists and product owners. In solving these challenges, many enterprises including governments' institutions and agencies employ enterprise architecture (EA).

The popularity of EA has increased in the last two decades, in both business and academic domains. Despite the cumulative interest from all sectors, the implementation and practice of EA have been entangled with numerous challenges and complexities. Consequently, some organisations continue to theorise the concept, which has ramifications on practice and ROI. This has led to many studies that have been conducted to understand the complexities impacting the implementations and practices of EA. Yet, the trajectory of some convolutions remains mystery in many quarters. This attributes to the struggle to articulate the value of EA in environments. Hence, many organisations find it difficult to apply EA for strategic management of modern IT solutions.

The book provides detailed insights on applying EA for strategic management of modern IT solutions from three main fronts. First, it explains the implications that lack of understanding of EA have on organisational activities and processes.

Second, it examines the challenges and complexities that hinder the implementations and practices of EA in organisations. Third, it proposes models and frameworks on how EA can be applied for strategic management of modern IT solutions in organisations.

Through a model, the author identifies and comprehensively explains the implications of theorising EA in an organisation. Structuration theory (ST) is applied as a lens to reveal and address the factors that influence complexities in the implementations or practices of EA in organisations. A readiness assessment model that explicitly focuses on enterprise business architecture (EBA) is provided in the book. It removes ambiguity from the influencing factors and rationalises the weight of the assessment factors in the deployment of EBA in an organisation. Based on actor-network theory (ANT), a conceptual framework is provided, to guide the deployment of EA as an agent of change, in transforming goals and objectives to realisation. Also, a unified architecture framework is proposed, to guide, govern and manage the use of mobile systems in accessing big data for service delivery towards competitiveness. Towards the end of the book, a model that can be used to assess and measure the value of EA in an organisation is presented, to provide a formal guide in assessing the value of the EA in an organisation. The author recognises the need and vital role of skill set in the implementations and practices of EA in organisations. Thus, provides a model for assessment and retention of the available skill sets, which allows individuals claim to expertise in a highly specialised discipline.

This book is significantly useful to business managers, postgraduate students, researchers and academics in the fields of information technology, information systems and enterprise architecture. It guides them on how to examine the complexity and assess the value and benefits of EA in an organisation. Methodologically, the use of ANT and AT will be of interest to academics.

Acknowledgement

I am thankful to the Department of Information Technology, Cape Peninsula University of Technology. Graciously, I extend my humble appreciation to current and past members of the Research Forum at the IT department that I have been fortunate to work with over the years. Tony Ekata, I thank you immensely for painstakingly proofreading the manuscript, you are one of a kind.

To my valued friends, Zwelakhe Sithole, Emmanuel Sotomi, Ayo Obisanya, Fred Eboka and Motsamai Nduna, thank you for always being there for me. You have made so many experiences joyful and satisfying for me in my journey.

Gratefully, I offer warmth and profound appreciation to my older cousin, IK Ediae, and my uncle, Thomas Odemwingie, for their continued guidance and support. Tony Uwagbafor and Osagie Omoregbee, special thank you for always having faith in me.

I feel a deep sense of gratitude to my siblings, particularly Ikpomwenosa (IK) and Austin, for their constant love and interest in what I enjoyably do. To my mother and late father, the wisdom that you shared with me has been my light and rock. I am deeply indebted to my family for their consistent and constant love and care; Ruvimbo, thank you for being a trusted confidant, and for your patience and support while I burn the midnight candle.

I dedicate this book to my young son, Osagie.

Author

Tiko Iyamu holds a PhD in information systems from the University of Cape Town, South Africa. Currently, Iyamu is research professor at the Faculty of Informatics and Design, Cape Peninsula University of Technology (CPUT), Cape Town, South Africa. Previously, he was with the Tshwane University of Technology, South Africa, and Namibia University of Science and Technology, Namibia. Iyamu served as a Professor Extraordinaire at the Department of Computer Science, University of the Western Cape, Cape Town, South Africa, from 2006 to 2015. In 2014, he was a visiting professor at the Flensburg University of Applied Sciences, Germany. Professor Iyamu's areas of focus include enterprise architecture, health informatics, big data analytics and mobile computing. In addition, he has keen interest in the application of sociotechnical theories, such as actor-network theory, structuration theory and diffusion of innovation for information systems research. He has authored 6 books, and over 150 peer-reviewed research articles in journals, conference proceedings and book chapters. He has received several awards in research and excellence in supervision of postgraduates.

Chapter 1

Introduction

Introduction

This book covers the application of enterprise architecture (EA) for the strategic management of information technology (IT) solutions. First, it identifies the IT solutions and highlights their relevance and usefulness in organisations. Secondly, it introduces EA and examines the concept through its domains; from business to technical architectures, and within the contexts of practice and theory. This includes the 'disconnects' that exist in technology deployment, information flow, business and IT alignment. With this, a better understanding of why things happen the way that they do in the computing environments of various organisations is gained. Also, the book provides empirical insights into the concept's capacity and skill set. It explains how capacity influences and affects the development, implementation and practice of EA in an organisation.

There are two fundamental challenges for many organisations: return on investment (ROI) and how IT solutions are used or can be used to address constraints and enable goals. In achieving ROI, organisations increasingly rely on IT solutions to enable and support their goals and objectives. Many organisations progressively make the deployment (development and implementation), management and practice of IT solutions critical. Also, there continues to be a disconnectedness between what is a business need and what is an architectural constraint. This negatively affects the alignment and collaborative initiatives between the business and IT units in many organisations. For example, having a suite of mobile applications that aims to provide personalised value to an individual user may not be enough. Needless to say, the collaboration required amongst the many enterprise applications is substantial. The impact some of the challenges have on decisions requires analyses and methods in order to translate and align IT solutions with business objectives successfully and profitably.

DOI: 10.1201/9781003268420-1

As a result of the many challenges, organisations increasingly invest in IT solutions and allocate a substantial resource to enable and support operational and strategic processes and activities. Also, various approaches and methods, including EA, have been employed to maintain and govern the selection and use of IT solutions. Despite these efforts, some of the challenges persist in many organisations. It is worse in some organisations in that some of the challenges derail business process, information exchange and management and the deployment and governance of IT solutions. Despite numerous efforts, ROI and better outcome continue to be challenging for many organisations across the spectrum of industries.

In the last three decades, three fundamental things have happened to the concept of EA. One, the interest in EA continues to increase, which engenders a popular debate and discourse on both academic and business platforms. One of the major rationales for the increasing interest is the premised benefits, such as cost reduction, standardisation, design and process improvement and strategic differentiation (Niemi & Pekkola, 2019; Shanks et al., 2018; Syynimaa, 2016). Also, the pace of deployment within private and public enterprises is slow, which affects the actualisation of the benefits towards customer satisfaction and service delivery to communities. This, reflectively, can be associated with the complexity in conveying the intent and priorities of EA across the structures of organisations (Kotusev, 2019; Hendrickx, 2015). Thirdly, accepting the concept has been a major challenge in many organisations. This can be attributed to different factors, such as lack of ability to derive requirements, design and implement IT and business based-projects (Löhe & Legner, 2014), and the skill and competence to motivate the rationale and strategic intent of the concept.

These three vital issues can be attributed to confusions and misunderstandings about the concept, which manifest from the fact that the influential factors of the concept are not well known to the promoters. As a result, many enterprises continue to be hesitant about or dismissive of the concept, despite its potentialities. This book therefore focuses on the use of EA for the strategic management of modern IT solutions in achieving enterprises' goals and objectives.

The book provides readers with deep and comprehensive insights to gain a better understanding of how to employ EA in managing modern IT solutions for business, and to maintain sustainability and advance competitiveness. It draws on pragmatic roadmaps in deploying IT solutions in enabling business goals and objectives effectively and efficiently. In doing so, the book provides guidance on the adoption, management and use of modern IT solutions through business requirements, standardisation and governance. Irrespective of the industry or sector, the book enacts a rethinking of IT solutions as a collaborative capability through the concept of EA. It offers practical guidelines to organisations in the use of EA for the strategic management of modern IT solutions that take budget control into consideration.

Information Technology Solutions

Improved returns can be achieved by deploying active collaborative capability through the use of EA. This chapter introduces and identifies IT solutions and highlights how they can be managed to ensure that passive information sharing as well as active and participative decision-making are geared towards competitiveness. The aim is to significantly improve business process, information management, collaborative tools and efforts and technologies and systems' deployment and use in an environment. Another challenge is that there seems to be a lack of understanding of the extensiveness of information services for the deployment of rule-based IT solutions. This book provides fresh perspectives for an improvement without compromising competitive advantage.

Introduction to Enterprise Architecture

In this chapter, EA is systematically introduced through clarifications of terms that lead to the definition, and existing frameworks are recognised. This is to lay a foundation towards understanding why many organisations continually struggle to achieve their goals despite the deployment of an EA framework (Urbaczewski & Mrdalj, 2006). To this extent, some organisations combine EA frameworks from the available, such as Gartner Inc., Federal Enterprise Architecture (FEA) and The Open Group Architecture Framework (TOGAF) (Simon, Fischbach & Schoder, 2014), which is sometimes prohibitive. This chapter and the entire book focus on the concept of EA rather than any of the frameworks. This is done by focusing the objective and discussion on the factors that impact the development and implementation of EA; how EA is used as a tool for the integration of information systems and technologies within an environment and the role of EA in an environment for competitive initiatives. This leads to exploring some of the confusions.

Data and Information Architectures: the Confounded Confusion

Even though the terminologies are not new, and are clearly distinctive in many quarters and languages, there continues to be a loose and interchangeable use of the terms 'data' and 'information' within organisations (Grabara, Kolcun & Kot, 2014). This is a challenge that extends to the EA discipline, and which has an impact on how the domains of data and information architectures are defined, developed, implemented and practised in many organisations. The challenge leads to the misunderstanding of both technical and business requirements, as well as the confusion about differentiation between data and information architectures. This challenge affects the accomplishment of IT solutions in using either data or information in an organisation. Frequently, this is caused by the fact that data is referred to as information, meaning it has been refined; which is incorrect, and therefore affects the requirements. This chapter presents a solution to halt a further misconstruction of the architectures and avoid the confusing challenges it has for organisations for ease of contribution to managing IT solutions for business enhancement.

Business Analysis and Business Architectures: the Implications for Organisations

A similar spectacle of the confounded confusion of data and information in the preceding chapter applies to the coexistence of the concepts of business architecture and business analysis in an organisation. The concepts have many things in common, with ramifications for organisations. The commonalities bring a beneficiary synergy to the organisations that employ both concepts. However, the complementarity also imposes challenges, such as how the concepts align, integrate or complement each other within an organisation. This has not been discussed in any study or book. Also, some of the challenges lead to confusion, disorientation and defragmentation of IT solutions, processes and activities in many organisations where both concepts are employed in parallel. The challenges get even worse as they increasingly continue to impact the structures in some organisations. This happens through the allocation of roles and responsibilities between the business analysis and business architecture units. Thus, the parallelism of both concepts raises a fundamental question – whether business analysis and business architecture are roles or titles. The management and use of IT solutions is one of the beneficiaries in answering this vital question.

This confusion manifests in a power struggle and selective accountability of practical unconsciousness as actors exert their mandates and authorities within the organisation. These challenges and confusion happen at different levels and do influence the use and management of IT solutions, and ultimately affect the organisation's competitiveness and overall performance. In this chapter and other parts of the book, the distinction between business analysis and business architecture, from the perspective of the computing environment is examined, discussed and highlighted. The chapter reveals differentiation, functionalism and serviceability as some of the critical factors which influence the challenges and confusion that are posed by the concepts' parallelism. Also examined are the implications of parallelism that both concepts bring into an organisational environment. This is done to pave a clearer path and intendedly reduce the negative impacts that the confusion and challenges do unconsciously and in practice have on processes and activities in the use and management of IT solutions.

Theorising Enterprise Architecture into Practice

EA is more of an applied discipline than a theoretical framework. This is mainly because it is expected to guide an organisation's practices in areas such as IT solutions, business process design and information governance towards sustainability and competitiveness. However, this has not always been the case in many organisations, in that the concept of EA continues to gain more theoretical attention than implementation and practice. Inevitably, the prevalent situation triggered the question: What are the implications of theorising the concept of EA in organisations? This chapter puts in the spotlight the necessity to examine and gain an understanding of the implications which the theorising of EA has for both academic and business industries. The implications of theorising EA are identified and a model is developed. The model draws on, and shows the interconnectivity and interrelationship between the theory and practice (post implementation) of EA.

Structuration View of Enterprise Architecture

In the last two decades, particularly, the interest in EA from both the academic and business domains has grown tremendously. Despite the overwhelming increase and signs of support across industries in the world, many organisations continue to struggle and encounter challenges in the development, implementation and practice of the concept (Safari, Faraji & Majidian, 2016). The problem is that some of the areas where the challenges exist are not obvious to many quarters or organisations, as well as academics. This problem does, indeed, have an impact on how EA is deployed and supported in various organisations. Also, it has implications for the management of IT solutions and influences the achievement of the goals and objectives of an organisation. These circumstances lead many organisations to seek and employ different approaches to ascertain the challenges that persist despite the efforts. An understanding of EA complexities is therefore examined in this chapter from a different perspective by employing Structuration Theory. Based on the theory, this chapter presents a framework that can be used to gain a better understanding and address complexities as they manifest from their natural settings during the development and implementation of EA in an organisation.

Readiness Assessment Model for Enterprise Business Architecture Deployment

Enterprise Business Architecture (EBA) is an essential domain of EA and, as such, it critically deserves attention. Notwithstanding, many organisations fail to achieve the objectives of their EBA (Hadaya & Gagnon, 2017). According to Whittle and Myrick (2016), some of the challenges arise from the prioritisation of the business activities that constantly change. Also, some of the challenges of EBA include a lack of understanding of the success factors (Gromoff, Bilinkis & Kazantsev, 2017). The challenges often cause a misalignment between the requirements of the business and IT units. This chapter reveals that the challenges are attributed to lack of assessment of readiness. Also, it is because there are no models specific to EBA readiness assessment. The lack of readiness assessment before deployment often results in challenges such as uncoordinated business designs, lack of flow in processes and derailment of activities. These make it difficult to employ IT solutions. Consequently, the cost of operations becomes prohibitive and causes increased complexity in managing potential risks and service stagnancy. The chapter, therefore, proposes a solution through a model that can be used to assess the readiness of EBA in an organisation. This addresses EBA's deployment challenges that individuals and organisations have been grappling with for many years.

Enterprise Architecture as an Agent of Change for Enterprises

One of the objectives of EA is to facilitate change from the current to desired states within an organisation. Facilitation is synonymous with an agent. Despite the simplification approach, the deployment of EA to manage, govern and use IT solutions, including business process, continues to encounter challenges which either cause its failure or slow the pace of implementation. Some of the challenges were highlighted by Buckle et al. (2011) as follows: a gap between requirements and product; unclear time of product delivery; and the uncertainty of some actors. The challenges could be caused by factors such as how the EA was problematised by the promoters among the various stakeholders known as networks, which attract different types of interest and shapes of participation (Bui & Levy, 2017).

The actor-network theory (ANT) is used as a lens to examine the challenges and roles of the various actors in the deployment of EA. Criticality of networks, structural collaboration, the transformative process and the iterative approach were found to be of influence in the development, implementation and practice of EA. Also, the implications which the deployment of EA has on organisations' environments and other stakeholders are identified. Based on this, a conceptual framework is developed and presented in this chapter. The framework can be used to guide enterprises in facilitating activities and providing services towards transformative goals engineered by IT solutions.

Unified Architecture Framework for Enterprises

This chapter examines the challenges that hinder the use of mobile systems as an IT solution in accessing big data in enterprises. This is based on the growing negative effect that the challenges have on the use of mobile systems in accessing big data for organisations' purposes. Sayogo et al. (2015) explain how lack of architecture is the source of the different challenges that affect data sharing or access to data, which in turn has implications for an organisation's growth. First and foremost, the fundamental components of flexible and scalable mobile systems necessary for the systems' connectivity and process integration are identified. Thereafter, the study reveals the most significant factors that influence the use of mobile systems in accessing big healthcare data. This chapter presents a Unified Architecture

Framework (UAF) that guides, governs and manages the use of mobile systems in accessing big data to improve either customers' satisfaction or service delivery to the communities. In addition, the UAF is intended to address the challenges that confront secure access to big data, systems' integration and governance.

Assessing the Value of Enterprise Architecture in Organisations

EA is considered as a strategic approach that can be used to improve organisational governance and the management of information systems and technologies (IS/IT). Despite this significance, many organisations find it difficult to assess, articulate and implement EA that is effective in the context of their organisations. Also, the skill set is essential to the effectiveness and realisation of EA value (Shanks et al., 2018). Without understanding the value of EA, it is difficult to determine its contributions. This has been debated by practitioners and academics in recent years. Bradley et al. (2012) argue that studies that empirically focus on the assessment and maturity of EA are lacking. This chapter discusses the factors of influence and provides important insights for organisations. This includes a model to assess the value of EA in an organisation. The model can be customised in the context of individual organisations. This is intended to enhance the capability to successfully apply the concept.

A Capacity Maturity Model for Enterprise Architecture

One of the vital factors that consistently remains in the discourse of EA is the role of actors. It begins and stops as the criteria used to appoint enterprise architects in many organisations that remain unclear amidst the scarcity of skilled personnel in the field of EA. This is arguably attributed to the fact that some managers are not aware of the things that they do not know about EA, which affects the requirements for the skill set and has implications for the management of IT solutions. The implications are that it creates more challenges and widens the gap of the skill set in an environment, and many organisations do not know how to address this. The challenge emanates from the fact that there is no specific model for EA skill capacity assessment or maturity (Curtis, Hefley & Miller, 2009; Tiku, Azarian & Pecht, 2007; Paulk et al., 1993).

First, it presents factors on why and how many enterprise architects and IT architecture managers are appointed on the basis of their experience in the organisation and seniority in the field of IT, as opposed to architectural requirements and the skill set. Secondly, the chapter confirms that there is no capacity maturity model specific to EA. This chapter presents a model which is intended to guide advances in capacity building and a retention strategy that can yield improved productivity, quality and continuity.

Developing Enterprise Architecture Skills

EA intends to bridge the gap between the business and IT units and drive the strategies of an organisation. However, this cannot be done without competent skilled personnel. EA service delivery is founded on EA capability, which entails skill sets and knowledge. Skill sets are required to formulate, implement and practise EA models, which are often complex (Shanks et al., 2018). Unfortunately, EA skills are not easily available (Walrad et al., 2014). This is because many of the trainers do not have appropriate guidelines that suit organisations' needs due to the uniqueness and specialised nature of the concept (Gøtze, 2013; Wagter et al., 2012). Erosa and Arroyo (2009) argued that some skills that are of technical nature could be best developed through experience. This chapter provides skill and competence guidelines specific for training and developing skill sets for EA specialists.

Summary

As shown in the brief of the chapters, this book provides a pragmatic practice approach in the use of EA for managing modern IT solutions for organisations' purposes. Inversely, the book combines academic rigour with professional practice. In some of the chapters, activity theory, ANT and structuration theory are employed. This imbues rigour from an academic perspective. It emphasises the fact that the evolution of the EA concept is critical for IT solutions' advancement and business enhancement and competitiveness. Most importantly, it demonstrates how EA can be used to manage IT solutions to enable and support business goals and objectives. In addition, the book advances the concept of EA from both academic and business perspectives.

The audience of this book are postgraduates, researchers, academics and professionals (business people). These include IS researchers, government and industry policymakers, directors and other decision-makers in organisations, business architects, information architects, technical architects and enterprise architects. Furthermore, the book can be prescribed for postgraduate programmes as material for classroom teaching and research in Information Technology and Information Systems fields. The book would sell to the international academic library primarily because of the rapidly increasing interest in, and need for EA.

References

Bradley, R. V., Pratt, R. M., Byrd, T. A., Outlay, C. N., & Wynn, D. E. Jr (2012). Enterprise architecture, IT effectiveness and the mediating role of IT alignment in US hospitals. *Information Systems Journal*, 22(2), 97–127.

Buckle, S., Matthes, F., Monahov, I., Roth, S., Schulz, C., & Schweda, C. M. (2011). Towards an Agile Design of the Enterprise Architecture Management Function. In

Proceeding of Enterprise Distributed Object Computing Conference Workshops (EDOCW). (pp. 322–329). 29 August-2 September, Helsinki, Finland. IEEE.

Bui, Q., & Levy, M. (2017). Institutionalization of Contested Practices: A Case of Enterprise Architecture Implementation in a US State Government. In *Proceedings of the 50th Hawaii International Conference on System Sciences.* 4-7 January, Hawaii. Waikoloa.

Curtis, B., Hefley, B., & Miller, S. (2009). *People capability maturity model (P-CMM) version 2.0*(No. CMU/SEI-2009-TR-003). Carnegie-Mellon University Pittsburgh Pa Software Engineering Institute. Url: ADA512354.

Erosa, V., & Arroyo, P. (2009). Technology Management Competences Supporting the Business Strategy. In *Proceedings of Portland International Center for Management of Engineering and Technology (PICMET).* (pp. 2190–2199). 2-6 August, Portland, Oregon USA. PICMET.

Gøtze, J. (2013). The Changing Role of the Enterprise Architect. In *Proceedings International Enterprise Distributed Object Computing Conference Workshops.* (pp. 319–326). 9-13 September, Vancouver, BC, Canada. IEEE.

Grabara, J., Kolcun, M., & Kot, S. (2014). The role of information systems in transport logistics. *International Journal of Education and Research, 2*(2), 1–8.

Gromoff, A., Bilinkis, Y., & Kazantsev, N. (2017). Business architecture flexibility as a result of knowledge-intensive process management. *Global Journal of Flexible Systems Management, 18*(1), 73–86.

Hadaya, P., & Gagnon, B. (2017). *Business architecture: The missing link in strategy formulation, implementation and execution.* Montreal: ASATE Publishing, 1–254.

Hendrickx, H. H. (2015). Business architect: A critical role in enterprise transformation. *Journal of Enterprise Transformation, 5*(1), 1–29.

Kotusev, S. (2019). Enterprise architecture and enterprise architecture artifacts: Questioning the old concept in light of new findings. *Journal of Information Technology, 34*(2), 102–128.

Löhe, J., & Legner, C. (2014). Overcoming implementation challenges in enterprise architecture management: A design theory for architecture-driven IT management (ADRIMA). *Information Systems and e-Business Management, 12*(1), 101–137.

Niemi, E., & Pekkola, S. (2019). The benefits of enterprise architecture in organizational transformation. *Business & Information Systems Engineering, 62*(6), 585–597.

Paulk, M. C., Curtis, B., Chrissis, M. B., & Weber, C. V. (1993). Capability maturity model, version 1.1. *Software, IEEE, 10*(4), 18–27.

Safari, H., Faraji, Z., & Majidian, S. (2016). Identifying and evaluating enterprise architecture risks using FMEA and fuzzy VIKOR. *Journal of Intelligent Manufacturing, 27*(2), 475–486.

Sayogo, D. S., Zhang, J., Luna-Reyes, L., Jarman, H., Tayi, G., Andersen, D. L., & Andersen, D. F. (2015). Challenges and requirements for developing data architecture supporting integration of sustainable supply chains. *Information Technology and Management, 16*(1), 5–18.

Shanks, G., Gloet, M., Someh, I. A., Frampton, K., & Tamm, T. (2018). Achieving benefits with enterprise architecture. *The Journal of Strategic Information Systems, 27*(2), 139–156.

Simon, D., Fischbach, K., & Schoder, D. (2014). Enterprise architecture management and its role in corporate strategic management. *Information Systems and e-Business Management, 12*(1), 5–42.

Syynimaa, N. (2016). Method and Practical Guidelines for Overcoming Enterprise Architecture Adoption Challenges. In *International Conference on Enterprise Information Systems*. (pp. 488–514). 25-28 April, Rome, Italy. Springer, Cham.

Tiku, S., Azarian, M., & Pecht, M. (2007). Using a reliability capability maturity model to benchmark electronics companies. *International Journal of Quality & Reliability Management, 24*(5), 547–563.

Urbaczewski, L., & Mrdalj, S. (2006). A comparison of enterprise architecture frameworks. *Issues in Information Systems, 7*(2), 18–23.

Wagter, R., Henderik, A., Proper, & Witte, D. (2012). Enterprise Architecture: A strategic specialism. In *Proceedings of the 14th International Conference on Commerce and Enterprise Computing*. (pp. 1–8). 9-11 September, Hangzhou, China. IEEE.

Walrad, C., Lane, M., Wallk, J., & Hirst, D. (2014). Architecting a profession. *IT Pro,* 42–49.

Whittle, R., & Myrick, C. B. (2016). *Enterprise business architecture: The formal link between strategy and results.* London: CRC Press.

Chapter 2

Information Technology Solutions

Introduction

Information technology (IT) solutions are classified in this book into three main categories, namely; software, hardware and network. Each of these categories has a variety of components or products which allow for options in their selection, deployment and practice. On one side of the coin, this is a boundless situation which removes monopolistic constraints and enables an organisation to exercise its capacity and ability to seek different options and approaches for optimisation purposes. From another angle, the rapid changing needs of organisations and the increasing variety of IT solutions continue to pose challenges for IT managers in their pursuits to enable and support business goals and objectives. The challenges are common phenomena in the stages where IT solutions have to be selected, deployed, used or managed for organisations' operations.

Each or a combination of IT solutions is employed to enhance, enable and support organisations' goals and objectives in order to promote effectiveness and efficiency. These efforts are primarily to ensure competitiveness and sustainability. Based on this premise, the reliance on IT solutions by both large and small organisations has increased immensely in the last two decades (Gabriel et al., 2014). Despite the numerous and vast opportunities and benefits, there are persistent challenges in the selection, deployment and use of IT solutions in many organisations (Carayon & Hoonakker, 2019). Some of the challenges are of standardisation, deployment, interoperability, information management and integration. Many of the challenges adversely impact sustainability and business performance (Haseeb et al., 2019).

DOI: 10.1201/9781003268420-2

The obstinate nature of the challenges motivates organisations to seek a redeemable approach such as enterprise architecture (EA). EA comprises domains which include business, information, application and technical (Iyamu, 2015). The concept has evolved over the years and is practised by mostly large organisations (Gampfer et al., 2018). EA is increasingly deployed and practised in many organisations across sectors, including financial, health, insurance, manufacturing and government sectors. The use of EA is vast; from governance, management and transformation in the areas of information and business, to data and technologies (Anthony Jnr, 2020).

This chapter is structured into five main sections. It begins with introduction, which draws on the focus of the chapter. Thereafter, the categories and components of IT solutions are covered. These are followed by problematisation of the challenges. Next, EA and its strategic nature are discussed, respectively. At the end, the chapter is summarised.

Information Technology

IT solutions consist of software, hardware and network, including processes (or approaches), which act as the connective scheme between artefacts. Ghobakhloo et al. (2011: 54) describe IT as "capabilities offered to organisations by computers, software applications, and telecommunications to deliver data, information, and knowledge to individuals and processes." The solutions entail the planning, design, development, use and management of technologies. The IT solutions are deployed for various reasons, using diverse approaches for organisations' purposes. Fundamentally, IT solutions are deployed for either strategic intent or operational efficacy, or both. The solutions often aim to provide structure, enablement, manageability, control and governance for diverse and rapidly changing needs and activities of the business and IT units in an environment.

Software – software is the computer programme that runs routinely for specific tasks to be performed. Generally, software can be classified into two categories: systems software and application software. The systems software includes operating systems, device drivers, firmware and utility. Word processors, databases, multimedia and web browsers are some of the prevalent application software.

The most common operating systems are Microsoft Windows, macOS, Linux, iOS, Android, CentOS, Ubuntu and Unix. Device drivers include BIOS drivers, motherboard drivers, display drivers, ROM drivers, printer drivers and sound card, essentially for hardware functionality. Computer peripherals, embedded systems, UEFI, and BIOS are categorised as firmware software. They are embedded in computer systems' read-only memory (ROM). Examples of the Utility software are Norton Antivirus, McAfee Antivirus, WinRAR, WinZip, Piriform C Cleaner, Windows File Explorer, Directory Opus and Razer Cortex. This group of software is for analysis, configuration, maintenance and optimisation of computer systems.

Application software include word processors, databases, multimedia and web browsers. Word processors include MS Word, Apple iWork Pages, Corel WordPerfect and Google Docs, used for documentation. Databases are used to create and manage a database, often referred to as database management system (DBMS). Examples are MS Access, FileMaker, dBase, Clipper, MySQL and FoxPro. Some of the multimedia software include Adobe Photoshop, Picasa, VLC Media Player, Windows Media Player and Windows Movie Maker. They focus on creating and recording images, audio and even video files. Some of the web browsers software are Google Chrome, Mozilla Firefox, Internet Explorer, Opera, UC Browser and Safari.

Software can be either proprietary or open source; see Zhu and Zhou (2012). According to Farshidi, Jansen and van der Werf (2020), the role of architecture in software is indispensable in that it influences the success or failure of software. The architecture defines the structure, subsystems, coexistence and interactions of software (Clements & Shaw, 2009).

Hardware – hardware is the tangible component parts of computer systems. Hardware includes servers, PC, wireless access points and cables. Some of the common computer hardware are server, personal computer (PC) and laptop. Each of these devices consists of a central processing unit (CPU), which hosts the motherboard, random access memory (RAM), video card, drives (hard drive, solid-state drive and optical drive) and card reader. Other hardware accessories include monitor, keyboard, mouse, battery backup (UPS), printer, sound card, network interface card (NIC), expansion card (firewire, USB, etc.), hard drive controller card, fan (CPU, GPU, case, etc.), heat sink, data cable, power cable, CMOS battery and daughterboard.

The hardware is physically connected to each other through cabling or wireless access points to wide area network (WAN) and internet. The interconnectivity of the hardware and internet components are configured to transport data between networks.

The network and security artefacts include the switch, router and firewall. A network switch provides connectivity between devices on a local area network (LAN), such as routers, firewalls, servers and PCs. A switch can contain several ports used to connect with other networks and devices. Routers allow connectivity between devices on different networks, thereby enabling and supporting enterprises' business continuity. Firewall is a security wall; through it, network traffic is scrutinised between devices. It is thus embedded with an enterprise's rules and requirements. Firewall can be complicated for reasons such as compatibility with other technologies in the same environment and unique rules of the organisation. This has led to many different types of firewalls over the years, which makes it critical to adopt standards and principles for selection and deployment.

A network server is simply another computer, but usually larger in terms of resources than what most people think. A server allows multiple users to access and share its resources. There are different types of servers; notably, file server, directory server, web server and application server: (1) File servers store and manage access to all types of files; (2) Directory servers provide the database of users' accounts and enable the management of the accounts as they access resources; (3) Web servers enable access to files through browsers; and (4) a variety of servers, including application servers, database servers and print servers.

Approach – owing to the criticality of the strategic management of IT solutions, different approaches have been explored and employed in various environments and organisations. Despite these efforts, challenges remain immense in many organisations. From the support and management perspectives, IT solutions are strategically and operationally deployed to increase systems' availability and maintain business productivity. Control and governance focus on the efficiency and effectiveness of processes, policies, standards and principles in the deployment and use of IT solutions for organisational purposes. This vastly helps to monitor and evaluate processes and activities towards enhancing business goals and objectives.

IT solutions are getting sophisticated, increasing in number, and more complicated. Hence, strategic management is crucial at all times if the business objectives are to be fulfilled. Strategic management entails the understanding of the strategic intent of each of the IT solutions and how to operationalise each of the solutions. Operationalisation combines implementation and practice with a process of translating concept into reality. The successful implementation of both the strategy and operationalisation depends on human competence and skills, to avoid artificially limiting the capabilities of the IT solutions to the detriment of the organisation.

IT solutions are diverse; from software to hardware, including security, antiviruses and content management. Modern IT solutions engage with business needs and processes through support and enablement. This necessitates a rheostat mechanism in the selection, deployment and evaluation of the technologies. This is because many factors are influentially involved. Thus, a controlled environment results in the stability of both business and technology solutions. Stability manifests from the actions intentionally enacted by both humans and technology, and solidly facilitates IT solutions in an environment.

Organisations employ the services of PCs, supercomputers and business applications, including collaborative (applications). These hardware and software are connected through protocols and switches. Some challenges arise when an organisation requires better and faster systems to execute complex and huge datasets. For smooth operation and continuity purposes, a reliable network is required. It is often difficult to come by an architecture which defines the network, its reliability, connectivity and governance of an environment. The architecture optimises the design and manageability of the hardware and software, including granularity enhancement of data processing.

The action of intentionality relies on governance and control to ensure uniformity, consistency and manageability. This ultimately promotes reliability.

Governance and control are some of the strengths of EA. Simon, Fischbach and Schoder (2014) explicate the concept of EA as a strategic management approach which covers the strategy and governance of business processes, information flow, application development and infrastructure technology deployment.

Information Technology Challenges

Many information systems and technology (IS/IT) practitioners, including managers, find themselves struggling and challenged with the selection, seamless deployment and evaluation mechanism of IT solutions. This includes the integration, consolidation, configuration, development and management of software, hardware and processes. Many of the challenges emanate from information flow and exchanges, capacity to store data, ability to manipulate data towards usefulness, security efficiency and network enablement. These are widely-known problems that have remained over the last decade across the globe. Private companies and government administrations, as well as academic institutions, have come to recognise the need for EA as a possible approach to addressing the above-mentioned challenges.

IT solutions are increasingly employed as an effective approach and means of managing businesses' aims, objectives and transformation. However, the enablement of IT solutions for the fulfilment of business events and activities is increasingly challenging as competitiveness intensifies. As a result, many organisations proactively seek various curative methods and approaches to address this challenge and bridge the gap between business strategy and operations.

Organisations directly and indirectly generate data from and for their service offerings. This is an iterative routine, as data are continuously processed for organisational use. Thus, data storage is critical for both business and IT managers. However, the storing of data is an immense challenge for many organisations. Also, lost, corrupted or compromised data can be recovered if the environment is well architected to do so. This is about an architecture that defines and designs systems and servers' backups to ensure and promote business continuity. Primarily, this is because the predictive volume, variety and transaction of data often do not align with the infrastructure provided. One of the implications is that the unstable state of the data shakenly accommodates a variety of applications. This challenge happens because there is no architecture for data storage. Data architecture is beyond space and cost; it enables flexibility, scalability and integration, which are critically necessary as data increases in size, variety and velocity. This gets worse when the high volume of data requires virtualisation and automation, which is a major challenge for many IT managers as they strive to simplify and speed up these processes.

Despite the increasingly heavy reliance on information, many modern businesses are struggling with the management and control of its flows and exchanges. The assimilation of information is intended to enhance the scalability of an organisation for sustainability and competitiveness purposes. The challenges

are attributed to factors such as lack of governance, standardisation and policies. The challenges are cost-prohibitive from both business and IT perspectives.
From the business viewpoint, incomplete or haphazard information affects the
productivity and manageability of projects. It is implausible for IT to provide
cost-effective and scalable alternative solutions that are conveniently capable of
ensuring a high frequency of information flows. This ultimately affects the processes
and activities.

Modern businesses are continuously alert for attacks that are carried out by
internal and external agents (or actors). Prevalently, the attacks are via emails, applications and web browsing. Also, attacks lead to the loss of important data and
significantly reduce the performance of the network and this affects online collaboration. In addition, data loss can occur as a result of insecure switches and routers.
Thus, a security architecture is required to guide the design, deployment and governance of security applications, such as firewalls. This is to protect the network and
its protocols (TCP/IP) from attacks and data loss.

Information Technology Solutions' Main Challenges

The usefulness of IT solutions for organisational purposes and value is influenced
by both technical and non-technical factors. As highlighted in Table 2.1, there are
six main critical challenges that modern businesses and IT solutions frequently
encounter. They are: (1) lack of alignment between business and IT units; (2) lack
of availability of IT solutions; (3) lack of integration of IT solutions; (4) challenges
of IT governance; (5) IT strategy; and (6) impediments in the operations of IT
solutions. The table should be read with the discussion that follows in order to
gain a better understanding of how the factors influence IT solutions in many
organisations.

The challenges, as highlighted above, can be traced to similar implications
which commonly include prohibitive cost, complexity, inefficiency and lack of optimum use of resources. The factors are discussed as follows.

Lack of Alignment

Despite the conceptual, empirical and theoretical advances in the area of alignment
between business and IT, there are consistently persistent challenges, which affect
the enabling of goals and objectives towards competitiveness (Ilmudeen, Bao &
Alharbi, 2019). A lack of alignment between the business and IT units results in
increasingly unceasing situations and events that need much more attention and
focus than ever before. This is a challenge that is getting more pressing in many
organisations and can be attributed to the growing competitiveness. Jia, Wang and
Ge (2018) explain how business-IT alignment has consistently been a highly-rated
challenge for both the business and IT units in the last three decades.

Table 2.1   Challenges of IT Solutions

Factors	Business and IT Solutions	Implication
Lack of Alignment	Disconnectedness between business and IT in the areas of: i. Goals and objectives ii. Resources iii. Strategies iv. Business processes and IT solutions	Negative effects: i. Redundant solutions ii. Increases in total cost of ownership iii. Duplication of efforts iv. Prohibitive operations v. Low or slow productivity
Lack of Availability of IT Solutions	i. Service level agreement ii. Business continuity assessment	i. Low level of competitiveness ii. Ineffectiveness of operations iii. Halt in access to services and operations
Lack of Integration	Lack of integration of: i. Business systems ii. IT solutions iii. Business process and IT solutions	Silo systems i. Duplication of solutions ii. Duplication of resources and capacity iii. Manipulations of data sets
IT Governance	Lack or low levels of: i. Control ii. Uniformity iii. Standards iv. Principles v. Policies	i. Complex and prohibitive environment ii. Duplication of IT solutions iii. Subdued organisational structure iv. Consistent inconsistency in selecting, deployment and management
IT Strategy	i. Lack of cohesion ii. Lengthy process	i. Repetitive development ii. Hardly operationalised iii. Cost-prohibitive
IT Operations	i. Prohibitive enablement ii. Low level support	i. Disenfranchised processes and activities. ii. Subdued roles and responsibilities

By implication, it is difficult to minimise the total cost of ownership (TCO) when business objectives and IT solutions are aligned. It is therefore highly imperative to align both the business and IT units and strategies to be more flexible and agile. An enterprise-wide view of processes, and underlying technologies are essential to the understanding of information flows, application deployment and infrastructure management, which enable traceability across the business units (Avison et al., 2004). Traceability enables strategic intent and operational decisions in improving response time. Thus, redundancies can be reduced or eradicated, productivity improved and TCO reduced.

Availability of IT Solutions

To ensure the availability of IT solutions and consistently do so is a challenging task. This is because the factors that can bring down IT solutions are many. Some are known and others are not empirically known. It therefore requires a continuous assessment to detect potential influencing factors. Franke et al. (2012) suggest EA for such an assessment. It is important that IT solutions, such as servers, mobility and cloud storage, have high availability levels in an organisation. One of the rationales is that a high availability of cloud storage ensures more reliable and efficient solutions that can reduce cost and improve competitiveness.

In many organisations, small and large, the availability of IT solutions is a concern of utmost criticality. This is primarily so, in that many organisations increasingly rely on IT solutions for their businesses. Thus, there is the prerequisite of availability with concerns about its levels of adherence. In this type of circumstance, EA is critically needed because it fortifies the control of IT solutions to ensure improved availability of solutions for business needs in a more effortless and efficient manner. Availability can also be seen or considered as the ability of an organisation to retain its IT strategy more effectively and efficiently.

Lack of Integration

Integration enables the coexistence of heterogeneous technologies at multiple layers (Qadri et al., 2020). In many computing environments, the integration of IT solutions has been faced with challenges, sometimes leading to the termination of some projects (Ismail & Abdullah, 2017). Many IT managers struggle to identify the influencing factors. This is attributable to lack of standard; as a result, managers employ different approaches inconsistently. When and where IT solutions are involved, many business and IT managers struggle with two fundamental factors; an understanding of TCO, and how to reduce the TCO. As a result, it becomes challenging to reduce the TCO. The main implication is that it affects competitive advantage and growth.

It has never been easy to manage IT solutions because of factors such as the disintegration of functions, silos of systems and lack of cohesiveness. These challenges are often caused by the heterogeneity of IT solutions and the complex nature of facilities such as data, servers, systems, networks and security. All these components form the core of every business.

IT Governance

The increasing reliance on IT solutions for enablement, support and sustainability, and its pervasive use, makes IT governance excessively significant. In the absence of IT governance, it intensifies challenges such as complexity and increased TCO. These manifest from the duplication of IT solutions and lack of business and IT alignment. When this happens, the operationalisation of strategies is impacted, resulting in business underperformance (De Haes & Van Grembergen, 2009). The emergence of online-based business and activities has increased the diversity of data into unprecedented high volumes, variety and velocity. This new norm continues to be challenging for many large and small enterprises in different sectors. The challenges include the capability of technology infrastructure to handle the new norm, compatibility and the governance of various IT solutions in an attempt to enable and support data usefulness.

IT Strategy

In the quest to enable decision-making and increase sustainability and competitiveness, managers continue to develop IT strategies that support business strategy. IT strategy is intended to bridge the gap between business processes and IT solutions (Kitsios & Kamariotou, 2019). IT strategy encompasses environmental uncertainty and various (business and technology) complexities. An IT strategy is more effective and adds value if its alignment with business goals can be measured (Jia et al., 2018). Thus, repetitiveness can be eradicated and, by so doing, some costs can be saved.

The development of an IT strategy facilitates holistic short- and long-term detailed plans to enact the usefulness of IT solutions for organisations' purposes. When this does not fulfil an organisation's needs and requirements, challenges arise. These challenges have been for many years attributed to the rapid changing nature and advancement of IT solutions and business requirements (Cascio & Montealegre, 2016). Many organisations either repeat or revisit the development of IT strategies; therefore, wasting resources, time and funds (Almalki, Al-fleit & Zafar, 2017). According to Batyashe and Iyamu (2020), this vicious circle is caused by the lack of an IT strategy or the inability to implement the current one. When this happens, it does not equate to operationalisation.

IT Operations

Organisations operationalise IT solutions in order to realise specific goals and objectives (Cascio & Montealegre, 2016). However, until an IT solution is measured to be a valuable asset, it remains a cost. Grant (2016) argues that the operationalisation of IT solutions for business usefulness is influenced by numerous factors which are either unknown or ignored. Consequently, alternative IT solutions are acquired. In most cases, the same problems are encountered in the process of implementation. Consequently, the objectives for using IT solutions to enable and support business needs towards competitive edge are, in such cases, not achieved (Batyashe & Iyamu, 2020). Therefore, little or no problem is solved. This often leads to disenchantment, in the course of which roles and responsibilities are subdued.

The operationalisation of IT solutions means it at least fulfils an objective in an organisation (Almalki, Al-fleit & Zafar, 2017). Otherwise, it is an unnecessary cost to the organisation and heightens low productivity. This has been the case in many organisations; hence, the IT unit (division or department) is considered a cost centre in some organisations. In the last three decades, IT units in many organisations have struggled to evade such a stigma.

Addressing the Challenges of IT Solutions

In addressing the challenges highlighted above, there are fundamental factors that need to be embraced and taken into cognisance. In no chronological order, they include an understanding of:

i. Modern management – managing IT solutions is no longer something an organisation can avoid or reduce its priority. The management is structurally carried out by domains' experts to streamline services.
ii. Capability – EA is used to develop capabilities for managing IT solutions in organisations in order to remain sustainable, take advantage of opportunities and improve competitiveness.
iii. Service offering – the services that are offered by an organisation are influenced by different factors, including information flow, business processes and logics, information (business) systems and technology governance.
iv. The fact that the influencing factors enable TCO and collaborative operations from both internal and external perspectives. Also, the factors are business-centric through a strategic and operational approach.
v. Emerging technologies – the emerging technologies as have been experienced in the last decades in the forms of virtualisation, big data and cloud computing. Also, IT solutions can be elusive, in that understanding them is not always straightforward. Thus, the flexibility and scalability of an environment is crucial. A static environment cannot accommodate the emergence and evolution of technologies. EA iteratively guides the selection of appropriate IT solutions to enable a stable operating environment in supporting business needs.

vi. Leveraging – understanding the necessity and essentiality of leveraging rapidly evolving business and technology ecosystems from both internal and external perspectives. Without appropriate leveraging, changes to hardware and software can ignite disruptions to availability of business systems. Also, the flow of information across the networks without appropriate security is a potential risk to business continuity.

vii. Regulation and governance – have major implications for business and IT requirements. EA provides governance for the synchronisation of emerging technologies such as big data analytics, cloud computing and mobility in their rapidly changing nature. Among other things, this addresses a poor integration and imbalance of IT solutions and results in an ineffective support for business goals, and high TCO.

The said points justify the deployment and practice of EA in an organisation. The practice ensures TCO effectiveness and the efficiency of technologies and systems for competitive edge. Efficient IT solutions lead to high productivity, increased reliability of systems' availability, improved decision-making and enhanced capabilities of IT specialists.

EA guides the strategic deployment of networks and their protocols, including the security of information. Also, the configuration or reconfiguration of servers adheres to EA standards and principles. This is to readily optimise these solutions for performance, integration and availability purposes. The EA approach is intended to improve optimisation and reduce prohibitive operationalisation of business processes and IT solutions in an environment. This is done through the segmentation of activities via EA domains. As discussed and demonstrated in the chapters that follow, EA facilitates the deployment of distributive systems, a standards-based framework, easy data transfer between different tools and layers, including the selection of tools and better data analysis (Iyamu, 2020). The analytics tools are primarily for the analysis of big data and activities on the network. This includes descriptive, predictive, prescriptive and detective analytics (Nakashololo & Iyamu, 2019).

Disasters can happen, such as earthquakes, fire or flood. Attacks can occur such as cyberattacks. These challenges are often sudden or unexpected. This is when an architectural design that allows and supports flexibility, scalability and ultimately enables business continuity becomes critically essential. The architecture enables systems that monitor and identify threats before the damage is done. For example, to monitor an unusually high number of changed files to detect ransomware viruses. The use of IT solutions to enable and support a business for continuity purpose creates an environment of a better experience. This includes uptimes rather than the technology mystics' downtimes which are typically associated with costs. Mystic situations are often unexpected and in turn attract unexpected costs. An IT environment that is not architected is unpredictable and faces challenges of manageability. This type of design employs a reactive approach and leads to challenges such as frequent and lengthy downtimes; data loss, redundancy; duplication of solutions; and lack of integration of solutions. EA is synonymous with proactiveness in governing and managing business processes, information flows and the application and technology infrastructure, towards continuity, sustainability and competitiveness.

Summary

The chapter provides an overview of the benefits of IT solutions, including the challenges that come with some of the solutions. This includes the complex nature of the systems. The deployment and practice of EA is linked to both the benefits and challenges as an approach for better governance and management of IT solutions in an organisation. The overview is intended to draw on the efficacy of EA in managing modern IT solutions across domains. This includes its flexibility in the management of IT solutions for improved reliability, scalability and the optimisation of complex tasks and processes.

References

Almalki, M., Al-fleit, S., & Zafar, A. (2017). Challenges in implementation of information system strategies in Saudi business environment: A case study of a bank. *International Journal of Computer Trends and Technology, 43*(1), 56–64.

Anthony Jnr, B. (2020). Managing digital transformation of smart cities through enterprise architecture – A review and research agenda. *Enterprise Information Systems, 15*(3), 299–331.

Avison, D., Jones, J., Powell, P., & Wilson, D. (2004). Using and validating the strategic alignment model. *Journal of Strategic Information Systems, 13*, 223–246.

Batyashe, N. R., & Iyamu, T. (2020). Operationalisation of the information technology strategy in an organisation. *Journal of Contemporary Management, 17*(2), 198–224.

Carayon, P., & Hoonakker, P. (2019). Human factors and usability for health information technology: Old and new challenges. *Yearbook of Medical Informatics, 28*(1), 71–77.

Cascio, W. F., & Montealegre, R. (2016). How technology is changing work and organizations. *Annual Review of Organizational Psychology and Organizational Behaviour, 3*, 349–375.

Clements, P., & Shaw, M. (2009). The golden age of software architecture revisited. *IEEE Software, 26*(4), 70–72.

De Haes, S., & Van Grembergen, W. (2009). An exploratory study into IT governance implementations and its impact on business/IT alignment. *Information Systems Management, 26*(2), 123–137.

Farshidi, S., Jansen, S., & van der Werf, J. M. (2020). Capturing software architecture knowledge for pattern-driven design. *Journal of Systems and Software, 169*, 110714.

Franke, U., Johnson, P., König, J., & von Würtemberg, L. M. (2012). Availability of enterprise IT systems: An expert-based bayesian framework. *Software Quality Journal, 20*(2), 369–394.

Gabriel, M. H., Jones, E. B., Samy, L., & King, J. (2014). Progress and challenges: Implementation and use of health information technology among critical-access hospitals. *Health Affairs, 33*(7), 1262–1270.

Gampfer, F., Jürgens, A., Müller, M., & Buchkremer, R. (2018). Past, current and future trends in enterprise architecture – A view beyond the horizon. *Computers in Industry, 100,* 70–84.

Ghobakhloo, M., Sabouri, M. S., Hong, T. S., & Zulkifli, N. (2011). Information technology adoption in small and medium-sized enterprises: An appraisal of two decades literature. *Interdisciplinary Journal of Research in Business, 1*(7), 53–80.

Grant, R. M. (2016). *Contemporary strategy analysis: Text and cases edition.* London, UK: John Wiley & Sons.

Haseeb, M., Hussain, H. I., Ślusarczyk, B., & Jermsittiparsert, K. (2019). Industry 4.0: A solution towards technology challenges of sustainable business performance. *Social Sciences, 8*(5), 154–178.

Ilmudeen, A., Bao, Y., & Alharbi, I. M. (2019). How does business-IT strategic alignment dimension impact on organizational performance measures. *Journal of Enterprise Information Management, 32*(3), 457–476.

Ismail, N. I., & Abdullah, N. H. (2017). Malaysia health information exchange: A systematic review. *Business and Economic Horizons, 13*(5), 706–721.

Iyamu, T. (2015). *Enterprise architecture from concept to practice.* Victoria, Australia: Heidelberg Press.

Iyamu, T. (2020). A framework for selecting analytics tools to improve healthcare big data usefulness in developing countries. *South African Journal of Information Management, 22*(1), 1–9.

Jia, Y., Wang, N., & Ge, S. (2018). Business-IT alignment literature review: A bibliometric analysis. *Information Resources Management Journal (IRMJ), 31*(3), 34–53.

Kitsios, F., & Kamariotou, M. (2019). Strategizing information systems: An empirical analysis of IT alignment and success in SMEs. *Computers, 8*(4), 74–88.

Nakashololo, T., & Iyamu, T. (2019). Understanding big data analytics and the interpretive approach for analysis purposes. *Journal of Contemporary Management, 16*(1), 272–289.

Simon, D., Fischbach, K., & Schoder, D. (2014). Enterprise architecture management and its role in corporate strategic management. *Information Systems and e-Business Management, 12*(1), 5–42.

Qadri, Y. A., Nauman, A., Zikria, Y. B., Vasilakos, A. V., & Kim, S. W. (2020). The future of healthcare internet of things: A survey of emerging technologies. *IEEE Communications Surveys & Tutorials, 22*(2), 1121–1167.

Zhu, K. X., & Zhou, Z. Z. (2012). Research note – Lock-in strategy in software competition: Open-source software vs. proprietary software. *Information Systems Research, 23*(2), 536–545.

Chapter 3

Introduction to Enterprise Architecture

Introduction

The concept of enterprise architecture (EA) was first introduced over 30 years ago; to be more precise, in the late 1980s (Gampfer et al., 2018; Zachman, 1987). The concept has since evolved into a reliable practice for the management and governance of information technology solutions, business processes, information flows and systems in alignment with business interests (Iyamu, 2015). The evolution of EA reflects in the hundreds of organisations showing interest and the thousands of scientific publications (Gampfer et al., 2018). The increasing interest spans public (government) and private institutions (Shah & El Kourdi, 2007).

In the last three decades, many frameworks have emerged, including The Open Group Architecture Framework (TOGAF), Gartner, Forrester and the Federal Enterprise Architecture Framework (FEAF). Each of these frameworks has models as a deterministic approach to assess data, manage solutions and facilitate the engineering and deployment of technologies and processes. Gong, Yang and Shi (2020) developed an EA-based model to facilitate the chronological analysis of transformation in a government administration. Some of the models guide data access and enterprise systems' deliverables.

This chapter introduces the concept of EA from four main angles. First, it provides a few definitions because there seems to be no universal definition of EA. This helps to gain an understanding of some challenges that confront the concept. Secondly, it provides an overview of EA, which covers its domains. Then, it explains the strategic nature of EA and how it can be employed to manage IT solutions for

DOI: 10.1201/9781003268420-3

an organisation's purposes. Finally, the significance of EA in an environment on which interested organisations can base their motivations is covered.

Definition of Enterprise Architecture

Individuals and organisations view EA from different perspectives from which they associate meaning and value to the concept. The significance of EA is encompassed in the definition. The definition of EA can be complicated, more so, because of its constituent words 'Enterprise' and 'Architecture'. The multifaceted nature and vastness of the concept, two words put together, has therefore contributed to making it difficult to have a single universal definition. "Enterprise is used to refer to a defined geographical location of incorporated business units with a system of culture, process, and technology components which are seen as one legal entity" (Iyamu, 2015: 1).

In the context of this book, Enterprise is defined as a "legal entity that envisions specific needs, consisting of people and other resources such as information, processes, and technologies." It has input and produces output in the form of services or products, entails various activities and passes through different stages. Also, in a sense, an enterprise can be a government institution or agency, an entire corporation or a division of a corporation or a chain of physically separated organisations, but linked together by a single ownership.

The term architecture has its original meaning in building and construction. IEEE 1471 defines architecture as: "the fundamental organisation of a system embodied in its components, their relationships to each other and to the environment and the principles guiding its design and evolution" (IEEE 2000: 9).

This definition can be viewed as the sequential procedure and arrangement of the components and attributes that make up a system and its relationships, and which shapes the interaction between the components in executing processes and procedures in an enterprise. In this book, the IEEE definition of architecture is adopted primarily because it is universal and it incorporates the components, relationships and principles which are fundamental to design and governance.

Having defined the terms enterprise and architecture separately, the definition of the concept of EA follows. Currently, there are many definitions of EA by both academics and practitioners. Some of the most popular definitions are presented here: Ross, Weill and Robertson (2006: 241) define EA as "the organising logic for core business processes and IT infrastructure reflecting the standardisation and integration of a company's operating model." This emphasises the match between IT and business.

The concept of EA goes a bit beyond business processes and IT infrastructure in the holistic sense of an enterprise. It covers the intended operating model of an enterprise and most significantly, it encompasses building a transformative scheme to realise a desired state from the perspectives of both the business and IT units. It is therefore a means of enabling change, governance and alignment. "Enterprise

Architecture is a complete expression of the enterprise; a master plan that acts as a collaborative force between aspects of business planning, such as goals, visions, strategies, and governance principles; aspects of business operations, such as business terms, organisational structures, processes, and data; aspects of automation such as information systems and databases, and the enabling technological infrastructure of the business such as computers, operating systems, and networks" (Schekkerman, 2004: 13).

This definition tries to cover every angle that, at the end, it becomes difficult to understand. This can be attributed to the complex nature of the structure. It is not an easy read, particularly for some architects, aspiring researchers and many businesspeople. The use of many generic and characteristic elements contributes to the complexity of the definition.

Gartner defines EA as the "process of translating business vision and strategy into effective enterprise change by creating, communicating, and improving the key requirements, principles and models that describe the enterprise's future state and enables its evolution." (Lapkin et al., 2008: 1).

From the definition, it entails the use of IT solutions by people through established processes for enterprises' purposes and advantages. This includes an entanglement between these components, as well as external factors. There are omissions of key components of the concept, such as design, governance and transformation.

Based on the definitions above, EA appears to be specifically concerned with the level of an entire organisation where business aspects are included. Also, it means that EA defines the desired state (future) and provides a plan for achieving this target from the current state (as-is) (Tamm et al., 2011). EA provides a holistic description of an enterprise from business process to IT solutions' perspectives. It is therefore intended to bridge integration, communication and alignment gaps between the business and IT units in an organisation (Kotusev, 2019). Subsequently, it improves organisations' sustainability, competitiveness and growth.

The above is an indication that there are many more definitions; also see Wegmann et al. (2007); Pereira and Sousa (2004); and Shaanika and Iyamu (2015). A further definition is provided by Iyamu (2015: 2), who defines EA thus: "EA is the holistic classification of the processes and activities of an enterprise into domains, and it provides fundamental governance to manage and bridge the gap between strategic planning and implementation efforts, iteratively." This is an enterprise-wide description that embeds both business processes and IT solutions into a common pragmatic direction. Another impetus for the focus of EA is the desire to enable and support enterprises towards achieving their goals and objectives in a more unified approach. The definitions conclude that EA focuses on the alignment of IT and business processes, operations and strategies, primarily for competitiveness. The foregoing analysis suggests that the definitions incorporate the integration of components, governance of artefacts and transforming an enterprise from as-is to a to-be state.

Enterprise Architecture

From the definition, it is clear that the scope of EA extends beyond multifaceted IT solutions and covers architectural elements of business capabilities and information assets and systems' components (Lankhorst, 2017; Rahimi, Gøtze & Møller, 2017; Ross et al., 2006). The concept of EA emerged three decades ago from John Zachman's effort to ease the challenges that exist between the strategy and implementation of complex systems in organisations (Zachman, 1987). The concept has evolved over the years to the point where it is employed to transform the activities of entire organisations, from business to information technology perspectives (Kaisler & Armour, 2017). The increasing interest in the concept motivated the emergence of other frameworks, such as the Zachman, Gartner, TOGAF and the FEAF.

The frameworks are briefly described as follows. TOGAF focuses on business applications and information management. Similar to other frameworks, TOGAF provides guidelines for formulating rules and principles for developing architectures. The Zachman framework provides the elements on how an organisation should organise its planning, documentation and processes, including the pivotal role of humans. The Zachman framework is generic and thus not limited to a certain industry. The Gartner EA process focuses on connecting the domains in planning and migrating from the current to desired future states. The FEAF constitutes various reference models which focus on facilitating communication between the stakeholders. This is purposely to reduce or eliminate duplications of resource and processes and to identify opportunities for growth.

The significant evolution of the concept, from a narrow focus on information systems, to extended domains of business, application and technical architectures, can be ascribed to the influence of rapid change and requirements in both the business processes and development of IT solutions. EA consists of domains, which include business, information, application and technical architectures. The domains are interrelated and depend on each other to deliver aggregates in achieving the goal and objectives of EA (Gampfer et al., 2018). The EA's holistic approach comes from the connectedness of the domains and their detailed models. Each of the domains has distinct deliverables (Iyamu, 2015). The connectedness of the domains is the backbone that ensures integration between, on one hand, technologies solutions and, on another hand, IT solutions and the business processes and information.

The field of EA is influenced by the fields of computer science and engineering, primarily because of their problem-solving focus (Lapalme et al., 2016). Even though the concept emerged over 30 years ago, there is currently no common definition of EA (Ajer & Olsen, 2019; Rahimi et al., 2017). It is on this basis that a definition is provided in the context of this book as follows: EA is a holistic approach for the integration and governance of the business and technology processes and activities in an organisation. It is therefore a strategic approach that integrates other components such as structure, information, processes, applications and infrastructure.

Numerous benefits of EA have been revealed and discussed in literature over the years (Niemi & Pekkola, 2017; Tamm et al., 2011). Seppänen, Penttinen and Pulkkinen (2018) discussed the benefit from a digital transformation perspective. The majority of potential benefits are either strategic or operational and can be indirect or intangible. In achieving the objectives of EA, Gellweiler (2020) suggests that the technical goals, including constraints from IT, should be regularly aligned with business strategies and constraints. Despite these studies, benefits realisation and value assessment of EA are challenging to demonstrate in many organisations. Niemi and Pekkola (2019) argued that studies are either abstract or contradictory, which contributes to making it unclear where the EA benefits are actually realised.

The phenomenon of EA is still poorly understood and indorses significant challenges (Alwadain et al., 2016). The evaluation challenge poses a problem of alignment between business and IT strategies (Pérez-Castillo, Ruiz & Piattini, 2020). It is critical to have sufficient available skilled personnel, in that architects are primarily responsible for the implementation and practice of EA in organisations. This has implications for the inexplicit view on why, how, when and by whom EA artefacts are used in order to realise its full potential always (Niemi & Pekkola, 2017). A study by Gampfer et al. (2018) revealed that the lack of integration among strategy, business and processes is one of the major challenges of EA frameworks encountered by organisations.

Domains of Enterprise Architecture

EA consists of four main domains: enterprise business architecture (EBA), enterprise information architecture (EIA), enterprise applications architecture (EAA) and enterprise technical architecture (ETA) as shown in Figure 3.1 (Iyamu, 2015). Each of the domains has distinctive deliverables which cover both technical and non-technical aspects and components of the organisation where it is deployed. Thus, the deployment, which is the development and implementation of EA, is carried out at the domains' levels.

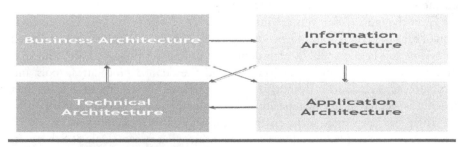

Figure 3.1   EA domains (Iyamu, 2015).

Enterprise business architecture (EBA) – EBA provides the outlines of the mission, goals and objectives of an organisation. Thereafter, the architecture defines and designs the processes and activities through which the goals and objectives can be achieved. The architecture provides the key components that guide the development of business initiatives and identify the constraints, including the determinism to forecast business elements and attributes. EBA offers the foundation that leads to the development and implementation of other domains.

Enterprise information architecture (EIA) – EIA provides a design approach for defining, categorising and classifying various information required in order to execute processes and activities in an organisation. This entails the definition of information and how it is used, communicated, managed and accessed by stakeholders. Through the definition, EIA clarifies what types of information is needed, where it is needed, where it is processed and how it flows within and across an organisation. Based on these clarifications and understandings, the use and management of information can be effectively automated and supported by IT solutions. EIA leads to the development and implementation of EAA.

Enterprise applications architecture (EAA) – EAA focuses on the development, deployment and manageability of business and systems (computer) applications in an organisation. The architecture aims to ensure the integration and coexistence of applications within an environment. This includes interconnectivity and interactive processes. It therefore provides the principles, standards and policies that govern the selection, deployment and practice of applications in an organisation. Based on the EAA, the ETA is developed and implemented.

Enterprise technical architecture (ETA) – ETA focuses on technologies' capabilities to enable and support the goals and objectives of an organisation. It is on this basis the architecture defines the acquisitions, deployments and utilisation of hardware and networks infrastructure in an organisation. According to Iyamu (2015: 88), "technical architecture models the technology environment, including the infrastructure configuration standards and guidelines for the selection, deployment, integration, configuration and management." These are ETA governance patterns for supporting and enabling IT solutions through assessments and manageability, towards ensuring an organisation's competitiveness and sustainability. A clear understanding of an organisation's needs of IT solutions and the impact on business activities and processes is necessary for an ETA.

Even though the domains are interrelated, the development and implementation of each domain is done independently (Shah & El Kourdi, 2007). As explained by Niemi and Pekkola (2017), each domain is uniquely structured. What make it unique are the distinguished deliverables and the defined procedures, tools and structures of each domain (Iyamu, 2015). Every domain is structured to focus on a specific aspect having its own specific deliverables (Shaanika & Iyamu, 2018).

There has been more focus on the technical and social conditions associated with EA success and failure rather than the influencing factors (Dale & Scheepers, 2020). This book provides new empirically and theoretically grounded insights into the use of EA to address the strategic management of modern IT solutions in organisations. This enacts the provision for addressing the difficulties and challenges currently in the development, implementation and practice of EA – reducing the probability of risk and challenges in order to improve the efficiency of EA for organisational solutions. Readiness assessment is therefore critical. This includes an understanding of the inherent complexity in the strategic and operational management of IT solutions.

Enterprise Architecture as Strategy

In a nutshell, Porter (1996) defines strategy as the creation of a unique and valuable position, involving a different set of activities. It requires specifics and focuses on 'fit' in an organisation's context. Strategy is purposely for sustainability and competitiveness. EA is employed as a strategic tool focused on addressing and managing the increasing complexity, integrating the emergence and governance of IT solutions and the difficulty in business service delivery. It provides a common approach for the integration of business and IT strategies. Its strategic approach makes possible information as an asset and defines the futurism of the business goals that are operationalised through applications (information systems) and enabled by the determinism of necessary technologies.

There are four primary essentialities: (1) understand the rationale for needing EA in an environment. According to Gong and Janssen (2019), EA is not well understood in many organisations and, as a result, some promoters struggle to justify the deployment or intention to deploy the concept. This means that it must be put into context and relevance; (2) EA must be well understood. This includes the definition, scope and deliverables; (3) the design and development of EA must be well thought through. This is to ensure its alignment with the business objectives and strategies; (4) there should be a strategy for the implementation of the EA in an environment; and (5) EA must be measured in an organisation to ascertain the value and contributions to the organisation. This requires an assessment model.

Through an iterative approach, EA can be substantially deployed to enable and support factors and components that are essential for the human management of IT solutions, such as policies, processes, governance, information flow, data manipulation and software engineering. This allows for an enhanced performance, improved availability and better sustainability and continuity. EA is considered a strategy intended to improve the management and functioning of complex enterprises and IT solutions (Lapalme et al., 2016). This logically means that EA also covers the processes that are involved in creating, updating and managing IT solutions through its domains (Rouhani et al., 2015).

From both the strategic and operational perspectives, EA provides mechanisms, models and tools for the integration and governance of IT solutions in supporting and enabling business objectives and processes, and the communication and management of artefacts. This ultimately results in the creation of competitive advantage through effective IT solutions. Through models, EA enables communication, which focuses on making complex systems easier to deploy and manage (Närman, Buschle & Ekstedt, 2014). Also, EA provides the structure to model enterprises' business and IT entities. Organisations strive to align their strategic decisions with the operationalisation of IT solutions (Azevedo et al., 2015).

The development and implementation of EA for strategic purposes involve several interrelated artefacts, concepts and models, including organisational factors. It is also used to facilitate strategic management in an organisation. This includes the internationalisation and externalisation of the factors that influence both the business and IT strategies. Conversely, these are fundamental factors that make the benefits realisation and value measurement a complex phenomenon.

Futuristically, the concept of EA is an iterative measure for describing and updating the predictivity of the business process, IT solutions' complexity and change management (Lapalme et al., 2016). From a strategy context, EA is best focused on capability-based planning, management and governance. Hence, it is often used to initiate communication and interaction with business leaders in terms of business outcomes (Azevedo et al., 2015). The capabilities are used for the operationalisation of the IT solutions by deploying EA in achieving a desired state.

In many organisations, an IT strategy is developed but does not get operationalised before another one is embarked upon (Batyashe & Iyamu, 2020). It is easier to develop a strategy than to implement it. One of the objectives of EA is to facilitate the operationalisation of strategic plans in an enterprise (Hinkelmann et al., 2016). Due to the numerous known and unknown challenges, some organisations find it prohibitive to operationalise their IT strategy. The inability to operationalise strategies has implications for competitiveness, sustainability and business continuity (Batyashe & Iyamu, 2020). One of the rationales is that the concept is intended to integrate the components of an organisation, such as processes, artefacts, systems and structures (Simon, Fischbach & Schoder, 2014).

Significance of Enterprise Architecture

The magnifying challenges of IT solutions that this book seeks to address through the concept of EA are outlined in the preceding chapter. Before embarking on the process, it is essential to understand that EA also has its own challenges that must be addressed. This includes the following: (1) lack of thorough understanding of the root cause of EA challenges in an organisation. Based on this challenge, many organisations struggle to either deploy the concept or reap the value; (2) differentiation between the domains. There is often confusion between the domains, such as data and information architectures; (3) lack of sufficient skilled personnel; (4) lack of understanding in the transition of the concept from theory to practice; and (5) inability to assess the value of the concept.

Some fundamental rationales for employing EA in an organisation are (1) EA is purposely to govern, manage and make an organisation more efficient. (2) It provides a guide for an organisation's strategic goals. Also, it facilitates change, business design and management of information (Buckle, Matthes & Schweda, 2010). (3) It helps in maintaining uniformity and consistency, particularly in complex and constantly evolving IT solutions (Tamm et al., 2011). It focuses on identifying deficiencies in IT solutions and business process, which are potential risks to an organisation (Safari, Faraji & Majidian, 2016).

In addition to the above, there are three primary reasons why organisations need to have a clear understanding and address the challenges: (1) first, to be able to assess the returns of EA deployment; secondly, to align processes and activities including stakeholders with different values and expectations; and thirdly, a clear understanding is needed to determine whether EA can enable organisational strategy, goals and objectives. It is significant to note that EA does not provide value or benefits by itself, but by the capability which the organisation possesses (Shanks et al., 2018).

The concept of EA has been embraced by many organisations to improve the value of their business and IT solutions. According to Ahlemann, Legner and Lux (2020), EA is used mostly to create value through EA modelling, planning, implementation and governance. EA governance is purposely to ensure standardisation and guard against risk and complexity (Foorthuis et al., 2016). It entails internal directives and compliance with principles and policies, as detailed in the EA designed document.

Literature suggests that EA adds value to organisations, hence organisations are increasingly and significantly investing in the concept (Shanks et al., 2018). Despite this strong circumstantial evidence, EA continues to prove elusive in demonstrating its value in organisations. This is often attributed to the fact that the value of EA is intangible and indirectly gained. Gong and Janssen (2019) suggest that it is critical to understand and demonstrate the value of EA against the backdrop of return on investment (ROI) in order to justify the efforts.

In the midst of its significance, there are elements that contribute to its usefulness. These include alignment, change, convergence, heterogeneity, integration and transition. The usefulness comes from its support for and enablement of modern IT solutions for business purposes.

Alignment – The alignment between the business and IT units and their strategies is one of the main concerns of EA (Lapalme et al., 2016). Change – facilitates the transition from the current to the future desired state of the enterprise. According to Ross et al. (2006), a stable environment is needed to enable and support the rapidly changing business needs. Convergence – enables standardised IT solutions based on business and technology reference models. This is intended to create a stable environment of a common organisational language. Heterogeneity – through its domains, EA is heterogeneous in that components, including principle and policy statements, are replicated.

Integration – The connectivity of IT solutions and interoperability of rules, processes and information flow across an organisation. Transitional – it enables the processes of transition from the current to future states; that is, implementing new technologies and approaches in response to the changing needs of an organisation. The deployment and practice of EA is a continuous process. It builds, reassesses on its own existence and shapes the future determinations. In the light of this, the approach is used to examine the relationship between IT solutions, business processes, actors and structure towards change and transformation effectiveness.

However, there are challenges with EA. Some were identified by Roth et al. (2013). According to Löhe and Legner (2014), it is difficult to measure EA's success and it takes long to achieve the benefits. Tamm et al. (2011) argue that some of those challenges exist because many organisations lack an understanding of EA. In Espinosa, Boh and DeLone (2011), the challenges are due to lack of measurement metrics. This can be related to Iyamu (2012) who highlights lack of skill as a major challenge of EA. Despite the challenges the concept encounters, it is still considered a critical approach for governing and managing IT solutions in enabling and supporting rapidly changing business needs, evolving technologies and the increasing complexity in modern enterprises (Shah & El Kourdi, 2007).

Summary

This chapter provides a foundation for the understanding of EA and its capability, as well as the understanding to guide readers on how to systematically employ EA to facilitate change, and the operationalisation of strategy through IT solutions. Also, through an engineering of the change and transformation, challenges that are often engraved in IT solutions can be identified and resolved. The chapter therefore prepares the ground for the subsequent chapters which explore the deployment of EA from different angles, intentionally for enabling and supporting businesses through modern IT solutions.

References

Ahlemann, F., Legner, C., & Lux, J. (2020). A resource-based perspective of value generation through enterprise architecture management. *Information & Management, 58*(1), 103266.

Ajer, A. K. S., & Olsen, D. H. (2019). Enterprise architecture implementation is a bumpy ride: A case study in the Norwegian public sector. *Electronic Journal of e-Government, 17*(2), 79–94.

Alwadain, A., Fielt, E., Korthaus, A., & Rosemann, M. (2016). Empirical insights into the development of a service-oriented enterprise architecture. *Data & Knowledge Engineering, 105*, 39–52.

Azevedo, C. L., Iacob, M. E., Almeida, J. P. A., van Sinderen, M., Pires, L. F., & Guizzardi, G. (2015). Modeling resources and capabilities in enterprise architecture: A well-founded ontology-based proposal for ArchiMate. *Information Systems, 54*, 235–262.

Batyashe, N. R., & Iyamu, T. (2020). Operationalisation of the information technology strategy in an organisation. *Journal of Contemporary Management, 17*(2), 198–224.

Buckle, S., Matthes, F., & Schweda, C. M. (2010). Future research topics in enterprise architecture management – A knowledge management perspective. In Service-oriented Computing. ICSOC/ServiceWave 2009 Workshops (pp. 1–11). Berlin, Heidelberg: Springer.

Dale, M., & Scheepers, H. (2020). Enterprise architecture implementation as interpersonal connection: Building support and commitment. *Information Systems Journal, 30*(1), 150–184.

Espinosa, J. A., Boh, W. F., & DeLone, W. (2011). The Organisational Impact of Enterprise Architecture: A Research Framework. In *System Sciences (HICSS), 44th Hawaii International Conference.* (pp. 1–10). 4-7 January, Koloa Kauai. IEEE.

Foorthuis, R., Van Steenbergen, M., Brinkkemper, S., & Bruls, W. A. (2016). A theory building study of enterprise architecture practices and benefits. *Information Systems Frontiers, 18*(3), 541–564.

Gampfer, F., Jürgens, A., Müller, M., & Buchkremer, R. (2018). Past, current and future trends in enterprise architecture – A view beyond the horizon. *Computers in Industry, 100*, 70–84.

Gellweiler, C. (2020). Types of IT architects: A content analysis on tasks and skills. *Journal of Theoretical and Applied Electronic Commerce Research, 15*(2), 15–37.

Gong, Y., & Janssen, M. (2019). The value of and myths about enterprise architecture. *International Journal of Information Management, 46*, 1–9.

Gong, Y., Yang, J., & Shi, X. (2020). Towards a comprehensive understanding of digital transformation in government: Analysis of flexibility and enterprise architecture. *Government Information Quarterly, 37*(3), 101487.

Hinkelmann, K., Gerber, A., Karagiannis, D., Thoenssen, B., Merwe, A., Van Der, & Woitsch, R. (2016). A new paradigm for the continuous alignment of business and IT: Combining enterprise architecture modelling and enterprise ontology. *Computers in Industry, 79*, 77–86.

IEEE Std 1471-2000, IEEE Recommended Practice for Architectural Description of Software-Intensive Systems, 2000.

Iyamu, T. (2012). Institutionalisation of the enterprise architecture: The actor-network perspective. *Social and Professional Applications of Actor-Network Theory for Technology Development*, 144–155.

Iyamu, T. (2015). *Enterprise architecture from concept to practice.* Victoria, Australia: Heidelberg Press.

Kaisler, S., & Armour, F. (2017). 15 Years of Enterprise Architecting at HICSS: Revisiting the Critical Problems. In *Proceedings of the 50th Hawaii International Conference on System Sciences.* 4-7 January, Waikoloa, Hawaii.

Kotusev, S. (2019). Enterprise architecture and enterprise architecture artefacts: Questioning the old concept in light of new findings. *Journal of Information technology, 34*(2), 102–128.

Lankhorst, M. (2017). *Enterprise architecture at work: Modelling, communication and analysis.* (4th ed.). London: Springer.

Lapalme, J., Gerber, A., Van der Merwe, A., Zachman, J., De Vries, M., & Hinkelmann, K. (2016). Exploring the future of enterprise architecture: A Zachman perspective. *Computers in Industry*, *79*, 103–113.

Lapkin, A., Allega, P., Burke, B., Burton, B., Bittler, R. S., Handler, R. A., & Buchanan, R. (2008). Gartner clarifies the definition of the term' enterprise architecture'. Gartner research. https://www.gartner.com/en/documents/740712

Löhe, J., & Legner, C. (2014). Overcoming implementation challenges in enterprise architecture management: A design theory for architecture-driven IT management (ADRIMA). *Information Systems and e-Business Management*, *12*(1), 101–137.

Närman, P., Buschle, M., & Ekstedt, M. (2014). An enterprise architecture framework for multi-attribute information systems analysis. *Software & Systems Modelling*, *13*(3), 1085–1116.

Niemi, E., & Pekkola, S. (2017). Using enterprise architecture artefacts in an organisation. *Enterprise Information Systems*, *11*(3), 313–338.

Niemi, E., & Pekkola, S. (2019). The benefits of enterprise architecture in organizational transformation. *Business & Information Systems Engineering*, *62*(6), 585–597.

Pérez-Castillo, R., Ruiz, F., & Piattini, M. (2020). A decision-making support system for enterprise architecture modelling. *Decision Support Systems*, *131*, 113249.

Pereira, C. W., & Sousa, P. (2004). A Method to Define an Enterprise Architecture Using the Zachman Framework. In *The Proceedings of the ACM Symposium on Applied Computing* (pp. 1366–1371). 14-17 March, Nicosia, Cyprus.

Porter, M. E. (1996). What is strategy?. *Harvard Business Review*, *74*(6), 61–78.

Rahimi, F., Gøtze, J., & Møller, C. (2017). Enterprise architecture management: Toward a taxonomy of applications. *Communications of the Association for Information Systems*, *40*(7), 120–166.

Ross, J., Weill, P., & Robertson, D. (2006). *Enterprise architecture as strategy: Creating a foundation for business execution*. Harvard Business Press.

Roth, S., Hauder, M., Farwick, M., Breu, R., & Matthes, F. (2013). Enterprise Architecture Documentation: Current Practices and Future Directions. In *Wirtschaftsinformatik* (p. 58).

Rouhani, B. D., Mahrin, M. N. R., Nikpay, F., Ahmad, R. B., & Nikfard, P. (2015). A systematic literature review on enterprise architecture implementation methodologies. *Information and Software Technology*, *62*, 1–20.

Safari, H., Faraji, Z., & Majidian, S. (2016). Identifying and evaluating enterprise architecture risks using FMEA and fuzzy VIKOR. *Journal of Intelligent system Manufacturing*, *27*(2), 475–486.

Schekkerman, J. (2004). *How to survive in the jungle of enterprise architecture frameworks: Creating or choosing an enterprise architecture framework*. Trafford Publishing.

Seppänen, V., Penttinen, K., & Pulkkinen, M. (2018). Key issues in enterprise architecture adoption in the public sector. *Electronic Journal of e-Government*, *16*(1), 46–58.

Shaanika, I., & Iyamu, T. (2015). Deployment of enterprise architecture in the Namibian government: The use of activity theory to examine the influencing factors. *The Electronic Journal of Information Systems in Developing Countries*, *71*(1), 1–21.

Shaanika, I., & Iyamu, T. (2018). Developing the enterprise architecture for the Namibian government. *The Electronic Journal of Information Systems in Developing Countries*, *84*(3), e12028.

Shah, H., & El Kourdi, M. (2007). Frameworks for enterprise architecture. *It Professional*, *9*(5), 36–41.

Shanks, G., Gloet, M., Someh, I. A., Frampton, K., & Tamm, T. (2018). Achieving benefits with enterprise architecture. *The Journal of Strategic Information Systems, 27*(2), 139–156.

Simon, D., Fischbach, K., & Schoder, D. (2014). Enterprise architecture management and its role in corporate strategic management. *Information Systems and e-Business Management, 12*(1), 5–42.

Tamm, T., Seddon, P. B., Shanks, G., & Reynolds, P. (2011). How does enterprise architecture add value to organisations?. *Communications of the Association for Information Systems, 28*(10), 141–168.

Wegmann, A., Regev, G., Rychkova, I., Lê, L. S., De La Cruz, J. D., & Julia, P. (2007). Business and IT Alignment with SEAM for Enterprise Architecture. In *11th International Enterprise Distributed Object Computing Conference (EDOC 2007).* (pp. 111–111). 15-19 October, Annapolis, MD, USAIEEE.

Zachman, J. (1987). A framework for information systems. *IBM Systems Journal, 26*(3), 276–283.

Chapter 4

Data and Information Architectures: The Confounded Confusion

Introduction

The focus of this chapter is to address the confusion caused by the loose and interchangeable use of the concepts 'data architecture' and 'information architecture'. The topics had to be spread in such a manner because both academics and practitioners are not consistent in their use of the terminologies that are associated with the concepts. Commonly used terminologies or the semantics of meaning contributes to the confusion between the concepts of data and information (Iyamu, 2011). Each of the topics was expanded in relation to the context of the chapter, purposely to ensure a comprehensive coverage. The focus areas were intended to be more precise in comprehension. For example, it would not have been possible to address the confusion without an understanding of the definitions (descriptions), scope (boundaries) and use of these concepts.

There is no business, government or social environment where data and/or information are not required or accessed for various reasons (Vick, Nagano & Popadiuk, 2015). Many organisations wholly depend on data and information for the competitiveness, sustainability and manageability of their activities (Grabara, Kolcun & Kot, 2014). However, the use of data or information can be confusing and complicated, specifically from design and support viewpoints. Such a confusion may affect the requirements gathering, development and implementation of systems and technologies (IS/IT) solutions (Fisher, 2016). Thus, it is critical to

DOI: 10.1201/9781003268420-4

understand the differences between the terms 'data' and 'information', particularly when employed from an architecture angle.

In the Oxford English Dictionary, the term 'data' is defined as "facts and statistics used for reference or analysis" (Soanes, 2002: 275). Data are therefore facts that have little or no meaning. Fisher (2016) describes the term as meaningless facts that are neither right nor wrong, but processed and put into an understandable context. Kitchin (2014) argues that data is not a simple entity, as it seems to be more about the ideas, techniques, technologies, people and contexts that are necessary for the existence, processing, management, analysis and storage of data. Grabara et al., (2014) empirically admit that data is most of the time confused with information. However, it is very difficult to distinguish them. Although Rein and Biermann (2013) also agree to the concept of confusion, they state that despite the use of the terms in an interchangeable fashion, the real meaning of data and information depends on the context.

The refinement or transformation of data into meaningful entities is information. Again, in the Oxford English Dictionary, 'information' is defined as "facts or knowledge that are provided or learned" (Soanes, 2002: 573), which can be considered epistemological. Grabara et al., (2014) argue that information is the means by which people obtain knowledge that leads to wisdom and understanding and is fundamental for the proper management of organisational operations. Similarly, Vick et al., (2015) argue that information is the fundamental input for the innovation and promotion of knowledge for both individuals and organisations.

From the viewpoint of fundamental vitality, governance and standardisation of data or information, it is important for an organisation to employ the architecture of the concepts. However, the architecture is even more complicated since the two concepts are closely related, and therefore interchangeably used. In this type of confusion, architecture becomes even more critical because it defines an aggregate of consistent and well-defined principles that are used to guide an enterprise design (Hoogervorst & Dietz, 2015). Additionally, the architecture is used to define the management structure, which includes how the components and elements of an enterprise are interrelated, interconnected, organised and managed for an enterprise's purposes (Safari, Faraji & Majidian, 2016). Thus, it is important to always differentiate between the data architecture and information architecture of an enterprise.

Enterprise architecture (EA) is already a complex concept necessitating the simplification of and distinction between data and information architectures (Iyamu, 2015). Hinkelmann et al. (2016: 79) argue that the ISO/IEC/IEEE 42010 standard defines EA as the "fundamental concepts of properties of an enterprise in its environment, embodied in its elements relationship and in the principle of its design and evolution." Similarly, Saint-louis, Morency and Lapalme (2017) explain that there are many definitions of the term EA, which sometimes causes confusion when attempting to employ the concept. The confusion between data and information can only make the concept of EA more complicated. Additionally, this can make things more challenging for many organisations that depend on data and information for their businesses.

Moreover, information is crucial in the development and implementation, mainly because it aids and provides necessary elements during the analysis towards addressing the goals of the EA (Farwick et al., 2013). Thus, the question is, what are the factors that differentiate data architecture from information architecture? The objective is therefore to address the confusion caused by the interchangeable use of the concepts in providing IS/IT solutions and management in an environment. Additionally, a better understanding of the implication of practice can assist in clarifying the differentiation between the concepts towards adding value to an organisation.

The remainder of this chapter is divided into four main sections. Sequentially, the concepts of data and information from architecture perspective are explained; the distinction between the concepts is discussed. This includes the attributes, influencing factors and how the concepts evolve. Thereafter, the implications of the confusion caused by the loose and interchangeable use of the concepts in an organisation are explained. This includes the implication of practice. At the end, the chapter is summarised.

Understanding Data and Information Architectures

The goal to address the confusion caused by the interchangeable use of data and information architectures in an environment is intended to, in three vital different ways, help gain: (1) a balanced view of how the terms have been used and applied, as well as the meanings that have been associated with the concepts of data and information architectures over the years; (2) more knowledge of reality in our consciousness or unconsciousness in the construction of the architectures; and (3) an understanding of the consistency of meanings associated with a concept, including the challenges and confusions that are manifested. Thus, it is necessary to gain an understanding of the concepts from the scope and description to confusion viewpoints.

Data Architecture

Data is a critical aspect of individuals', organisations', systems' and technologies' activities, as has been demonstrated through the social media and networking in the last decade (Grabara et al., 2014). According to Inmon and Linstedt (2014), data is the gasoline that fuels the computer since the first computer programme was first written. The use, storage and management of data have shaped and transformed many organisations over the years through the support and enablement of architectural design. Thus, data architecture is singled out for academic studies (Inmon & Linstedt, 2014). You et al. (2015) suggest that the concept of 'data architecture' is defined as a composition of models, policies, rules and standards that define the collection, storage, management, integration and organisation of data. These tasks are performed by a data architect, based on the requirements of the business (Shaw et al., 2016). The definition of data architecture enables and guides the employment of architects.

In some organisations, the scope of data architecture has expanded from determining the collection, storage and organisation of data to big data architecture, which involves a design for large-scale big data solutions (Miller, 2014). Mohammad, Mcheick and Grant (2014) claim that the scope of data architecture is not only limited to design, but also to identifying and planning for communication with external and internal stakeholders. The above seems clear enough. However, Brose et al. (2014) argued that some of the roles of the data architect include the design, development and implementation of information architecture and data warehouses.

How are the above different from information and information architecture? This is the main question that led to this chapter; to clarify the confusion and misunderstanding between the two concepts from architecture and computing perspectives. Only then the architectures can be distinctively developed and implemented to support and enable business goals and objectives.

Information Architecture

Information architecture is a discipline that determines how information is presented in an appropriate way based on users' and environmental contexts (Toure, Michel & Marty, 2016). In the context, the term 'appropriate way' simply means the form in which information is organised or structured; this includes the flow, exchange and use (Pessoa et al., 2015). The authors went further to describe the organisation of information as defining the levels of details in a set of information which involves identifying the components and grouping them into categories. Toure et al. (2016) are of the opinion that the organisation of information is done purposely to identify, classify and determine how it can be used most effectively to achieve business goals and objectives. Thus, information architecture becomes very useful in many areas, such as the management of information challenges and ensuring that knowledge is presented in a structured and understandable manner to increase its purpose and usefulness within contexts (Iannuzzi et al., 2016). This is a task that is performed by an information architect from both organisational and technological perspectives.

The information architecture is not limited to designing single information spaces, such as websites and software applications; it also includes the strategic use, aggregation and integration of multiple information spaces and their channels, modalities and platforms (Ding, Lin & Zarro, 2017). Additionally, the information architecture includes providing standards that enable an organisation in their use, exchange and management (archives and libraries) of information (Joudrey & Taylor, 2017). In addition, in terms of development, information architecture can lead to the contextual inquiry and support for the process of keeping track of the development and implementation of IS/IT artefacts and solutions (Rojas & Macías, 2015).

Understanding the Confusion

The confusion between data architecture and information architecture starts with the definition and the attributes of the concepts. According to Pras and Schönwälder (2002), it is often difficult to separate the attributes of data from that of information, which brings about grey areas, as both concepts continue to overlap. Rossi and Hirama (2015), on the other hand, claim that it is within information architecture that data is reviewed to have meaning, value and usefulness. Despite this confusion, Molnár and Vincellér (2013) suggest that both information and data architecture are fundamental to any business and represent the structure of the information that is required and used by an organisation. Such a lack of clear distinction wholly contributes to the confusion which both businesspeople and IS/IT personnel encounter in the course of their duties, as well as career development.

In the management of networks, as well as defining objects within computing, there has always been confusion due to the misunderstanding between data and information artefacts (Pras & Schönwälder, 2002). Aamodt and Nygård (1995) acknowledge that there was confusion between the terms 'data' and 'information' from the perspective of computing. The relationship between data and information is the main contributing factor to the confusion and misunderstanding (Kanehisa et al., 2013). From a modelling angle, Pras and Schönwälder (2002) explain that there has been ongoing confusion about the differences between information and data.

Even though this only refers to data and information, and not the architectural aspect of the subjects, that is where the confusion and misunderstanding start. Kanehisa et al. (2013) argue that the concept of 'data' and 'information', including knowledge, contributes to improving architecture from a database viewpoint. Even though the misunderstanding between data and information has long been identified, no proposed solution has yet been put forward. The few models that have been presented are abstracts. According to Aamodt and Nygård (1995), if a model leaves out many details, it is clearly an abstraction. It should be regarded as a foundation and a basis for further discussions and development that can lead to a possible solution.

Distinction between Data and Information Architectures

The hermeneutics technique from an interpretivist perspective was employed in the analysis of the data. This allows for subjective reasoning towards achieving the objective of the chapter. The analysis focused on three main components: (1) Attributes; (2) Influencing factors; and (3) Evolution, as shown in Figure 4.1.

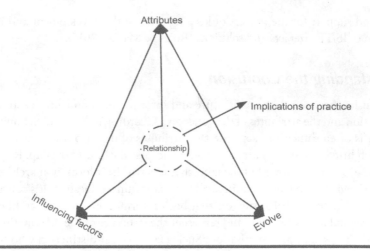

Figure 4.1 Connecting the confusion between data and information architectures.

These components help to connect the confusion between the data and information architectures through an understanding of the relationship that they share. As discussed further later, the three components can be fundamental in gaining a better understanding about the confusion between the data and information architectures in an organisation.

The three components are briefly discussed, followed by a detailed analysis:

i. The attributes of the concepts – the attributes of both data and information architectures were identified. This helped to understand what each concept comprises. The attributes are the state of originality, associated terms and catalogue.

ii. Evolving characteristics of the concepts – from the analysis, reproduction and refinement were the two main factors through which both data and information architectures evolve. This is particularly from the perspectives of development, use and management.

iii. Influencing factors – six factors were found to be the main influence in the ways in which the concepts of data and information architectures are developed, used and managed. The factors were identified from the three attributes discussed in Table 4.1. The factors are requirements, differentiation, confusion, source, characteristics and purpose. The factors are discussed here, and they should be read with the attributes (Table 4.1) to gain a better understanding of the concepts towards clarifying the confusion about them.

Attributes of Data and Information Architectures

As shown in Table 4.1, there are three main attributes in the course of differentiating data architecture from information architecture: state of originality, associated

Table 4.1 Data and Information Architectures

Attribute	Data Architecture	Information Architecture
State of originality	The original state of data is rawness. Based on the rawness of data, the architecture is used to describe a set of models, standards and principles which dictate the collection, storage, usage and integration of data in a data system (You et al., 2015). In an organisation, the data architecture is designed in a way that it can describe artefacts about the systems, and how the artefacts share the resources and interaction between them within an environment (Nielsen & Parui, 2011).	Information begins from the state of refinement. Information architecture is a set of several elements of the information about infrastructures and activities of a business, which include the business model and processes. Information architecture is defined by, and developed based on an organisation's data, to rapidly and consistently provide the stakeholders with the necessary information (Affeldt & Junior, 2013). Alhefeiti and Nakata (2017) explain how information architecture is the collection of rules and regulations that guide the collection, storage, processing, usage and sharing of information within an organisation.
Associated terms	There are big data, which mean that we could soon have big data architecture. Data architecture covers the flow of data in an organisation. Hoven (2003) states that data architecture is fundamental in an enterprise or organisational environment where there are several data sources to be managed. Thus, the focus of data architecture is to understand the flow of data across multiple systems in the organisation, the source, maintenance, sharing, updates and storage of the data (Fleckenstein & Fellows, 2018).	The questions are: can information be big? Can we say big information architecture? The answer, at least for now, is no. Information architecture is often developed to facilitate the management, access and use of large amounts of information available to an organisation (Resmini & Rosati, 2012). The architecture covers the design of single and multiple information spaces and provides standards for information usage and management (Ding et al., 2017; Joudrey & Taylor, 2017).
Catalogue	Each business has its own policies and needs that guide how data is organised by using architecture (Crespo & Santos, 2015). Therefore, the elements of data architecture will most often depend on the type of business activities and its needs. Thus, in an organisation, data architecture catalogue should include data glossary, models, data lifecycle diagrams, standards, policies, rules and data asset inventory (Fleckenstein & Fellows, 2018; You et al., 2015).	Information architecture is an umbrella term that covers all elements of data architecture and other architectures. The key elements of information architecture are: (i) data architecture, (ii) system architecture and (iii) computer architecture. In software development, information architecture includes models for the activities to be carried out during the development of the technologies, with the focus on usability to facilitate the development of useful software (Rojas & Macías, 2015).

terms and catalogue. These attributes, as presented in Table 4.1, help to differentiate between the concepts of data and information architectures.

Evolving Nature of Data and Information Architectures

In the context of architecture, data and information continue to evolve through refinement and reproductive approaches. As shown in Figure 4.2, the relationship between data and information architectures implies that the concepts wholly depend on each other and neither one can exist by itself. At the same time, by virtue of the concepts' nearness to each other, they cannot coexist in an environment.

The evolving nature of both data and information architectures is transformative, in that the refinement of one leads to the other. The transformation has no end, as long as one of the entities (data or information) exists. The two components, refinement and reproduction that form the transformative approach, are discussed here.

Refinement

As stated many times in this chapter, the term 'data' is different from information even though they have often been used interchangeably. According to Grabara et al., (2014: 1) very often the term data has been defined as "information processed by a computer," and information has been defined as "data processed by a computer." This interpretation can be misleading because if we look at these concepts in a hierarchic structure, data exists before information (ibid). Therefore, data needs to be refined in order to be considered information (Vick et al., 2015).

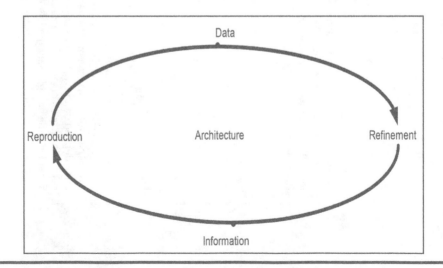

Figure 4.2 The evolving nature of data and information.

Data are raw facts which are meaningless; therefore, they cannot be considered right or wrong (Fisher, 2016). So, in order to draw meaning out of the data, the refinement process takes place. Refinement of data is basically transforming raw facts into meaningful entities which are then considered information. This involves processing or analysing the data in a way that it results in an understanding of what is meant by what we read or listen to (Rein & Biermann, 2013).

Reproductive

Refined data is considered information because they result in meaningful facts. However, what is considered information (meaningful facts) in one environment is not necessarily information within another environment. This is mainly because the meaning of data or information depends on the context in which it is used (Rein & Biermann, 2013). Fisher (2016) claims that data is often processed and put into an understandable context and is only then considered information. Therefore, depending on the context, there is a possibility that whatever has been processed and considered information in one environment may be considered data in another. Therefore, it will be required to be processed again in order to be considered information within a different environment; making the distinction very difficult (Grabara et al., 2014). Additionally, Kitchin (2014) states that context is one of the influencing factors in the existence, processing, management, analysis and storage of data. Thus, there is a loop in which data becomes information and information becomes data again, depending on the context. This is also known as production and reproduction within the context of structuration theory.

Structuration theory emphasises the production and reproduction of social systems (Chang, 2014). This happens through the interaction between agents (technical and non-technical) and structure (rules and resources). This means that agents make use of rules and resources for the production and reproduction of social systems which then influence the interaction between agents and structure (Iyamu, 2013). This influence can either be a constraining or enabling factor for agents' actions (Giddens, 1984). Thus, it creates an endless loop similar to the refinement and reproduction of data and information which makes differentiating between the terms even more complex (Grabara et al., 2014). This complexity affects the understanding of data and information architectures (Rossi & Hirama, 2015). However, these two terms (data and information architectures) can be clarified and understood by clearly laying out their requirements, purpose and characteristics.

Factors of Influence between Data and Information Architectures

Based on the attributes, as summarised in Table 4.1, four factors were found to influence the differentiation between data and information architectures. This helps to understand the confusion between the two concepts. The factors are requirements, purpose, source and characteristics. Through a subjective understanding and examination of the confusion, we were able to differentiate between the architectures in the discussion that follows:

Requirements

Based on the similarity between data and information architectures, the same requirements can with ease be gathered and used for the concepts, even though that might not be the intention. An example and reference can be drawn from Colati (2018) who argued that policies can be combined for data architecture and information architecture to develop a strategic framework. Despite this possibility, both data architecture and information architecture have different types of requirements for an organisation's purposes (Crespo & Santos, 2015).

Through systems and technologies, information is obtained from multiple data sources (Affeldt & Junior, 2013), which confirms that data exists before information. However, information may become data, as shown in Figure 4.2, depending on the phenomenon being monitored or studied. The evolving nature of both data and information can be influenced by factors such as time. This shapes the requirements which define the architecture.

Over the years, the volume of data has increased and new requirements for data architecture have emerged (Bakshi, 2012). In the same line of thought, You et al. (2015) suggested that the following could be the emerging requirements for data architecture: large capacity, high interactive speed, high reliability and well-designed metadata. In addition, Fleckenstein and Fellows (2018) claim that some of the critical data architecture requirements for an organisation include data governance, privacy and security. However, privacy and security are also critical requirements for information architecture. This is mainly because data architecture is one of the elements of information architecture.

In general, information architecture focuses on facilitating access to and the management of information in an organisation (Resmini & Rosati, 2012). Chen and Lin (2014) state that usability and accessibility are some of the main requirements of information architecture. This means that the information should be easy to access and of high quality (Toure et al., 2016). These requirements should be met to make the information usable for the users.

Purposes

In today's digital world, a large amount of data is stored in digital libraries and often accessed through search engines. Chen and Lin (2014) claim that the digital library is the entity that enables the growth of information. Digital libraries are established and enhanced by information architecture by reducing the search time (ibid). Thus, Dillon and Turnbull (2010) state that information architecture optimises the search engines and accessibility to information. This current situation helps to reshape the purpose of information architecture in an environment.

Based on the details provided in the scope, as presented and discussed earlier, data cannot be used to achieve the organisation's goal and objectives because it is raw. The question is, how is architecture developed or provided for a raw data entity? Information architecture is increasingly being developed and implemented to achieve the needs of an organisation and promote its competitive advantages (Resmini & Rosati, 2012). According to Pessoa et al. (2015), this is possible because information architecture facilitates strategic decision-making within organisations by turning the complex into clear and understandable information. The architecture, therefore, enables standardisation, ease of access, increased usefulness and ease of management (ibid).

Similar to information architecture, organisations generally make use of data architecture to facilitate the management of a large amount of data. In the view of Bakshi (2012), the purpose of data architecture is not limited to the storage and management of data. The author suggests that the data architecture should provide tools to analyse and extract meaning out of the data (information). Hoven (2003) claims that a data architecture enables the effective use of data and enhances the integration of data in two ways: (1) To get a better understanding of the organisation's performance, and (2) to provide a better combination of the organisation's customers and stakeholders' data. However, Fleckenstein and Fellows (2018) claim that the purpose of data architecture is a deeper concept, including the ability to extract trusted information from a network of architectures.

Confusion

The confusion often begins with a question that is consciously asked: when is data, data, and when does it become information? Data remains data, a set of data or big data when it is impossible or difficult to make sense of it. Once meaning can be generated from, or associated with the data, it becomes a piece of information. Thereafter, the architecture is defined.

Additionally, the term 'information architecture' is used within two different contexts, namely; websites and organisations. Within the website context, the term information architecture refers to the way digital information is structured in order to optimise search engines and speed up the access to information online (Chen & Lin, 2014). This is different from the organisational context. Within the organisational context, information architecture is a much deeper concept. Information architecture in the organisation involves data standards for well-structured and accessible information to facilitate decision-making (Pessoa et al., 2015). This is not different from data architecture. In fact, both information architecture and data architecture involve providing a structure for the information that is used within an organisation (Molnár & Vincellér, 2013).

However, it is confusing whenever one is referring to information architecture for websites or in the organisational context. This confusion comes from the use of the term information architecture within two different contexts without clearly stating the context. This is what makes some aspiring architects and those who are not IT specialists think that information architecture and data architecture are two different subject areas.

As stated many times in this chapter, data architecture is a subset of information architecture. Therefore, the two terms cannot be referred to on their own. However, the terms are often used interchangeably to mean the other. For example, many times data architecture is used to refer to information architecture and vice versa. This confuses aspiring architects, non-IT specialists and the people who write about information and data architecture.

Characteristics

The characteristics of a data or information architecture vary from business to business, depending on the need and objectives. However, in general, a data architecture is constituted by models, data standards, principles for data management, policies, rules, data glossaries, data lifecycle diagrams and data storage (Fleckenstein & Fellows, 2018; You et al., 2015). Information architecture constitutes all the same elements of data architecture plus other subsets. Information architecture consists of data architecture, system architecture and computer architecture.

Implications for Practice

The loose and interchangeable use of the terms, 'data architecture' and 'information architecture', has implications in practice for IS/IT managers, architects, as well as business managers. As revealed from the analysis, the primary implications in practice are in the areas of information systems design and management, as discussed in Table 4.2.

As summarised in Table 4.2, an understanding of the characteristic elements that differentiate and create confusion between the terms data and information can help define a clearer architecture for an organisation. This includes having an appropriate resource to develop and manage the concepts.

Additionally, architects will be appropriately employed and assigned roles and responsibilities, which limit confusions and conflicts within the organisational structure.

Table 4.2   Implications of Practice

Factor	Description
Evolve	Information comes from data, which makes the latter original. The relationship between data and information is iterative. With this understanding, the requirements for information or data architectures can be better sourced, and the definition, development and implementation of the architectures can be clarified for an organisation's purposes. Thus, in practice, this has implications for how the artefacts of the terms are classified and categorised.
Development	In practice, the confusion about data and information architecture has implications for both an organisation and individuals, from a development perspective. In an organisation, the implication affects the structure and allocation of roles and responsibilities to the specialists, data architecture or information architecture. At the individual level, the confusion hampers career development in that some of the specialists are not convinced on the path to follow.
Enterprise architecture	Many organisations are confused on whether to include data or information architecture as a domain in the development and implementation of enterprise architecture (EA). As a result, the terms are often loosely or interchangeably used or referred to in EA. The implication is that each domain (data or information) stands on its own. Therefore, the content of one domain affects other domains, such as application, business and technology, in their development and implementation.

Summary

This chapter examined the implication for practice of the loose and interchangeable use of the terms 'data' and 'information' architectures within an organisation. Four factors are found to be influencing the differentiation between data and information architectures. The factors are requirements, purpose, source and characteristics. Thus, this chapter provides a clear differentiation between 'data' architecture and 'information' architecture to overcome the loose and interchangeable use of the terms. The chapter proposes a solution to halt a further misconstruction of the architectures and avoid the confusing challenges it has for organisations, including aspiring architects and managers. The chapter will be of benefit to organisations, in that it will facilitate decision-making, definition, development and implementation of the domains of data and information architecture. It also contributes to the academia through its addition to existing literature and as a teaching and learning material.

References

Aamodt, A., & Nygård, M. (1995). Different roles and mutual dependencies of data, information, and knowledge – An AI perspective on their integration. *Data Knowledge. Engineer, 16*(3), 191–222.

Affeldt, F. S., & Junior, S. (2013). Information architecture analysis using business intelligence tools based on the information needs of executives. *JISTEM-Journal of Information Systems and Technology Management, 10*(2), 251–270.

Alhefeiti, A., & Nakata, K. (2017). A Framework for Information-sharing Analysis Based on Activity Theory. In *Proceedings of the 3rd International Conference on Communication and Information Processing.* (pp. 151–157). 24-26 November, Tokyo, Japan. ACM.

Brose, M. S., Flood, M. D., Krishna, D. & Nichols, B. (eds). (2014). *Handbook of financial data and risk information I Illustrate.* London: Cambridge University Press.

Bakshi, K. (2012). Considerations for Big Data: Architecture and Approach. In *Aerospace Conference.* 3-10 March, Big Sky, USA. IEEE.

Chang, C. L. (2014). The interaction of political behaviours in information systems implementation processes – Structuration theory. *Computers in Human Behaviour, 33*(21), 79–91.

Chen, C. M., & Lin, S. T. (2014). Assessing effects of information architecture of digital libraries on supporting e-learning: A case study on the digital library of nature & culture. *Computers & Education, 75*, 92–102.

Colati, G. (2018). A data architecture for library collections. *Journal of Library Administration, 58*(5), 468–481.

Crespo, P., & Santos, V. (2015). Construction of integrated business management systems for micro and small enterprises. *Iberian Association for Information Systems and Technologies,* (15), 35–50.

Dillon, A., & Turnbull, D. (2010). Information architecture. *Encyclopaedia of Library and Information Science, 1*(1), 2361–2368.

Ding, W., Lin, X., & Zarro, M. (2017). Information architecture: The design and integration of information spaces. *Synthesis Lectures on Information Concepts, Retrieval, and Services, 9*(2), 152.

Farwick, M., Breu, R., Hauder, M., Roth, S., & Matthes, F. (2013). Enterprise Architecture Documentation: Empirical Analysis of Information Sources for Automation. In *System Sciences (HICSS), 46th Hawaii International Conference.* (pp. 3868–3877). 7-10 January, Wailea, Hawaii. IEEE.

Fisher, M. (2016). Develop a data system for your pilot plant. *Chemical Engineering Progress, 112*(10), 43–47.

Fleckenstein, M., & Fellows, L. (2018). *Modern data strategy.* Cham: Springer.

Giddens, A. (1984). *The constitution of society: Outline of the theory of structuration.* Berkeley: University of California Press, CA.

Grabara, J., Kolcun, M., & Kot, S. (2014). The role of information systems in transport logistics. *International Journal of Education and Research, 2*(2), 1–8.

Hinkelmann, K., Gerber, A., Karagiannis, D., Thoenssen, B., Merwe, A., Van Der, & Woitsch, R. (2016). A new paradigm for the continuous alignment of business and IT: Combining enterprise architecture modelling and enterprise ontology. *Computers in Industry, 79,* 77–86.

Hoogervorst, J. A., & Dietz, J. L. (2015). Enterprise architecture in enterprise engineering. *Enterprise Modeling and Information Systems Architectures, 3*(1), 3–13.

Hoven, J. V. D. (2003). Data architecture: Blueprints for data. *Information Systems Management, 19*(4), 90–92.

Iannuzzi, D., Grant, A., Corriveau, H., Boissy, P., & Michaud, F. (2016). Specification of an integrated information architecture for a mobile teleoperated robot for home telecare. *Informatics for Health and Social Care, 41*(4), 350–361.

Inmon, W., & Linstedt, D. (2014). *Data architecture: A primer for the data scientist: Big data, data warehouse and data vault.* (1st ed.). S. Elliot (ed). Waltham: Morgan Kaufmann.

Iyamu, T. (2011). The architecture of information in organisations. *South African Journal of Information Management, 13*(1), 1–9.

Iyamu, T. (2013). Underpinning theories: Order-of-use in information systems research. *Journal of Systems and Information Technology, 15*(3), 224–238.

Iyamu, T. (2015). *Enterprise architecture from concept to practice.* Victoria, Australia: Heidelberg Press.

Joudrey, D. N., & Taylor, A. G. (2017). *The organization of information.* (4th ed.). ABC-CLIO.

Kanehisa, M., Goto, S., Sato, Y., Kawashima, M., Furumichi, M., & Tanabe, M. (2013). Data, information, knowledge and principle: Back to metabolism in KEGG. *Nucleic Acids Research, 42*(D1), D199–D205.

Kitchin, R. (2014). The real-time city? Big data and smart urbanism. *GeoJournal, 79*(1), 1–14.

Miller, S. (2014). Collaborative approaches needed to close the big data skills gap. *Journal of Organization Design, 3*(1), 26–30.

Mohammad, A., Mcheick, H., & Grant, E. (2014). Big Data Architecture Evolution: 2014 and Beyond. In *Proceedings of the Fourth ACM International Symposium on Development and Analysis of Intelligent Vehicular Networks and Applications.* (pp. 139–144). 21-26 September, Montreal, Canada. ACM Press.

Molnár, B., & Vincellér, Z. (2013). Comparative Study of Architecture for Twitter Analysis and a Proposal for an Improved Approach. In *Proceedings of the 4th International Conference on Cognitive Infocommunications (CogInfoCom).* (pp. 11–16). 2-5 December, Budapest, Hungary. IEEE.

Nielsen, P., & Parui, U. (2011). *Microsoft SQL server 2008 bible.* Canada: John Wiley & Sons.

Pessoa, C. R. M., Baracho, R. M. A., Erichsen, M. N., & Jamil, G. L. (2015). Information architecture: Case study. In: G.L. Jamil (ed). *Information architecture and management in modern organizations.* 625.

Pras, A., & Schönwälder, J. (2002). *On the difference between information models and data models* (No. RFC 3444).

Rein, K., & Biermann, J. (2013). Your High-Level Information Is My Low-Level Data a New Look at Terminology for Multi-Level Fusion. In *Proceedings of International Conference on Information Fusion (FUSION), 16th.* (pp. 412–417). 9-12 July, Istanbul, Turkey. IEEE.

Resmini, A., & Rosati, L. (2012). A brief history of information architecture. *Journal of Information Architecture, 3*(2), 33–45.

Rojas, L. A., & Macías, J. A. (2015). An Agile Information-Architecture-Driven Approach for the Development of User-Centered Interactive Software. In *Proceedings of 16th International Conference on Human Computer Interaction.* 7-9 September, Villanova, Spain. New York. ACM.

Rossi, R., & Hirama, K. (2015). Characterizing big data management. *Issues in Informing Science and Information Technology, 12,* 165–180.

Safari, H., Faraji, Z., & Majidian, S. (2016). Identifying and evaluating enterprise architecture risks using FMEA and fuzzy VIKOR. *Journal of Intelligent Manufacturing, 27*(2), 475–486.

Saint-louis, P., Morency, M. C., & Lapalme, J. (2017). Defining enterprise architecture: A systematic literature review. In *Enterprise distributed object computing workshop (EDOCW), IEEE 21st international.* pp. 41–49. *10-13 October. Quebec, Canada.* IEEE.

Shaw, S., Vermeulen, A. F., Gupta, A., & Kjerrumgaard, D. (2016). Hive architecture. In *Practical hive.* pp. 37–48. Berkeley, Apress.

Soanes, C. (2002). *The compact Oxford English dictionary of current English.* (2nd ed.). London: Oxford University Press, UK.

Toure, C. E., Michel, C., & Marty, J. (2016). Re-designing knowledge management systems: Towards user-centred design methods integrating information architecture. *Computer Science Human Computer Interaction, 1,* 7–8.

Vick, E., Nagano, S. M., & Popadiuk, S. (2015). Information culture and its influences in knowledge creation: Evidence from university teams engaged in collaborative innovation projects. *International Journal of Information Management, 35*(3), 292–298.

You, S., Zhu, L., Liu, Y., Robertson, R., Liu, Y., Shankar, M., & King, T. (2015). Data Architecture for the Next-Generation Power Grid: Concept, Framework, and Use Case. In *Information Science and Control Engineering (ICISCE), 2nd International Conference.* (pp. 679–682). 24-26 April, Shanghai, China. IEEE.

Chapter 5

Business Analysis and Business Architecture: The Implications for Organisations

Introduction

Business and information technology (IT) units are increasingly inseparable in many organisations. This could be attributed to the fact that both units share a common interest in achieving the organisation's goals, including sustainability and competitiveness. This has raised the need to gain a better understanding of the alignment, which includes the structure, connective scheme and the successful nature of the alignment by both business and academic domains.

For over three decades, there have been numerous studies about business and IT alignment. For example, Aier and Winter (2009) found the need to examine the integration between business and IT artefacts from which they developed an alignment architecture. Due to the potential benefit of such a common interest, professionals and academics continue to advocate for the alignment between the business and IT units within organisations. Zhang, Chen and Lyytinen (2020) explain how organisations control the alignment trajectory. According to Silvius (2009), the alignment between IT and business strategies is one of the factors used by successful companies to effectively enable and efficiently support their activities and operations. Alignment is supported and enabled by business analysis and business architecture through their roles, responsibilities and functions within

DOI: 10.1201/9781003268420-5

organisational structures and processes. It does not stop either the business or IT unit from having distinctive deliverables (Queiroz et al., 2020).

For many years, some organisations have employed the concept of business analysis to analyse their processes and activities with the intention to bridge the gap between their business and IT units. Hence, business analysis is primarily focused on the processes of IT and business units within an organisation (Clare, 2011). The International Institute of Business Analysis defines a business analyst as a liaison between stakeholders in order to elicit, analyse, communicate and validate business and IT requirements. The business analyst focuses on both business problems and opportunities within the context of requirements and recommends solutions that can enable the organisation to achieve its goals and objectives (Clare, 2011).

The emergence of business architecture over two decades ago began to change the landscape of the roles and responsibilities of business analysis in many organisations. The positioning of business analysis or analyst became a challenge and, as such, started to dominate in some organisations. This could be attributed to the similarity and contrasting nature of the two concepts. On similarity, both concepts focus on the business domain of an organisation. Business architecture is used to define the business design and strategy, process governance and the management of artefacts in an organisation. Pereira and Sousa (2004) suggest that the business architecture aids in defining the business strategies, processes and functional requirements. This means that some of the activities of business architecture are to model business process and define scope and boundaries of the organisational events. Also, it enacts processes and other architectural elements, including overseeing the allocation of resources in an environment. McKeen and Smith (2008) argue that it is necessary for business architects to understand the overall strategy, goals and business models in extracting the requirements for the purposes of the integration of skills (people), processes and technologies that are needed to reproduce a comprehensive architectural plan for the enterprise.

The concepts of business analysis and business architecture do have individual and complementary significant contributions to the organisation that employs them. This is because each of the concepts has unique contributions to an organisation. However, there are challenges in how the concepts are complementarily employed. The challenges have persisted for many years. Versteeg and Bouwman (2006) argue that business architecture receives the least attention, as compared to the significant role it plays in translating the business strategy of the IT domain of the organisation. Some of the interactions, confusions and conflicts that happen between the concepts of business analysis and business architecture could be of conscious or unconscious nature by people who are directly responsible for the processes and activities. This is due to the subjective interpretation and understanding that people have about their roles, responsibilities and functions, in accordance with their personal or organisational interest.

In the context of this chapter, business analysis and business architecture are interchangeably referred to as subject, and business analyst and business architect as object, respectively. Both subject and object can hardly be separated in practice. Hence, the terms subject and object are often interchangeably used by practitioners, including the academia. I have therefore followed suit in this chapter. Also, there are many similarities between the two concepts which make it difficult to distinguish one from the other, from both theoretical and practical perspectives. This chapter answers the question that is often posed: "what is the distinction between business analysis and business architecture?" Whether business analysis and business architecture are roles or titles is also examined. The chapter therefore focuses on clarifying the confusion and overlapping factors between the two concepts when they are employed complementarily in an organisation.

The chapter is sequentially divided into four main sections. It began with discussion that covers the concepts of business analysis business architecture. Next, the problem which the chapter addresses is explained, and the distinction between the two concepts is discussed. This includes the influencing factors and the implications. Finally, the chapter is briefly summarised.

Business Analysis and Business Architecture

Many organisations are constantly challenged with change caused by various factors, such as processes, supplies, events, partnership and customers' connectivity in their business environments. These factors often manifest from lack of understanding or interpretation based on personal rather than organisational interest. Also, many of the employees do not have a clear view of the artefacts that constitute the challenging factors. Kurpjuweit and Winter (2009) emphasise the fact that an understanding of all relevant business-related artefacts, as well as their relationships, is a prerequisite for managing changes that constantly occur within an environment. The relationship between the business and IT units is critical for the benefit of the organisation's interest since the alignment enables and supports achieving organisational goals. However, alignment is increasingly complex, in that it consists of factors that operate in a heterogeneous manner, such as people-to-people, artefacts-to-artefacts and people-to-artefacts. Hendrickx et al. (2011) argue that the developments and rapid changes within IT and business environments make it necessary to have a role that has a comprehensive view and understanding of the implications of both concepts.

From the IT perspective, business analysis focuses on the requirements that originate from business processes, activities and events, including the liaison between the business and IT units. Evans (2004) describes business analysis as the process of specifying business requirements, followed by the specification of the technical requirements and designs. Requirements gathering and their analysis are efforts engineered towards finding business solutions for competitiveness and sustainability. Business improvement is procedurally carried out through analysis to detect both negative and positive potentialities, such as deficiency, strengths and benefits, and to determine possible improvements for organisational growth. The analysis covers processes, activities and events twofold: business and IT. Thus, an analyst is considered to be an expert who studies data or facts to detect gaps and problems in order to recommend or propose solutions. A business analyst is considered to be a problem solver, as argued by Blais (2011). However, business analysis is not the only considerable approach for business designs, processes, activities and events. Some organisations complementarily employ the concept of business architecture in their operations and strategic intents.

Even though so much has been said about business architecture in the context of enterprise architecture (EA), we echo it one more time that business architecture is a domain of EA. Business architecture focuses on processes, activities, events and the connectivity of designs in an organisation (Gøtze, 2013). The concept is used to define, design and guide the development of business strategies, process governance and integrations. The requirements are extracted from the organisation's business events and functional requirements. Based on the scope of the business architecture, its roles are critically important to the organisation that deploys it to achieve its goals and objectives.

The primary role of business architecture is to provide a definition to gain a holistic view and an understanding of the business direction and strategies within context and relevance. This includes communication with various stakeholders through the structures of the organisation. According to Aier and Winter (2009), business architecture is designed to achieve organisational process effectiveness and process efficiency, over time. Thus, it is a prerequisite for the architects to have a deep understanding of the organisation's business strategy. This is to be able to explain the rationale behind the architectural principles and standards.

There are distinctions; similarities and differences between the concepts of business analysis and business architecture. For example, while the business analysis models organisational processes, sometimes there is little or no consideration for the underlying technologies and applications. Business architecture has the holistic view of the entire organisation and manages the relationships between strategies, technologies and operations. This chapter seeks to clarify the similarities and distinctions between business analysis and business architecture in an environment.

Understanding the Problem

The chapter poses two fundamental questions: (1) what is the distinction between the concepts of business analysis and business architecture? (2) Are the concepts roles or titles? In an attempt to answer the questions, the factors that induced the questions are first established. These are definition, scope, focus and function. These factors are crucial in that they influenced the concept of business analysis and business architecture to be practised and experienced. Table 5.1 describes each

Table 5.1 Data Collection

Area	Description
Definition	Definition concisely explains the meaning related to object or subject within context. It is used to clarify and give precise meaning to terms. This helps to unambiguously convey thoughts and ideas in a given circumstance. Both the Oxford and Collins English dictionaries define 'definition' the same way. In Oxford, it states, "an explanation of the meaning of a word or phrase", while in Collins: "a formal and concise statement of the meaning of a word, phrase, etc." Thus, the definitions of both business analysis and business architecture assist to clarify the distinctions and their overlapping nature. Also, the definition guides the essentiality and understanding of the concept and provides the platform for managing its activities within an environment.
Scope	Scope simply refers to the work that has to be done in order to achieve goals and objectives. It specifies the boundaries of the entire work to be completed. It includes requirements and involves process. The scope clarifies the timeline, outcome, as well as delineation. It is the centre of interest that provides the management with a guide of activities.
Focus	Focus refers to a centre of activity, event or attraction. It is a Latin word *for* "hearth, fireplace". It gives stakeholders the ability to be attentive and time conscious in a particular activity. Focus is a cause to converge on a specific point, a metaphor that describes "fireplace", which can be seen as a centre of activity. It is intended to enable organisations to see their goals, objectives and requirements clearly.
Function	Function refers to an executable set of tasks in an environment. It is used to express the performance of objects or subjects. It draws on a relationship between inputs and outputs, including rules, procedures and processes. This means that functions can be ubiquitous and are essential for the relationships between artefacts and variables.

of the factors in the context of this chapter and book. The description is idiosyncratic, in that it provides a holistic cover of the factors. The examples of references of studies in the third column are not referenced in the table.

The concepts, business analysis and business architecture, are defined in certain ways, within the scope that is of relevance and context, to ensure a specific strategic and operational focus that clarifies the functions that have to be executed for an organisation's competitiveness and sustainability. This helps to provide answers to the questions: (1) what are the distinctions and similarities between business analysis and business architecture in practice? (2) What are some of the implications or impacts of the overlapping nature of the concepts to an organisation?

Evidently, as shown in column 3 of Table 5.1, many studies have been conducted separately about the concepts of business analysis and business architecture, venturing on the aspects of definition, scope, focus and functionalities. Different meanings are drawn from the studies, often based on the interpretivist approach because it allows multiple realities and insights. In this way, there is a greater possibility of gaining a better understanding of reality about the factors, definition, scope, focus and functionality.

Reality, and an understanding and knowledge about a factor or subject, are social products that cannot be understood independently of those who construct and make sense of them (Howcroft & Trauth, 2005). The understanding refers to the researcher's subjective view as influenced by his or her experience of the subject that is being studied. The interpretive technique is therefore recognised for its value in providing contextual depth (Bryant, 2011). Thus, the interpretive approach was employed to gain a better understanding of the distinction between business analysis and business architecture by examining their definitions, focuses and functionalities in a subjective manner. The subjective reasoning was informed by the author's tacit and explicit knowledge acquired over many years of practice, as well as academic rigour.

Distinction between Business Analysis and Business Architecture

Over the years, the concepts of business analysis and business architecture have been loosely and interchangeably used, particularly from an IT perspective. This has had a confusing impact on how the concepts are employed and practised in some organisations. The confusion reflects in the definition and design of business processes, process integration and solution management, which manifest in the outcome of organisations' events and activities. Also, it shapes many individuals' career through the training and education that they undertake. This section sequentially covers the influencing factors, differentiating factors and the factors that manifest into implications.

Influencing Factors

The confusion between the concepts of business analysis and business architecture in an organisation is attributed to many different factors, of both conscious and unconscious natures. Consciously, individuals and groups, academics and

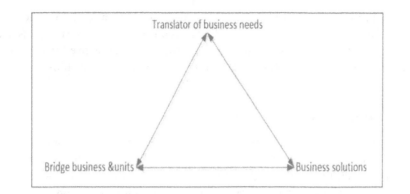

Figure 5.1   Factors of business analysis and business architecture.

non-academics interpret and communicate the definitions and functions of the concepts based on their interest, which is often influenced by their roles and responsibilities in the organisations. Similarly, the unconscious action is often based on how the concepts are understood, making it difficult to draw a distinction between the thin lines that exist in their similarities.

There are three main critical factors that draw the two concepts close to each other. The factors are (1) the translation of business needs; (2) a bridge between business and IT units; and (3) the development of business solutions. These three factors are interlinked as shown in Figure 5.1. For example, it is difficult or near impossible to bridge the gap between the business and IT units without an understanding, and impossible to translate their individual requirements. Similarly, the development of business solutions is based on the understanding of business needs and the ability to detect gaps in both the current and future states.

Translates Business Needs

The translation of business needs is critical to organisations. One of the primary roles of both business analysis and business architecture is to translate and interpret the business requirements towards providing solutions for the organisation. This includes the translation of business needs and desires into a technical specification. This is done *vice versa* in order to ascertain the fulfilment of organisational objectives. Translation begins by identifying the strategic direction and vision of an organisation, based on which an analysis is conducted. From the analysis, business requirements and needs are translated into requirements for a design, which ultimately produces IT solutions.

The analysis and translations are carried out through various techniques and modelling. According to Deutscher and Felden (2010), the business analyst and the business architect undertake the tasks of business processes and activities with the aim of finding the coherent understanding that is needed in order to deliver business solutions for competitiveness. For some individuals and organisations, the thin lines between the concepts make the confusion even more prevailing, as managers and other practitioners continue to have their own subjective interpretations of both business analysis and business architecture roles in various projects.

Bridge Business and IT

Evidently, there are gaps between the business needs and IT solutions in many organisations. Hence, there is the need to bridge those gaps in order to foster operational efficiency and effectiveness to improve sustainability and competitiveness. Both the business analyst and the business architect are considered to be the 'middle entity' between the business and the IT units of an organisation. As such, it is critical for them to have a deep understanding of the business and IT strategies. According to Clare (2011), in addition to being business oriented, business analysts and business architects are required to have a good understanding of IT solutions.

The role of the analyst and architects is crucial in bridging the gap between the business and the IT units, in pursuit of the common goals and objectives of the organisation. In Hendrickx's (2015) study, the positions of the business analyst and the business architect are responsible and have the capability to bridge the aligned business and IT strategies in an organisation. Business analysis and business architecture assess and analyse IT strategic supports and enablement for business strategy. The current state is analysed to detect deficiencies and gaps, based on which the future state of the processes and activities are formulated for consideration.

Develop Business Solutions

Another major similarity between business analysis and business architecture is their roles and responsibilities, which includes to develop business solutions for an organisation. Organisational solutions can be a business process, a business model, a system to be developed or a combination of them. System in this context does not mean computer system, but rather business system, which entails and encapsulates input and output. This can however overlap, as both concepts are mandated with business solutions.

The development of business solution is derived from a collaborative approach that entails internal and external factors that focus on improving strengths and addressing weaknesses and constraints for competitiveness. Thus, the business analyst develops the business requirements while the business architect develops the architectural requirements. Both business requirements and architectural requirements focus on non-functional requirements and eliminating constraints in an organisation.

Differentiating Factors

There are similarities and differences at the same time, between the concepts. As much as there are similarities and overlaps, conflicts and confusions will continue to exist between the concepts. That does not ignore the fact that there are differences between business analysis and business architecture.

Exploring the differences will enhance an understanding of the roles of each of the concepts. This will alleviate and clarify the confusion between the concepts to academics, researchers and practitioners. There are two main differences between the business analysis and business architecture concepts: (1) user requirements driven; and (2) initiator of business processes and logics. As shown in Figure 5.2, both differentiating factors also contribute to the similarities, but from different perspectives. The differences are later expanded as shown in Figure 5.3

Business Analyst: User Requirements Driven

The main focus of the business analyst is to collect, manage and communicate business requirements within the organisation. A business analyst is therefore more concerned with understanding business requirements through interaction with a variety of stakeholders, mostly users (Wever & Maiden, 2011; Schreiner, 2007; Wetzstein et al., 2007). Arguably, stakeholders do not always know how to explain or articulate their needs within contents and contexts for the IT specialists to gain a good understanding of their requirements. This has an impact on the IT solutions that are selected or developed and implemented in an organisation.

The business analyst therefore translates the needs from a natural and basic language as presented by the users into requirements for the technical people to process

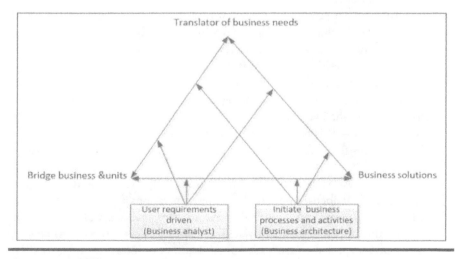

Figure 5.2   Differentiating factors.

further. According to Kaisler, Armour and Valivullah (2005), various stakeholders do require different perspectives which often reflect their needs within the IT solutions. Thus, the business analyst acts as an interactive channel among the three communities, which are the business architect, users and IT in the organisations (Vashist, McKay & Marshall, 2014). The analyst carries out an analysis to assess the connection between the requirements and the IT solutions that are developed or selected by IT architects.

Business Architect: Initiate Business Processes and Activities

The business architect initiates projects by developing solutions for strategic purposes on behalf of the organisation. This entails the design and development of the business architecture, based on the organisation's vision and analysis of the current state ("AS IS") that is against the future state ("TO BE") (Kaisler et al., 2005). The business architecture calls for the infusion of the overall strategy and directions into the design and operation of an enterprise (Hendrickx et al., 2011). The architect operates at a strategic level and focuses more on business continuity. The business architect also ensures that business needs align with the vision or strategic mission. Significantly, the architect ensures that business needs and requirements are clearly understood for the selection and implementation of appropriate IT solutions.

In organisations, the business analyst carries out activities that are based on architectural solutions. Hendrickx et al. (2011) argued that business analysts add value at the solution level, and that the organisational structure and architectural levels are out of their reach. This is attributable to the differentiation associated with the roles. Nevertheless, the analyst does contribute to the architectural solutions. The analyst's activities and tasks are focused on the operationalisation of the architectural solutions.

The distinction between the concepts of business analysis and business architecture, as revealed in this chapter, manifests from their roles and responsibilities. Another significant aspect is the implications that the concepts linearly have on each other. This is reflective from two main perspectives: (1) service domain; and (2) functional domain, as illustrated in Figure 5.3. The remainder of this section should be read with the figure to gain better clarification and understanding of the distinction between the two concepts.

Service domain – This is categorised into operational and strategic levels. The categorisation helps to distinguish the two concepts in an organisational context:

i. Business analysis is the role in which responsibilities are exercised at an operational level. It focuses on the day-to-day operations for effectiveness and efficiency purposes. This is intended to enhance processes and activities for the sustainability and competitiveness of an organisation. A business analyst is therefore expected to analyse an organisation's processes in order to align them with the systems that are in operation at the time. According to Dawson

(2000), organisational strategy defines its strategic positioning and direction, which distinguishes it from its competitors and contributes to growth.

ii. Business architecture is considered to be strategic. It focuses on the future as business changes. According to Iyamu (2011), the business architecture expresses the organisation's key business strategies and tactics, and that typically consists of the current and future state models of business functions, processes and information value chain. It is dependent on the organisation's vision and requirements.

Functional domain – This domain is further classified into two categories of ownership and contributor. This is to specifically distinguish their roles and responsibilities. As shown in Figure 5.3, the dotted and solid lines connecting the entities represent the contributor and ownership, respectively, as they point to the different functions.

i. Contributor – This means that the primary role and responsibility of a stakeholder is to contribute to the organisational processes and activities towards

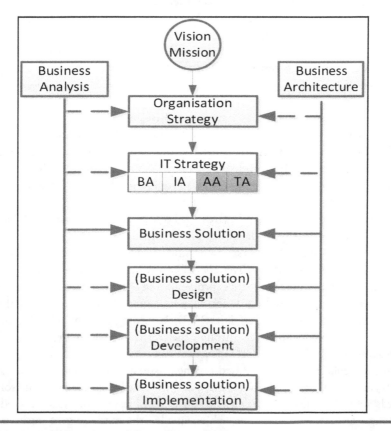

Figure 5.3 Solution ownership and contributor.

sustainability and competitiveness. The contributions are therefore driven by the users' requirements on both periodic and *ad hoc* bases.

ii. Ownership – Unlike the "Contributor", it is not only responsible, but it is also accountable for the activities that are involved in the processes. It therefore takes ownership of any activities that they are involved in and exerts their leadership in the process. Based on the leadership bestowed on the role, the owner has the mandate to initiate activities and processes within the organisation.

Organisational strategy – The organisational strategy is developed at the senior management and executive levels. As a result, neither the business analysis nor the business architecture is able to take ownership of the organisational strategy activity. However, both business analysis and business architecture contribute directly or indirectly, depending on the size of the organisation, to the organisational strategy. In smaller organisations, structures are a bit flat, with a reduced number of levels in the hierarchy. As a result, business analysts as well as business architects could be more involved at the organisational level rather than divisional levels. The organisational level refers to the holistic organisational activities, while the divisional level refers to the departmental units, such as marketing, human resources and IT.

IT strategy – Similar to the organisational strategy, both business analysis and business architecture are contributors to the IT strategy. Their contributions are carried out directly. This could be related to the fact that they are categorised as one of the primary and focal actors of the IT division. In many large organisations, as viewed by Iyamu (2011), as well as Ross, Weill and Robertson (2006), EA is the main contributor of value to the IT strategy. Both business analysis and business architecture focus more on the business and information domains of the EA. Other domains of the EA include application and technical architectures. In smaller organisations, the business analysis unit often takes the centre stage in the formulation of the IT strategy.

Business solution – The objectives of both business analysis and business architecture are primarily to deliver solutions that are derived from the business requirements. As such, they take ownership through their accountability and responsibility to initiate and deliver the solutions for the organisation. The business analyst understands the business problems and opportunities from the context of their requirements, based on which they recommend solutions that enable the organisation to achieve its goals (Clare, 2011). According to Iyamu (2013), the business architect arrives at solutions through the translation of the organisation's key business strategies.

Business solution design – Based on the business solutions that are obtained, both business analysts and business architects partake in the design of the solution towards achieving the organisation's objectives. Business architects are tasked with the design of high-level solutions, which involve the modelling of business processes and activities in the organisations. According to Iyer and Gottlieb (2004), the architecture design specifies how the overall functionality of business solutions is decomposed into individual functional components, and the way in which these components are to interact, in order to provide the overall functionalities. The business analyst and business architecture are the main actors in the design of solutions; therefore, they take ownership of the activities.

Business solution development – A team of different experts is involved in the development of business solutions in organisations. Both the business analyst and the business architect are co-owners of the development of business solutions. This is iterated in Johri (2010), where it is stated that the business analyst is accountable for the alignment between organisational needs and solutions development. The author further argues that once a design for solution has been agreed upon, the business analyst assists the technology team with a detailed design work, including splitting a large project into phases, reviewing technical design deliverables and building usability into application software.

Business solution implementation – Development is not the end of the means to actualising business solutions (Iyamu, 2013). If organisational mission and vision are to be achieved, implementation is critical to solutions. Implementation is about practising conceptual ideas, processes and activities. In many organisations, implementation is a challenging process likely to overrun time and financial budgets that are duly allocated. This could be attributed to the transitioning of phases from theoretical to practical. During the implementation of business solutions, both business analysts and business architects are contributors. The application and technology specialists are often tasked with implementation. As a result, they take ownership of the activities that are involved. However, they are supported by the business analysis and business architecture in the process, primarily to provide an interpretation through guidelines and governance.

Implications of the Distinction

As has been revealed in this chapter, it is necessary to establish and understand the distinction between business analysis and business architecture. However, there are implications in doing so, which are (1) alignment; (2) roles and responsibilities; and (3) organisational structure. These three components are interconnected and difficult to separate.

Alignment

The coexistence of both the business analysis and business architecture units can be a strategic and valuable asset but can also pose challenges to the organisation. Alignment between the concepts in an organisation is critical in order to streamline the challenges of coexistence. This has an impact on productivity. Also, alignment is significant due to the similarities that the concepts share, as well as the differences between them. This makes complementarity of both concepts even more critical within an organisation. The main implication of having both units in an organisational structure comes from how to manage the thin line between the concepts.

For effectiveness and efficiency, the business analysis and architecture need to align so as to collaborate, complement and support each other in achieving the goals and objectives of the organisation. However, within the collaborative environment, conflicts are bound to occur. Conflicts such as the ownership of ideas and processes between the business analysis and business architecture units limit communications and innovation among the team members. Conflicts about ownership manifest from organisational politics that is often inevitable. Architects must be able to resolve organisational politics and work with various stakeholders to influence and ensure the successful implementation of the architecture in the organisation. For this to happen, roles and responsibilities must be well understood and maintained for the benefit of the organisation.

Roles and Responsibilities

Based on the principles of division of labour, employees are assigned roles and responsibilities. Robbins et al. (2013) stated that division of labour describes the degree to which activities are subdivided in organisations. There is a common belief in many quarters that work can be performed more efficiently if employees are allowed to specialise in specific areas or disciplines. Yarnall (2007) highlights a critical point that, in order to achieve an organisation's strategies, roles and responsibilities of the employees must be clarified. This promotes focus and improves productivity.

However, the coexistence of both the business analysis and business architecture units in the same organisation is a serious challenge, particularly in the allocation of roles and responsibilities. This is primarily because of their overlapping nature. As a result, the coexistence invokes the power to control and dominate one another by the personnel who are involved in the activities of business analysis and business architecture. This challenge has the potential to affect the quest of achieving the organisational goals. According to Tang, Han and Chen (2004), the IT architect could take on the roles of the business analyst. This sort of argument propels a sense of superiority, manifesting from power to control, hence an organisational structure is critically required to define and clarify the roles and responsibilities of individuals and groups in the organisation.

Organisational Structure

Organisational structure provides the framework for order and control through which activities can be planned, organised, directed, managed and monitored (Craig & Campbell, 2012). Organisational structure is impacted by various factors, such as employees, size and functions (Robbins et al., 2013). The roles and responsibilities of employees, including business analysts and business architects, are thus determined by the size, functions and focus of the organisation. For example, the employees interpret the functions of the organisation in their own subjective ways or perspectives and determine how to structure the environment. Hence, the organisational structure is deterministic of the power to control.

The coexistence of both the business analysis and business architecture units has an impact on how the organisation is structured, and allocates workload as well as responsibilities to the units, teams and individuals. Due to the nature of business analysis and business architecture, as established in this chapter, the distinction between their roles and responsibilities remains a challenge. Also, some organisations are often confused on whether the business analysis and business architecture units should be in the IT division or better placed in the business division. There are some justifications on why both business analysis and business architecture need to be situated in the business rather than the IT division. According to Vashist et al., (2014), in some organisational structures, the business analyst resides in the IT division. It is even more challenging in smaller organisations that do not have the luxury of hierarchy and wide structures. Smaller organisations often merge multiple IT functions in a single job title (Evans, 2004). As long as the concepts of business analysis and business architecture are employed by the same organisations, it will continue to have an impact on the structure.

Summary

It is clear that the concepts of business analysis and business architecture are different. However, the concepts do have many things in common from the IT perspective. Even though the differences are not many, they are vital. The confusions and challenges that they do create and cause can be detrimental in their influences and impacts on organisational performance. Also, the confusion can have a significant impact on individuals' careers, in that some specialists struggle and are challenged on the decision to specialise in specific areas. This challenge is often caused by a lack of understanding of the roles and boundaries of each of the concepts. This chapter clarifies that confusion by drawing the distinction between business analysis and business architecture.

Other primary contributions of this chapter come from its clarification of the confusion regarding the lack of distinction between business analysis and business architecture in both the academic and business domains. Over the years, the roles and responsibilities of both concepts have been loosely referred to and interchangeably used in many quarters, including large enterprises. Another contribution of this chapter is that it will help managers to gain a better understanding of the distinct roles and responsibilities so that both the business analysis and business architecture units can coexist in the same organisation for common goals and objectives. It therefore would help to reduce the negative impacts that the confusion and challenges practically and unconsciously impose on the processes and activities in the organisations that employ both concepts in parallel.

Also, and very importantly, the clarification of the distinction of the concepts by this chapter raises a fundamental question of whether business analysis and business architecture are roles or titles. This could be for further discourse or study.

References

Aier, I. S., & Winter, R. (2009). Virtual decoupling for IT/business alignment – Conceptual foundations, architecture design and implementation example. *Business & Information Systems Engineering, 1*(2), 150–163.

Blais, S. P. (2011). *Business analysis: Best Practices for success.* Hoboken, NJ, USA: John Wiley & Sons.

Bryant, A. (2011). *Leading issues in business research methods. Leading issues in business research methods, volume 1.* United Kingdom: Academic publishing international limited, Reading RG4 9AY, United Kingdom.

Clare, R. (2011). *The new business analyst: Managing business analysts.* International Institute of Business Analysis (IIBA). www.iiba.org.

Craig, T., & Campbell, D. (2012). *Organisations and the business environment.* (2nd ed.). Oxford: UK: Elsevier Butterworth-Heinemann.

Dawson, R. (2000). Knowledge capabilities as the focus of organisational development and strategy. *Journal of Knowledge Management, 4*(4), 320–327.

Deutscher, J. H., & Felden, C. (2010). Concept for Implementation of Cost Effective Information Technology Service Management (ITSM) in Organizations. In *Proceedings of Network Operations and Management Symposium Workshops (NOMS wksps).* (pp. 167–168). 19-23 April, Osaka, Japan. IEEE.

Evans, N. (2004). The need for an analysis body of knowledge (ABOK)-will the real analyst please stand up. *Issues in Informing Science & Information Technology, 1,* 313–330.

Gøtze, J. (2013). The Changing Role of the Enterprise Architect. In *Proceedings International Enterprise Distributed Object Computing Conference Workshops.* (pp. 319–326). 9-13 September, Vancouver, BC, Canada. IEEE.

Hendrickx, H. H. (2015). Business architect: A critical role in enterprise transformation. *Journal of Enterprise Transformation, 5*(1), 1–29.

Hendrickx, H. H., Daley, S. K., Mahakena, M., & von Rosing, M. (2011). Defining the business architecture profession. In *Proceedings of the 13th Conference on Commerce and Enterprise Computing.* (pp. 325–332). 5-7 September, Luxembourg-Kirchberg, Luxembourg. IEEE.

Howcroft, D., & Trauth, E. M. (eds). (2005). *Handbook of critical information systems research: Theory and application.* Cheltenham, UK: Edward Elgar Publishing.

Iyamu, T. (2011). Enterprise Architecture as Information Technology Strategy. In *Proceedings of the 13th Conference on Commerce and Enterprise Computing (CEC)* (pp. 82–88). 5-7 September, *Luxembourg-Kirchberg, Luxembourg.* IEEE.

Iyamu, T. (2013). *Enterprise architecture: From concept to practise.* Australia: Heidelberg Press.

Iyer, B., & Gottlieb, R. (2004). The four-domain architecture: An approach to support enterprise architecture design. *IBM Systems Journal, 43*(3), 587–597.

Johri, A. (2010). *Business analysis*. New Delhi, India: Himalaya Publishing House Ltd.

Kaisler, S. H., Armour, F., & Valivullah, M. (2005). Enterprise Architecting: Critical Problems. In *Proceedings of 38th Annual Hawaii International Conference*. (pp. 224b–224b). 3-6 January, Big Island, Hawaii. IEEE.

Kurpjuweit, S., & Winter, R. (2009). March. Concern-oriented Business Architecture Engineering. In *Proceedings of the ACM Symposium on Applied Computing*. (pp. 265–272). 8-12 March, Honolulu, Hawaii. ACM Press.

McKeen, J. D., & Smith, H. A. (2008). Developments in practice XXIX: The emerging role of the enterprise business architect. *Communications of the Association for Information Systems, 22*(1), 261–271.

Pereira, C. M., & Sousa, P. (2004). A Method to Define an Enterprise Architecture Using the Zachman Framework. In *Proceedings of the 2004 ACM Symposium on Applied Computing*. (pp. 1366–1371). 14-17 March, Nicosia, Cyprus. ACM Press.

Queiroz, M., Tallon, P. P., Coltman, T., Sharma, R., & Reynolds, P. (2020). Aligning the IT portfolio with business strategy: Evidence for complementarity of corporate and business unit alignment. *The Journal of Strategic Information Systems, 29*(3), 101623.

Robbins, S., Judge, T. A., Millett, B., & Boyle, M. (2013). *Organisational behaviour*. Pearson Higher Education AU.

Ross, J., Weill, P., & Robertson, D. (2006). *Enterprise architecture as strategy: Creating a foundation for business execution*. Harvard Business Press.

Schreiner, K. (2007). The bridge and beyond: Business analysis extends its role and reach. *IT Professional, 9*(6), 50–54.

Silvius, A. G. (2009). Business and IT alignment. *International Conference on Information Management and Engineering (ICIME '09)*. 3-5 April 2009, Kuala Lumpur, Malaysia.

Tang, A., Han, J., & Chen, P. (2004). A Comparative Analysis of Architecture Frameworks. In *Proceedings of 11th Asia-Pacific Conference on Software Engineering* (pp. 640–647). 30 November-3 December, Busan, South Korea. IEEE.

Vashist, R., McKay, J., & Marshall, P. (2014). Learning at the Boundaries: An Action Agenda for Business Analysts. In *Proceedings 47th Hawaii International Conference on System Sciences (HICSS)* (pp. 4536–4545). 6-9 January, Waikoloa, Hawaii. IEEE.

Versteeg, G., & Bouwman, H. (2006). Business architecture: A new paradigm to relate business strategy to ICT. *Information Systems Frontiers, 8*(2), 91–102.

Wetzstein, B., Ma, Z., Filipowska, A., Kaczmarek, M., Bhiri, S., Losada, S., Lopez-Cobo, J. M., & Cicurel, L. (2007). Semantic Business Process Management: A Lifecycle Based Requirements Analysis. In *Proceedings of the Workshop on Semantic Business Process and Product Lifecycle Management (SBPM)*. (Vol. 251, pp. 1–11). 3-7 June, Innsbruck, Austria.

Wever, A., & Maiden, N. (2011). What Are the Day-to-day Factors that Are Preventing Business Analysts from Effective Business Analysis? In *Proceedings of 19th International Conference on Requirements Engineering (RE)*. (pp. 293–298). 29 August-2 September, Trento, Italy. IEEE.

Yarnall, J. (2007). *Strategic career management*. London: Routledge.

Zhang, M., Chen, H., & Lyytinen, K. (2020). Validating the coevolutionary principles of business and IS alignment via agent-based modelling. *European Journal of Information Systems*, 1–16.

Chapter 6

Theorising Enterprise Architecture into Practice

Introduction

Enterprise architecture (EA) is a concept that is used to organise the logics of business processes and IT artefacts in order to reflect on the integration and standardisation of the operating models of an organisation (Ross, Weill & Robertson, 2006). EA is comprised of architectural domains which cover the technical and non-technical activities of an organisation. The domains are traditionally business and information, application and technology (Iyamu, 2015; Wang & Zhou, 2009). The concept of EA has been debated for over three decades, since John Zachman's work of 1987 (Zachman, 1987) was first published. Thereafter, many EA frameworks (EAFs) have been developed and practised (Urbaczewski & Mrdalj, 2006). However, only a few of the frameworks, such as Gartner Inc., Federal Enterprise Architecture (FEA) and The Open Group Architecture Framework (TOGAF), remain common and available (Simon, Fischbach & Schoder, 2014).

Over the years, practitioners and consultants have registered their interest to develop and evolve the concept, but more from a theoretical front than actual practice. Academics have also shown interest through their trade of research and teaching. In addition, many individuals and groups in various organisations, including government institutions and agencies of different countries, continue to show interest in EA (Lnenicka & Komarkova, 2019; Tamm et al., 2011), such as Norway (Ajer & Olsen, 2020); Malaysia (Jayakrishnan, Mohamad & Abdullah, 2018); Namibia (Shaanika & Iyamu, 2018); India (Kaushik & Raman, 2015); and China (Zheng & Zheng, 2013). Despite the increasing interest, the rate at which organisations adopt or subscribe to the concept is slow and limited in practice. The

DOI: 10.1201/9781003268420-6

values and benefits of EA have therefore been more theoretically explained rather than experienced from a practice viewpoint. Foorthuis et al. (2016) argued that the practices and benefits of EA have not been extensively investigated from the perspective of empirical research.

Through practice, EA contributes to an environment from both technical and non-technical perspectives (Fritscher & Pigneur, 2015). Wang, Zhou and Jiang (2008) suggest that EA enables an alignment between IT and business strategies, through which IT vision and values are communicated and guidelines are provided for IT investments in an organisation. The alignment helps to achieve and increase business value. Over the years, practitioners and academia have made substantial contributions to the evolvement and advancement of the concept from practice and theory viewpoints. Many academic studies focus on how EA is developed and implemented, exploring and examining the interaction that happens among the actors that are involved in the concept (Niemi & Pekkola, 2017; Abraham, Aier & Winter, 2015). Some of the studies, such as Iyamu (2015), examine the factors that influence the institutionalisation of EA in an organisation. Based on this premise, EA has been widely thought through and well-researched. Yet, the concept falls short when it comes to implementation and practice (Iyamu, 2019; Franke, Cohen & Sigholm, 2018).

From the practice point of view, EA is an applied discipline in the field of IT (Azevedo et al., 2015). Within this context, academic research has been carried out towards advancing and evolving the discipline (Vargas et al., 2016; Närman, Buschle & Ekstedt, 2014). However, this has been done mainly as basic (theoretical) rather than applied (practical) research, which limits the knowledge that is required to apply the concept in the field of IT. The knowledge that is gained from theory is considered limited, in that there is little frame of reference from the practice point of view. Iyamu (2019) attributed this to various challenges, such as organisational structure, technology, social context and process associated with EA, which make the concept complex. Thus, practitioners' knowledge to act in their quest to add value to an organisation is also limited.

The challenges influencing the practice have been traced to the root, which increasingly makes the factors the focal points in the development and implementation of the phenomenon in the last decade. Tamm et al. (2011) argued that majority of the existing studies tend to focus on two main aspects: how EA could be used for planning, and to represent organisational artefacts. EA is used in organisations for both current and future states to create, communicate and improve key requirements, principles and models, for sustainability and competitiveness (Safari, Faraji & Majidian, 2016). Thus, Hiekkanen et al. (2013) emphasised how EA is used as a strategic tool to holistically address the gap between the business and IT units in many organisations. Some abstractions from existing frameworks suggest its practicality and applicability, which has often been theorised by academia and practitioners themselves. This makes it a challenge because its central function is to contribute effectively to an organisation's practices.

Examining and understanding the EA concept is intended to bring meaning to its theoretical premise and philosophical assumptions from a sociotechnical context and viewpoint, by using empirical evidence (Bradley et al., 2012). This includes an analysis of the frameworks, organisational context and theoretical perspectives (Franke, Johnson & König, 2014). Thus, without an understanding of such contexts and perspectives, the meaning of the concept of EA will slowly decline in practice.

The rationale for theorising EA rather than practice it can also be attributed to limited skilled personnel (Hiekkanen et al., 2013). Shortage of skilled personnel becomes more challenging in that not all the actors involved in the development stage participate in the implementation of EA in an organisation (Iyamu, 2015). This sort of challenge creates disjoints in practice, and this has been observed over the last two decades (Glissmann & Sanz, 2011). The shortage of skills can be attributed to a limited supply from academic institutions, caused by a recursive response of demand by the same organisations that require the skill set, as discussed in Chapter 12 of this book.

Thus, the question is, what are the implications of paying more attention to the theoretical (theorising) rather than the practical aspect of EA? Based on this question, two objectives were formulated: (1) to examine the implications of theorising the concept of EA; and (2) to gain an understanding of how the implications are interconnected and interrelated between the theory and practice of EA in organisations. The objectives form the basis of this chapter, structured into four main sections. It began with a review of literature. Next, are a holistic and detailed discussion on theorising EA, and the process of theorising EA, respectively. A model and the implications for theorising EA are presented and discussed. At the end, the chapter is summarised.

Review of Literature

The review of existing work and literature is covered in two parts; EA and frameworks. This is to draw more attention to how individual frameworks contribute to making EA more theoretical rather than practical, as organisations make efforts to employ the service of the concept.

Enterprise Architecture

EA is regarded as an important and strategic tool for the enablement, support, governance and management of processes and activities in many organisations (Al-Kharusi, Miskon & Bahari, 2018; Simon et al., 2014). Also, EA is viewed as the glue that holds the business and IT units together towards the reshaping and competitiveness of an organisation (Fritscher & Pigneur, 2015). There seems to be an ongoing debate on whether EA brings both business and technology together in a better and more effective working relationship in achieving an organisation's goals and objectives (Niemi & Pekkola, 2017; Safari et al., 2016). According to Ross et al. (2006: 41), "EA is the organizing logic for business processes and IT artefacts, to reflect the integration and standardization requirements of an organization's operating model".

EA comprises architectural domains from both technical and non-technical perspectives, which Wang and Zhou (2009) divided into four, namely; business, information, application and technology. The four domains were discussed in detail by Iyamu (2015) from the angles of theorisation and practice. Each of the domains has its deliverables through which they interconnect and interact with each other (Niemi & Pekkola, 2017). Usually, the development and implementation of EA follows a particular methodology or framework as adopted by the organisation. Mohamed et al. (2012) explain how the frameworks are considered as a conceptual structure of what it should contain and how to create the components. Frameworks provide the tools and guidance required by an organisation in order to develop and manage EA projects. Song and Song (2010) elucidate the usefulness of frameworks, give a comprehensive description of the relevant elements of EA, and provide a principle structure and classification schema that can be used as terms of reference for architecture development, but only from a theory viewpoint. From theoretical standpoints, many studies continue to explain how and why EA should be deployed, and not how it has been practised (Vallerand, Lapalme & Moïse, 2017).

Also, EAFs represent the structure that can be used to model an enterprise's business and IT processes and activities (Rouhani et al., 2015). Several EAFs, such as the Zachman Framework, TOGAF and the Gartner Enterprise Architecture Method do exist (Lapkin et al., 2008). However, not all the available frameworks can be easily applied in many organisations (Urbaczewski & Mrdalj, 2006). According to Lapkin (2005: 4), "A good framework will define the components of enterprise architecture and the relationships between them, providing the architecture team and the organisation a set of shared semantics and concepts with which to describe their architecture".

The suitability and applicability of EAFs are relatively different from one organisation to another, even though the purpose of the frameworks remain unchanged (Urbaczewski & Mrdalj, 2006). This could be attributed to many factors, such as an understanding of EA within an organisation's context and EAFs' own weaknesses and strengths. Tang, Han and Chen (2004) explain that the differences between EAFs are evident in the activities and outcomes produced through the frameworks. According to Song and Song (2010: 871), "However, without proper tuning, EA may not be as useful as it should, which means EAF may need to be customized according to the organization's own culture, policy and procedure". The EAFs can either provide a realisation or result in the neglect of the organisation's goals and concerns in the process of development and implementation (Lapalme et al., 2016).

Despite the promising rationale, organisations need to complement the EAFs with other factors not necessarily covered in EA literature (Rouhani et al., 2015).

Also, the EAFs must not be mistakenly considered as the sole driver of the EA process (Närman et al., 2014). Some of the factors that influence the development, implementation and practice of EA include environmental trends, people, process and technology (Iyamu, 2019). The factors influence and have an impact on EA through their interconnection and interrelationship, which makes the concept either theoretical or operationalised.

Overview of EA Frameworks

An overview of existing EAFs is presented with particular focus on those that have somehow survived the test of time and have remained popular over the last decade. This includes the Gartner EA Process, TOGAF and the Zachman Framework. The selection of the frameworks was based on two factors; context and consistency: the frameworks are difficult to apply in organisations because of the different contexts and uniqueness of environments. (Iyamu, 2015); and Wang et al., (2008) assert that several EAFs and methodologies have come and gone in recent years, and that only four of the frameworks remain dominant in the field: FEA, Gartner Inc. EA process, TOGAF and Zachman Framework for EA. The objective was not to compare the frameworks but to provide an overview in order to gain a better understanding of the implications of theorising EA for the industry.

Gartner Inc.: EA Methodology

Gartner Inc. defines EA as the process which transforms business requirements and vision into strategies through principles, standards and models that enable and support an organisation in its competitiveness and sustainability goals (Lnenicka & Komarkova, 2019; Lapkin et al., 2008). The EA process is carried out through four main different domains: business, information, application and technical (Iyamu, 2015). In the Gartner process, EA is a constituent of three components referred to as business owners, information specialist and technology implementers (Rouhani et al., 2015). Also, the concept of the EA approach is considered to be a multiphase, iterative and non-linear phenomenon (Al-Nasrawi & Ibrahim, 2013). These are some of the terms that many professionals struggle to identify with in reality and practice (Kappelman & Zachman, 2013). The approach also focuses on bridging the gap between the future and current states of an organisation that deploys it (Simon et al., 2014).

Some IT specialists, including researchers, share their experiences on how the Gartner methodology is rather an EA practice than a framework (Bente, Bombosch & Langade, 2012). This means that the method should rather be used to analyse the organisations' future business strategies. In Gartner's view, EA is more about establishing a shared business vision and strategy for an enterprise (Bente et al., 2012). This view is presented in the method which prescribes that environmental trends are first identified, and sequentially followed by other processes. However, no organisation seems to have executed EA within this theoretical recommendation (Azevedo et al., 2015; Bradley et al., 2012).

The Open Group Architecture Framework

TOGAF is an EA framework that is aimed "to denote both an entire enterprise, encompassing all of its information systems (IS), and a specific domain within the enterprise" (The Open Group, 2003: 14). The Open Group defines its framework as a tool that can be used to institute the development of different architectures in an organisation, while utilising methods and standards for designing information systems and technologies (IS/IT) solutions. TOGAF provides a foundation for decision-making, IT solutions guidance and architecture principles.

However, TOGAF seems to fall short in ensuring a solution architecture acceptance in many organisations (Kriouile & Kriouile, 2015). As a result, there are difficulties in the attempts to make use of the TOGAF method in the delivery of services that can improve an organisation's performance (Frampton et al., 2015). Such challenges can be attributed to the fact that the method is not a mainstream of the EA approach, as it is normally proclaimed. Kotusev (2016) argues that TOGAF is not purely an EA tool, hence the method has not been a success in many areas and organisations where it has been deployed.

The Zachman EA Framework

The Zachman Framework was developed by John Zachman and first introduced in the 1980s. The framework was initially intended for IS modelling but was later and gradually expanded to a more holistic approach for enterprise needs. The framework provides an organisation with the mechanisms to mitigate complexities of IS solutions from an EA viewpoint, by strongly advocating the importance of human involvement. Over the years, the Zachman Framework has proved to be efficient in the crafting of IS processes and activities because it allows an identification of the key stakeholders' area of interest, and their involvement in the processes, including the information needs of the stakeholders (Lapalme et al., 2016). Tang et al., (2004) also highlighted some points where the framework is capable of incorporating different EA analysis and modelling techniques, as well as the perspectives of the key stakeholders in the deployment of EA.

However, in practice, the framework is limited in some areas such as the alignment and documentation of units and artefacts (Rouhani et al., 2015). The Zachman Framework is well documented to support advanced development, but that is only in theory. Kriouile and Kriouile (2015) emphasise this point by arguing that the framework lacks in areas of documentation of the EA management process and does not support strategic alignment. Thus, the use of the framework only to collect artefacts does not add value to an organisation (Frampton et al., 2015).

In summary, many EAFs, including TOGAF and the Zachman Framework, are not practice-oriented. From theoretical viewpoints, the benefits are well researched and documented, including their theory building of artefacts (Foorthuis et al., 2016). Franke et al. (2018) argue that models from EA are propositions that have not rigorously been tested. Like many other studies, the results from Vallerand et al. (2017) theoretically explain how EA can be used in general terms.

Theorising Enterprise Architecture

The discussion in this section is based on the objective of the chapter, which is to understand the implications of theorising EA in organisations. This is split into three parts in order to gain a deeper understanding of the phenomenon, as follows: (1) factors of influence in the development of EA; (2) factors of influence in the implementation of EA; and (3) factors of influence in practising EA in organisations.

Factors of Influence in the Development of EA in an Organisation

There are objectives that guide the development of the EA in an organisation. Many organisations have similar objectives for their EA, as summarised as follows: The EA is intended to guide the capability to define and support an organisation's future, short- and long-term plan, from both business and IT perspectives. This is an important initial step in organisations, in order to avoid ambiguity. A business manager in one of the blue-chip organisations said to me in the course of writing this chapter that: "there is ambiguity about EA, which jeopardises the efforts in the attempts to contribute or execute some of our tasks in the development of the concept, in that the scope keeps changing and expanding".

Within this objective, EA activities are planned and the domains are defined, developed and operationalised (implemented and practised) in the organisations. In the process, there is always a wary situation because IT managers often think if they got it wrong, and the implementation and practice fail, it would become another theoretical exercise. Such circumstances must be acknowledged and a strategy provided to guard against failure.

As is the norm, the development stage is guided by the scope, and influenced by the organisations' requirements and objectives. However, the development stage is not always easy as sometimes claimed or thought. This is evident as the interest in the concept does not collaborate with the rate of its development in organisations. This is purely attributed to know-how, which comes from training and experience. Further, this is directly or indirectly reflective and echoed in many organisations. One of the challenges is that there is a gap in knowledgeability between IT architects and the managers. Some of the architects complain that the development of EA is not as easy as the managers think – because many of the architects have limited training and education about the concept, which they obtained at short courses from organisations such as Gartner Inc. and TOGAF. There are very few universities that offer EA as a degree programme.

Also, the challenges can be viewed from a tools' perspective: TOGAF is more of a theory than practical aiding approach. As a result, some of the inexperienced employees are often challenged in attempts to employ the approach. For example, in some large organisations that have many business units that are far apart from each other, it becomes more difficult to find a common ground. This often results in the development of separate architectures for each of the business units. Alternatively, some employees embark on a 'trial and error' type of approach until a reasonable or acceptable conclusion is reached. This adds to the challenge that makes it difficult to get sponsorship buy-in from business units.

In some of the organisations, the approach is, first theorise the concept of EA before considering it for operationalisation. This is primarily to gain a comprehensive understanding of the influencing factors from both technical and non-technical perspectives. Also, such an approach gives an organisation the chance to assess the existing EAFs against their business goals, objectives and requirements. In some organisations, the evaluation process of EAFs takes between 3 and 12 months, depending on the size of the organisation. Another aspect that poses a challenge is that many of the business managers struggle to understand the concept beyond theory. This process is common practice in many organisations. It results from the fact that EAFs are closely related. Also, EA is a concept that is often difficult to get buy-in from the management.

The process of evaluation gives the organisations an opportunity to get buy-in and strive towards a common understanding among the stakeholders. An understanding of EA is deeper than an overview knowledge of the concept. EA consists of four main domains, which are business, information, application and technical. Each of the domains requires a thorough understanding in order to achieve a successful development of the concept. This has been a challenge in many organisations for many years. This challenge was more of a consequence in that each of the domains requires different methods and skill sets in carrying out their distinct deliverables. The challenge was attributed to lack of skilled and trained personnel for the specific domains. This has escalated into a detrimental factor as revealed and discussed in this chapter, as it subsequently influences the operationalisation of the EA in the organisations. As discussed in Chapter 12, it is a growing challenge in some organisations to find and employ or retain EA domain experts.

Factors of Influence in the Implementation of EA in an Organisation

The development does not automatically lead to a successful implementation of EA in an organisation. After development, the focus has to shift to implementation, in pursuit of its value or benefit. At the implementation stage, the EA portrays its benefits and strengths within the organisational context. The implementation often encounters challenges with an impact on the realisation of the objective. Some of the challenges:

i. Some of the implementers are not involved in the development. As such, this group of specialists learn as they implement the concept, which is inevitably prone to errors and is costly to both business processes and IT solutions.
ii. Many employees, including business sponsors, see EA as any other project which starts and finishes within a short time. EA is not a once-off project. The implementation of EA is a process that is iteratively carried out over a period of time, as the organisation's goals, objectives and requirements continue to change.
iii. In addition, many employees, particularly those in the division, have expectations of tangible value from the implementation of EA. It gets worse as some IT architects struggle to explain or convince the stakeholders on the durability of EA.

Thus, the implementation stage remains a focal point for both the IT and business units. The major challenge lies in the fact that EA cannot be theorised at the implementation stage. The implementation is context-based, and the reality of the benefits must be observed and experienced. As a result, the implementation stage is considered to be a critical, integral and truly effective aspect of EA functionalities in an organisation. Thus, it is difficult to realise the functionalities of EA without proper implementation. This challenge has somehow made EA to be continually referred to as a theoretical concept, owing to implementation failures in many organisations. The challenge gets worse due to limited cases from which organisations can draw terms of reference. As a result, many organisations have developed EA, but only few have implemented the concept in various industries in many parts of the world.

The implementation of EA in organisations is influenced by technical and non-technical factors requiring buy-in and participation from stakeholders; both IT and business units in an organisation. This entails a process through which EA is understood beyond a theoretical concept. Also, the promoters of EA or the IT architects should be able to provide a detailed explanation and education to the stakeholders to ease awareness and have a common understanding to associate proper meaning and justification for EA investment.

A proof of concept (PoC) is necessary in getting buy-in from the stakeholders. As part of the planning, a stakeholder, preferably from the business unit, takes ownership of the PoC. The requirements for PoC must be formulated in collaboration with the business and IT units (or representative) to ensure ownership and foster understanding. The collaboration enhances alignment and, most importantly, it establishes factors of influence from both business processes and IT solutions.

Factors of Influence in the Practice of EA in an Organisation

As in the development and implementation stages, there are factors that influence the practice of EA in organisations. Some of the factors are known and others are not empirically known to the promoters of EA. Owing to lack of knowledgeability, organisations invest in different EAFs. It is clear that none of the EAFs seems to offer a step-by-step guidance from its theoretical concept to the practice stage. As a result, many organisations are often challenged at the post-implementation stage of EA in their various environments. This can be attributed to the question that is often asked by business stakeholders, post-implementation process: what is the next step after implementation? This is the realisation point that there is limited understanding and that there are more challenges ahead.

The limited understanding and lack of know-how at the post-implementation stage have an impact on assessing the benefits and value of EA in an organisation. In some organisations, many employees, particularly from the business units, expect a form of system to be deployed or installed in the server or their computer by the IT unit. When that does not happen, and the stakeholders are being trained on the steps and procedures of EA practice, disappointment arises.

Without demonstrating the results and assessment of the value EA adds to the environment, it is difficult to reach a conclusive statement about the benefits. The results manifest from the practice and are not a tangible thing. In the beginning, some IT architects and their managers do think that the development and implementation of EA is difficult, until they reach the practice stage; then, they subsequently realise that there were more challenges ahead. This is primarily because they are somehow compelled to show the business unit and other IT employees the tangible output from the development and implementation. Somehow, it feels like the entire process has been theorised.

There is no single method that can be used to practice EA, but the concept has specific and similar benefits to the organisations that deploy it. This is because of the varying nature of organisations' focuses, goals and objectives. Also, each domain of EA dictates its mode of practice. The practice of EA is influenced by context and relevance. It therefore requires more than theorisation of the concept. It includes the mapping of the organisation's culture and strategies with the EA, which is not a textbook approach.

The factors that influence EA practice in organisations are neither easy to detect nor understand. Also, the factors are neither straightforward nor easy to address. In practice, from an organisational context, it is important to recognise that EA is a path and not a destination; hence, it is essential to gain an understanding of the strengths and weaknesses of the frameworks towards operationalisation. This leads to the bottom line, which explicably indicates that the strengths and weaknesses of EA influence the selection of frameworks for an organisation's purposes. Thus, frameworks are continually customised based on the objectives and requirements of the organisation.

In order to limit customisation, the most appropriate framework should therefore be selected for increased benefits and suitability from an organisational perspective. Through this means, enablement and support can be improved for an organisation's goals and objectives. However, this has never been easy, and can be attributed to the fact that there are not many cases that can be used for comparison and as points of reference. This is an experience of explicit knowledge that IT architects and managers should gain in order to contextualise their roles, demonstrate the practice of EA and transform business and IT activities from the current to desired states in an organisation. Benefits and value, such as a stronger alignment between business and IT units, better decision-making and simplification of IT solutions begin to surface when the practice of EA is institutionalised in an organisation.

The Process of Theorising EA

Theorising EA is a process on its own. The three main stages (development, implementation and practice) that constitute the deployment evolve through a theoretical frame as shown in Figure 6.1. Even though EA has over the years evolved and matured to a certain degree of acceptance (Kappelman & Zachman, 2013), many organisations continue to struggle with one or a combination of EA deployment stages. This could be attributed to the fact that each of the stages is clearly different in its processes, requirements, resources and deliverables.

Despite the distinction that lies in the deployment stages, some organisations still plan to make use of the same requirements and processes for both the development and implementation phases of EA. That is one of the prohibitive exercises in the deployment of EA. It is crucially more difficult when employees in the business

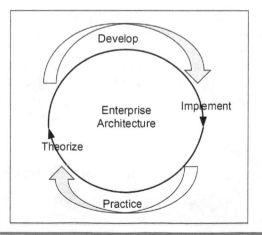

Figure 6.1   Theoretical frame of EA.

units, who were trained, get involved in the practice of EA. In those circumstances, the concerned employees would find it difficult to know exactly what to do, particularly as they were not involved in the process either at the development or implementation stage. However, specialists such as the enterprise architects can be assigned tasks across the domains, in both the development and implementation stages.

Essentially, the concept should be theorised to all stakeholders before the process is embarked upon. This entails awareness programmes and training at various levels; beginner, intermediary and advanced, which cover the main stages of EA deployment. Figure 6.1 depicts the iterative nature of EA in an organisation.

As shown in Figure 6.1, the theoretical frame is helpful, as it is the main instrument for gaining an understanding of the strengths and weaknesses of EAFs in an organisation. This plays a significant role in selecting EAFs for development, implementation and practice. The strengths and weaknesses form parts of the development and implementation procedures. Some of the weaknesses are often difficult to address, depending on the organisation's structure, objectives and culture. These factors influence employees' actions, and, at the same time, the formulation of the factors is influenced by employees' actions. The influence of organisational structure tends to make people explicitly consolidate their actions and behaviour in the manner that they do.

Some employees' behaviour is as a result of using technology as a source of power and dominance, thereby causing processes to be incorrectly interpreted against the objectives of the organisation. Thus, it is feasible for employees that nurse the use of power for personal gain to understand that selecting inappropriate frameworks could potentially have negative impacts on EA development, implementation and practice in the organisation. In addition, the reliance on domain experts is critical and should not be trivialised or substituted with political circumstances or factors.

The approach employed has to be critical because it has the capability to hinder EA's deliverables, specifically at the implementation and practice stages. The manifestations from the deliverables also have an impact on organisational optimum performances, sustainability and competitiveness. Through theorising of the concept, some of the challenges can be identified and addressed before they undergo the development and implementation stages, as the iteration process continues.

Understanding the Implications of Theorising EA

Although it is significant to understand the implications of theorising EA in an organisation, it is, however, not always easy to identify the factors. As revealed in this chapter, EA has been theorised more than it has been practised in organisations over the years. Based on the discussion as presented above, five factors were found to be of fundamental implications in theorising EA in an organisation. The factors are (1) limited case studies – there are limited case studies of EA implementation and practice that can be used as references for practitioners; (2) slow pace of evolvement – the pace at which practical knowledge about EA has advanced is slow; (3) lack of balance – there is a lack of balance between academic rigour and practical relevance, with the former being emphasised more heavily than the latter currently; (4) research materials – there should be a greater focus than what it currently is, in developing applied research materials that provide help and concrete directions for practitioners; and (5) ineffective practice of EA – practices surrounding EA are ineffective due to the inconsistencies among the extant EAFs.

Figure 6.2 shows how the factors relate to the main stages of EA, which include conceptualisation, development, implementation and practice. The discussion below should be read with the figure in order to gain a better understanding of how the implications are interrelated and can have an impact on the activities of an organisation.

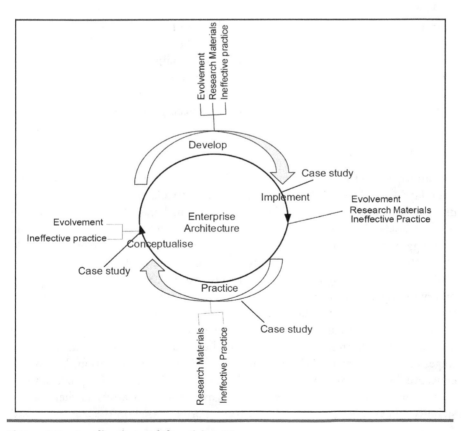

Figure 6.2   Implications of theorising EA.

Limited Case Studies

In relation to the number of medium and large enterprises in the world, including government institutions and agencies, it is clear that there are limited practical cases of EA. This makes cases for comparison and reference purposes, as learning about the concept evolves, scarce to find. It is important to know that the concept needs to be distilled into forms that practitioners can adopt as a guide for practice determination. The distillation of EA is an iterative process, as depicted in Figure 6.1 and expanded in Figure 6.2. The process starts from the conceptualisation of the concept. Thereafter, it is developed, implemented and practised. The practice of EA follows an iterative process that is enacted by recursive actions of the agents, which include human, process and technology. The iterative process is problematised through a theoretical phenomenon, conceptualised into an organisational context, developed into an operationalised artefact thereafter, and becomes the norm that is practised over a period of time. The norm that is practised can be re-theorised as the organisation continues to transform or seek a competitive advantage through innovative actions of agents.

However, this has not been the case as academics and postgraduate students continue to struggle to find organisations that can be suitably used as cases in IS studies. From practitioners' perspective, EA has been implemented and practised in some organisations, enabling them to be more competitive. Nonetheless, many organisations have fallen short in the area of know-how, during the implementation and practice of EA. Also, the limited cases of EA practice in organisations have an impact on the slow pace of evolvement and advancement of the concept.

Lack of Balance

EA undergoes a rigorous conceptualisation process through which scope and boundary are defined within the context and relevance of an organisation that deploys it. Khazanchi and Munkvold (2003) argued that there is a relationship between academic rigour and practical relevance, which has a negative connotation that suggests that practice can only be achieved at the expense of rigour in the field of IS. This is completely correct in the case of EA as an applied discipline. Iyamu (2013) highlights the significance of balancing relevance with practice, stating that, otherwise, rigour will continue to dominate. As a result, organisations will continue to gain little or no value from the concept.

Through conceptualisation, the stakeholders generally share meanings that they associate with EA, from which they gain a better understanding about the three stages of deployment in their environments. Within an organisation, EA can be conceptualised and re-conceptualised as it continues in its iterative process. Only then it produces and reproduces process, governance and artefacts that lead to stability and enact organisational values and norms. Based on the conceptualised frame, the context and tenets of EA are developed through theoretical investigations and explorations.

Slow Pace of Evolvement

The concept of EA has been theorised more than it has been put to practice for so long. Theorising EAFs has both positive and negative implications and challenges for an organisation. The implications are influenced by technical and non-technical factors. Some of the technical implications are of know-how and technologies factors. Examples of the non-technical factors include the constraints caused by the process and unpredictable roles and actions of stakeholders.

Theorisation helps to define the concept, as well as extract the benefits. Through the definition, boundaries are outlined and values are predicted. The benefits come from an understanding of actors' roles at the stages of deployment of EA. Also, theorisation provides guidance to practitioners, researchers and educators for further exploration, investigation and development of the concept, which helps with the evolution of EA as a discipline in the field of IS. Evolution is only possible if there is a duality between theorisation and practice. Giddens (1984) defines duality as the recursive interactive relationship between humans and structures, whereby structures shape human action, which in turn constitutes the structures. Duality enacts the iterative process through which actions are recursively reproduced to achieve the organisational goals and objectives over a period of time and space.

The theorisation of EA is favourable in terms of academic research and development. Based on the analysis that is presented above, it is safe to say that in its current status, the understanding that is gained from theorising EA is limited and slow. This has an impact on modifying the frame of reference within which practitioners can act in their quest to add value and promote competitive advantage in their organisations.

Research Materials

The analysis of past works, as well as the development of future works that concern EA should focus on how research may offer more concrete help and direction to practitioners and organisations from the standpoint of applicability and practice. It is significant to understand as a form of ethos that academia teach what they research and research what they teach.

The benefits of EA are realised through its operationalisation over a period of time, depending on the size and nature of the organisation. Also, operationalisation provides practitioners with a guide to achieving the organisation's return on investment from EA deployment. However, operationalisation of EA is influenced by other factors, some of which can be difficult. This is primarily because of the generalised nature of some of the EAFs. Urbaczewski and Mrdalj (2006) suggest that many of the frameworks are abstract due to their generality of terms, which raises questions of validity or their ability to work accurately within many organisations in a specific context.

Ineffective Practice

To practice is to sanction, which leads to organisational norms over a period of time and space. In recent years, EAFs have drifted apart from each other in terms of commonalities, making the practice even more challenging for practitioners in some organisations. Wang et al. (2008) argue that the EAFs are no longer consistent in terms of terminologies. However, some of the frameworks still share common goals. The question is whether the differences in terminologies affect the practice of EA. The answer is not far-fetched as the goals remain similar. However, the terminologies shape the meaning that architects and other stakeholders associate with the artefacts, which manifest in the outcome of EA deployment and make the practice sometimes ineffective.

Thus, it is unfavourable on the part of the practitioners, academic researchers and educators to draw references from ineffective practice. The implications and consequences arise from the fact that academia are expected to teach what they research and research what they teach. In the same vein, practitioners are expected to practice what has been theorised and apply what has been researched in order to enable and support their organisations' competitiveness and add substantial value.

Summary

Despite the increasing interest in EA, the rate of deployment in organisations is relatively slow, particularly in South Africa. This is one of the primary implications of the theorised nature of the concept which does not give confidence to potential sponsors and promoters in many organisations. Through this chapter, organisations and academics can gain a better understanding of the implications that continue to influence the deployment and practice of EA, from a theorisation viewpoint. Also, it will be of benefit to some organisations to understand from different perspectives, such as the types of relationships that exist in a societal context where EA is problematised before development and implementation are embarked upon. To academics, this contributes to motivation for more work in the area of EA deployment rather than more emphasis on theoretical viewpoints. This chapter adds to existing literature as one of its contributions. It is intended to conceptually advance the practice of EA in organisations through an understanding of the implications of theorising the concept.

The chapter therefore triggers more and further study in the advancement of EA from business development and enhancement perspectives not covered by it. Other areas of limitation for further studies are the relationship and interaction between technical and non-technical factors in the deployment of EA in an organisation. Proposed studies of this nature can be underpinned by sociotechnical theories, such as the structuration theory and actor-network theory. This can assist to gain fresh perspectives on why the pace of operationalisation of EA has been slow and complicated for many organisations over the years.

References

Abraham, R., Aier, S., & Winter, R. (2015). Crossing the line: Overcoming knowledge boundaries in enterprise transformation. *Business & Information Systems Engineering, 57*(1), 3–13.

Ajer, A. K. S., & Olsen, D. H. (2020). Enterprise architecture implementation is a bumpy ride: A case study in the Norwegian public sector. *Electronic Journal of e-Government, 17*(2), 79–94.

Al-Kharusi, H., Miskon, S., & Bahari, M. (2018). Enterprise architecture development approach in the public sector. *International Journal of Enterprise Information Systems (IJEIS), 14*(4), 124–141.

Al-Nasrawi, S., & Ibrahim, M. (2013). An Enterprise Architecture Mapping Approach for Realizing E-government. In The Proceedings of the 3rd International Conference on Communications and Information Technology: Digital Information Management & Security. (pp. 17–21). 19-21 June, Beirut, Lebanon. IEEE.

Azevedo, C. L., Iacob, M. E., Almeida, J. P. A., van Sinderen, M., Pires, L. F., & Guizzardi, G. (2015). Modelling resources and capabilities in enterprise architecture: A well-founded ontology-based proposal for ArchiMate. *Information Systems, 54*, 235–262.

Bente, S., Bombosch, U., & Langade, S. (2012). *Collaborative enterprise architecture: Enriching EA with lean, agile, and enterprise 2.0 practices.* Morgan Kaufmann Publishers.

Bradley, R. V., Pratt, R. M., Byrd, T. A., Outlay, C. N., & Wynn, D. E. Jr (2012). Enterprise architecture, IT effectiveness and the mediating role of IT alignment in US hospitals. *Information Systems Journal, 22*(2), 97–127.

Foorthuis, R., Van Steenbergen, M., Brinkkemper, S., & Bruls, W. A. (2016). A theory building study of enterprise architecture practices and benefits. *Information Systems Frontiers, 18*(3), 541–564.

Frampton, K., Shanks, G. G., Tamm, T., Kurnia, S., & Milton, S. K. (2015). Enterprise Architecture Service Provision: Pathways to Value. *In the Proceedings of Twenty-Third European Conference on Information Systems (ECIS),* 26-29 May, Münster, Germany.

Franke, U., Cohen, M., & Sigholm, J. (2018). What can we learn from enterprise architecture models? An experiment comparing models and documents for capability development. *Software & Systems Modelling, 17*(2), 695–711.

Franke, U., Johnson, P., & König, J. (2014). An architecture framework for enterprise IT service availability analysis. *Software & Systems Modelling, 13*(4), 1417–1445.

Fritscher, B., & Pigneur, Y. (2015). A visual approach to business IT alignment between business model and enterprise architecture. *International Journal of Information System Modelling and Design (IJISMD), 6*(1), 1–23.

Giddens, A. (1984). *The constitution of society: Outline of the theory of structuration.* Cambridge, UK: John Polity Press.

Glissmann, S. M., & Sanz, J. (2011). An Approach to Building Effective Enterprise Architectures. *In the Proceedings of the 44th Hawaii International Conference on System Sciences.* 4-7 January, Kauai, Hawaii.

Hiekkanen, K., Korhonen, J. J., Collin, J., Patricio, E., Helenius, M., & Mykkänen, J. (2013). Architects' Perceptions on EA Use – An Empirical Study. In *Business Informatics (CBI), 2013 IEEE 15th Conference.* (pp. 292–297). 15-18 July, Vienna, Austria. IEEE.

Iyamu, T. (2013). Underpinning theories: Order-of-use in information systems research. *Journal of Systems and Information Technology, 15*(3), 1–13.

Iyamu, T. (2015). *Enterprise architecture: From concept to practice.* Australia: Heidelberg Press.

Iyamu, T. (2019). Understanding the complexities of enterprise architecture through structuration theory. *Journal of Computer Information Systems, 59*(3), 287–295.

Jayakrishnan, M., Mohamad, A. K., & Abdullah, A. (2018). Digitalization approach through an enterprise architecture for Malaysia transportation industry. *International Journal of Civil Engineering and Technology (IJCIET), 9*(13), 834–839.

Kappelman, L. A., & Zachman, J. A. (2013). The enterprise and its architecture: Ontology & challenges. *Journal of Computer Information Systems, 53*(4), 87–95.

Kaushik, A., & Raman, A. (2015). The new data-driven enterprise architecture for e-healthcare: Lessons from the Indian public sector. *Government Information Quarterly, 32*(1), 63–74.

Khazanchi, D., & Munkvold, B. E. (2003). On the Rhetoric and Relevance of IS Research Paradigms: A Conceptual Framework and Some Propositions. *In the Proceedings of the 36th Hawaii International Conference on System Sciences.* 6-9 January, Big Island, Hawaii.

Kotusev, S. (2016). Enterprise Architecture Is Not TOGAF. British Computer Society (BCS). http://www.bcs.org/content/conWebDoc/55547

Kriouile, H., & Kriouile, A. (2015). Towards services-based enterprise architecture for cloud computing-opened information systems. *Journal of Computers, 10*(3), 195–203.

Lapalme, J., Gerber, A., Van der Merwe, A., Zachman, J., De Vries, M., & Hinkelmann, K. (2016). Exploring the future of enterprise architecture: A Zachman perspective. *Computers in Industry, 79*, 103–113.

Lapkin, A. (2005). *Business strategy defines enterprise architecture value.* USA: Gartner Research.

Lapkin, A., Allega, P., Burke, B., & Burton, B. (2008). Gartner Clarifies the Definition of the Term 'Enterprise. 1-5.

Lnenicka, M., & Komarkova, J. (2019). Developing a government enterprise architecture framework to support the requirements of big and open linked data with the use of cloud computing. *International Journal of Information Management, 46*, 124–141.

Mohamed, M., Galal-Edeen, G., Hassan, H., & Hasanien, E. (2012). An Evaluation of Enterprise Architecture Frameworks for E-Government. *In the Proceeding International Conference on Computer Engineering and Systems (ICCES '2012).* (pp. 255–261). 27-29 November, Cairo, Egypt.

Närman, P., Buschle, M., & Ekstedt, M. (2014). An enterprise architecture framework for multi-attribute information systems analysis. *Software & Systems Modelling, 13*(3), 1085–1116.

Niemi, E., & Pekkola, S. (2017). Using enterprise architecture artefacts in an organisation. *Enterprise Information Systems, 11*(3), 313–338.

Ross, J., Weill, P., & Robertson, D. (2006). *Enterprise architecture as a strategy: Creating a foundation for business execution.* USA: Harvard Business Press.

Rouhani, B. D., Mahrin, M. N. R., Nikpay, F., Ahmad, R. B., & Nikfard, P. (2015). A systematic literature review on enterprise architecture implementation methodologies. *Information and Software Technology, 62*, 1–20.

Safari, H., Faraji, Z., & Majidian, S. (2016). Identifying and evaluating enterprise architecture risks using FMEA and fuzzy VIKOR. *Journal of Intelligent Manufacturing, 27*(2), 475–486.

Shaanika, I., & Iyamu, T. (2018). Developing the enterprise architecture for the Namibian government. *The Electronic Journal of Information Systems in Developing Countries, 84*(3), e12028.

Simon, D., Fischbach, K., & Schoder, D. (2014). Enterprise architecture management and its role in corporate strategic management. *Information Systems and e-Business Management, 12*(1), 5–42.

Song, H., & Song, Y.-T. (2010). Enterprise Architecture Institutionalization and Assessment. *In the Proceedings of the 9th International Conference on Computer and Information Science (ICIS).* (pp. 870–875). 18-20 August, Yamagata, Japan. IEEE/ACIS.

Tamm, T., Seddon, P., Shanks, G., & Reynolds, P. (2011). How does enterprise architecture add value to organisations? *Communications of the Association of Information Systems, 28*(10), 141–168.

Tang, A., Han, J., & Chen, P. (2004). A Comparative Analysis of Architecture Frameworks. *In the Proceedings of the 11th Asia-Pacific Software Engineering Conference.* (pp. 640–647). 30 November-3 December, Busan, South Korea. IEEE.

The Open Group. (2003). The Open Group Architecture Framework Version 8.1 "Enterprise Edition". 1-12.

Urbaczewski, L., & Mrdalj, S. (2006). A comparison of enterprise architecture frameworks. *Issues in Information Systems, 7*(2), 18–23.

Vallerand, J., Lapalme, J., & Moïse, A. (2017). Analysing enterprise architecture maturity models: A learning perspective. *Enterprise Information Systems, 11*(6), 859–883.

Vargas, A., Cuenca, L., Boza, A., Sacala, I., & Moisescu, M. (2016). Towards the development of the framework for inter sensing enterprise architecture. *Journal of Intelligent Manufacturing, 27*(1), 55–72.

Wang, X., & Zhou, X. (2009). Information Resources Planning Based on Enterprise Architecture. *In the Proceedings of the International Conference on Service Operations, Logistics and Informatics (SOLI '09).* (pp. 230–234). 22-24 July, Chicago, Illinois.

Wang, X., Zhou, X., & Jiang, L. (2008). Method of Business and IT Alignment Based on Enterprise Architecture. *In the Proceedings of the International Conference on Service Operations and Logistics, and Informatics (SOLI 08).* (pp. 740–745). 12-15 October, Beijing, China.

Zachman, J. (1987). A framework for information systems. *IBM Systems Journal, 26*(3), 276–283.

Zheng, T., & Zheng, L. (2013). Examining e-government enterprise architecture research in China: A systematic approach and research agenda. *Government Information Quarterly, 30*, S59–S67.

Chapter 7

Structuration View of Enterprise Architecture

Introduction

Within organisational complexity, there exists a dynamic interplay between requests and demands for better services which, in turn, are enacted by competitiveness and sustainability. Demands for growth, service and competitive advantage set a periodic agenda for architectural design, development, implementation and practice within an organisation. Enterprise architecture (EA) is a tool and an approach that can be used to facilitate and enhance an organisation's goals, processes and activities. The approach can also be considered or referred to as an actor by its nature, primarily because it has the capability to make a difference as a change agent within an organisation. In essence, EA is influenced by requirements, and it is at the same time used to influence the activities, events and structures of an organisation.

Many organisations, including government institutions and agencies, have in recent years realised the significance of EA. This interest has evolved into employing the concept within the landscapes of industries in both developed and developing countries, purposely to support, govern and manage the variety of information systems and technologies (IS/IT) solutions in their environments. Some organisations rely on EA in developing their business designs, managing information flow and governing technical challenges and complexities.

The reliance is based on the premise that EA facilitates and manages IT solutions from one state to another, such as from strategy to operations, and from disparity to cohesion. This includes the integration of business and IT strategies towards a common goal. These efforts are executed based on EA's set of processes, tools and

DOI: 10.1201/9781003268420-7

structures that are necessarily needed to implement an enterprise-wide coherent and consistent IT architecture. This is primarily to support enterprises' business operations for competitive advantage. However, the deployment and practice of EA have never been easy or straightforward; they are filled with complexities, from both the perspectives of human and technology solutions.

Despite the growing interest in the concept of EA, it is difficult to find an organisation that has successfully designed, developed, implemented and institutionalised the concept. In some organisations, the implementation has been partly at domains' levels. This is attributed to the bogus and complex nature of the concept, which gets worse when amplified by a multifaceted environment. Some of the complexities could be ascribed to differences in understanding the concept, as opposed to what EA actually is, and bring to the fore the organisation. Despite the numerous explanations on how EA can be employed as an approach to facilitate organisational competitiveness, it has not worked in many organisations primarily because the trajectories of the challenges have not been addressed.

Based on the studies that have been carried out, it is clear that there will continue to be challenges in the development, implementation and attempts to institutionalise the concept of EA in organisations (Dang, 2021; Al-Kharusi, Miskon & Bahari, 2018; Sayogo et al., 2015). Some of the challenges are fairly covered in the literature of the last decade; see Lapalme et al. (2016), Safari, Faraji and Majidian (2016) and Kappelman and Zachman (2013). What has not been explored or covered is where the challenges manifest from or into. Some of the challenges have been revealed in studies such as Iyamu and Mphahlele (2010); Song and Song (2010); and Gutierrez, Orozco and Serrano (2009). Due to these growing challenges and complexities, many organisations are sceptical of fully engaging with the concept.

Thus, it is necessary to employ a different and fresh approach. The structuration theory (ST) of Anthony Giddens is selected and used as a lens to examine and gain a better understanding of how some of the challenges manifest into making EA a complex concept for individuals and organisations. The ST is selected primarily because it focuses on how agents' actions enable and at the same time constrain processes and activities, and how the actions are produced and reproduced within a social system. The theory's focus on social systems involves the interaction between structural properties, agent and structure. In ST, the agent is both technical and non-technical and the structure is rules and resources (Giddens, 1984). Iyamu and Roode (2010) emphasised that the word 'structure' must not be confused with its obvious connotation of organisational hierarchy in the English language.

The remainder of this chapter is divided into five main sections. First, EA and ST are discussed, respectively. Next, ST's view of EA complexity is presented. Thereafter, a model that depicts EA complexity is presented and the implications are discussed. Finally, the chapter is summarised.

Enterprise Architecture

EA is a holistic approach for the management and governance of strategic intent and operationalisation through the re-engineering of processes, control of information osteopathy and flow, systems deployment and technology management. EA consists of enterprise-wide domains, which are mainly business, information, application and technology architectures, as shown in Figure 7.1. Based on its ostensible and purported value for organisations, interests are shown, and investments are made by both public and private enterprises. Also, the complexities of some information systems, their enablers and supporting technologies are the primary reasons many organisations employ EA. In addition, EA acts as an agent of change, and provides organisations with the capacity to identify and make appropriate changes, thereby providing stability and flexibility within the environment.

The emphasis on EA is mainly because of the premise that the concept can be used to facilitate the development of strategies and as well incorporate them within existing processes, implementation and governance of IT solutions, design and operationalisation of business processes and the transformation of other organisational activities and modules. However, in achieving some of these anticipated benefits of EA, the organisation is required to commit to strict mechanisms and best practices in gathering the requirements for the deployment (development and implementation) of the concept. The scope of EA has an influence and impact on its development and implementation in the organisation that deploys it. In defining the scope of EA, emphasis should be put on the fundamental factors, which include processes, people and IT solutions, as well as the relationships and connections between these factors.

With the extensive spread of EA, from business logics of processes and activities to IT operations and strategies, there are bound to be complexities and challenges with its deployment and practice. The complexities of EA are not drawn or encountered from one particular angle or perspective. They cut across domains, including business, information, application, technology, infrastructure and service-oriented architecture (SOA). Also, within the domains, other activities take place which can have different dimensions of influence and weight on the deployment of EA in an organisation. Another strength of EA is that it organises the logics of the business processes and IT solutions, thereby reflecting the integration and governance of an organisation's operating models and frames of work. The development and implementation of EA domains are carried out separately, but they do depend on each other in the process, owing to their common goal and interest.

Based on the complex nature of EA, different EA frameworks (EAFs), such as The Open Group Architecture Forum (TOGAF), Gartner Inc., and Zachman Framework (Zachman, 1996) are employed in its development and implementation in different organisations. As illustrated in Figure 7.1, the domains of EA are interconnected and interdependent. Each domain has a distinctive area of focus with

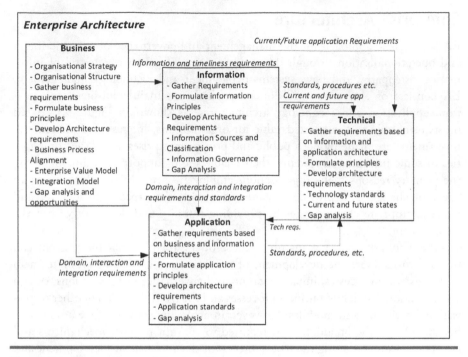

Figure 7.1 Enterprise architecture domains.

a set of deliverables. The deliverables inform the dependency and characteristics of each domain. For example, the business architecture informs the development of the information architecture. Some of the characteristics of the dependency include information and technology categorisation, business objective variables and organisational structures. As exemplified in the development stage, the relationship among the domains is also evident in the implementation and practice of EA. Categorisation, variables and structures are synonymous with complexities because they are often based on and associated with subjective reasoning.

The development and implementation of EA are process-oriented and are carried out through the domains: business, information, application and technical architectures. The EA domains are linked and interrelated with each other, as shown in Figure 7.1. Thus, a challenge with one domain influences and affects others. However, the challenges are not always clear or obvious, as the agents of complexity include non-technical factors, such as inconsistency of procedures, principles and standards. In order to gain a better understanding of why things happen the way that they do in the deployment of EA, the ST was selected and used as a lens to examine the processes and activities of influence.

Structuration Theory

ST is a sociotechnical theory in which both technical and non-technical factors are social constructs. It is a constructivist theory mainly because it focuses on humans as social constructs and institutions as constructs sustained by human actions in reality. Another constructivist aspect of the theory is its consideration as a process that continues between structures and human action, in a duality rather than two separate entities. The theory has agents and structure as its main tenets. Structures in the theory of structuration enable and at the same time constrain agencies (MacKay & Tambeau, 2013). In ST, technologies can possibly change social structures while at the same time the social structures shape how humans develop and use technologies (Nicholson, Tsagdis & Brennan, 2013). Giddens (1984) describes agents not only as persons, but also as anything that has the capability to exert power and can have influence over others in a social context, such as an organisation. This means that agents are associated with some form of power. Structure is rules and resources in ST, as opposed to organisational hierarchy in the English language (Iyamu & Roode, 2010).

Power is viewed as a representative of subjective actions to govern and monitor, from which results make a difference in various contexts. Power is therefore a manifestation of actions of individuals or groups to influence a desired or intended outcome in an organisation. In structuration, agents exert the power to exercise control within a social system, purposely to explore how the exercise of power manifests in a dialectical interplay between agents and structure. This is often a two-way approach. Giddens (1984) describes power as the capability of actors to encourage decisions to favour them and to mobilise biasness. This means that in structuration, according to Giddens (1984), power is not a resource, but resources are used mainly as a medium for power. The capacity to make a difference in a social context endorses structures as the means through which power is exercised during interaction and legitimate actions.

Structures do not exist independently of agents. Rather, structures exist as they are enacted by human agents. Thus, the actions of human agents continually produce and reproduce structures. The theory offers deep insights into how relationships within social systems are reflexively and recursively structured by drawing on rules, regulations and resources. The recursive (repeated) relationship between people and structures, whereby structures shape human action, which in turn constitutes (forms) the structures, is defined as Duality of Structure (Giddens, 1984). This is significantly critical in understanding how events and factors manifest in the iterative process of EA development, implementation and practice. The duality of structure, therefore, is a process through which legitimated structures evolve and are reconstituted by actions.

Duality of Structure

The Duality of Structure as shown in Figure 7.2 depicts the relationship between interaction and structure to produce and reproduce human actions through modality, which consists of interpretative scheme, facility and norms. The duality of structure constitutes an opposition to the continuity and transformation of activities within a social system (Sztompka, 2014). Through this duality, structure enables and constrains at the same time, but does not wholly determine human actions and their influence. Therefore, human actors have the ability or power to act according to their free will within a social structure, which Akaka and Vargo (2014) describe as the composition of two interrelated layers of structures and systems.

Thus, if a person acts differently and their actions are institutionalised as a broader and acceptable pattern, other actors, such as people, follow the pattern of action over a period. This becomes the norm until such a time when the pattern is no longer sanctioned or legitimated. This acceptance is based on their interpretation of the action. The new pattern becomes the norm and a new operating structure emerges from the changed structure. This means that the actions of human agents have the ability to produce and reproduce or re-engineer social structure. Archer (2010) refers to this reproduction of human actions as essential and recursive of social life, in which structure is both the medium and outcome of the reproduction of practices.

When human actors interact, they explore the interpretative scheme to construct a logical framework from it and make differences through their interactions. According to Giddens (1984: 22), *"all human beings are highly 'learned' in respect of the knowledge which they possess and apply in the production and reproduction of day-to-day social encounters"*. Thus, the interaction of human actors facilitates the modification and reproduction of the interpretative scheme in which many ontology-based realities are at play. This informs the structure of significance in a dualistic form.

The interpretative scheme outlines the structure of promoting and indorsing significance or meaning (Orlikowski, 1992). In attempts to gain a better

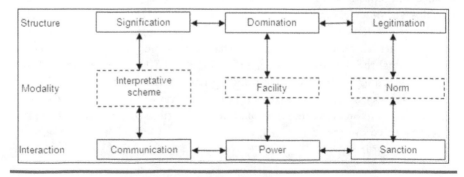

Figure 7.2 Duality of structure. (Giddens, 1984)

understanding of the factors that cause or influence EA complexity, the duality of structure was particularly helpful; specifically, as Iyamu (2015) explains, the structure of significance in its turn represents the rules and regulations that facilitate and ground the communication of actors. Resources are facilitated and allocated, using power, thus informing the structures of domination among actors in the course of transformation of events (Nyella & Mndeme, 2010). The structure of domination can be altered or changed by agents, based on the ability to do so, which in a way, applies to how people carry out actions in the deployment of EA in different organisations. This type of change to dominance by agents is referred to by Giddens (1984) as the dialectic of control. Norms facilitate constructive human actions and inform the structure of legitimation through sanctions. Norms, therefore, present rules that catalyse legitimate or generally acceptable behaviours within a social system or organisation.

The duality of structure or ST was employed as a lens, from an interpretive perspective, primarily because the theory provides a useful method for analysing the interaction that happens between humans and technologies within an environment. This was essentially critical in gaining insights into the complexities of EA in an organisation. Also, the theory is often applied in studies or environments where the interpretivist approach is employed to examine complex phenomena (Woodside & Baxter, 2013). This is attributable to the fact that the use of the theory has long been established as a valuable method in interpretive paradigms (Walsham & Han, 1991). It is within this context that duality of structure was applied as a lens to examine and understand the complexity of EA in organisations.

Structuration View of EA Complexities

The duality of structure, from the perspective of ST, was employed as a lens to examine and understand the factors that reproductively manifest into complexities in the deployment of EA in organisations. Based on the theory, a summary of events and activities is presented in Table 7.1. It includes the interconnection and how actions are reproduced during the development and implementation of EA, in a recursive manner. The summary should be read with the discussion that follows to gain a better understanding of EA complexities.

Structure: Signification/Domination/Legitimation

The concept of EA is considered significant by individuals and organisations due to its focus on synergy, strategy, alignment, governance and operationalisation. First and foremost, EA is aimed at achieving a synergy of elements and events that help to formulate and articulate the goals and objectives of an organisation that deploys it. Based on requirements, EA drives strategic and operational activities executed by people, through processes and the use of various IT solutions to enhance competitiveness.

Table 7.1   EA Complexity

	Signification	Domination	Legitimation
Structure	Organisational requirements drive and determine the selection, deployment and practice of EA, which in turn determine its importance. This influences employees' interest about the concept within their organisation.	On one hand, managers make use of resources, such as technologies and processes to control and enable activities in the deployment of EA. On the other hand, architects employ their stock of knowledge about EA to assert their stance and influence processes and activities.	The deployment of EA in an environment including the allocation of its tasks, from development to practice, is based on the approval by relevant authorities within the organisational structure.
	Interpretive scheme	*Facility*	*Norm*
Modality	Employees' subjective interpretations of EA requirements are based on their understanding, which in turn influences and impacts processes and activities in its deployment and practice in the organisation.	Different resources, which include organisational rules, regulations and technologies are employed as facilities to guide the deployment and practice of EA in an organisation.	The architects define the processes and procedures that are used for the deployment and practice of EA in the organisation.
	Communication	*Power*	*Sanction*
Interaction	Communication is carried out based on an understanding, which is influenced by interest and knowledge. An understanding is based on how communication is delivered in both the deployment and practice of EA in an organisation.	Rules and regulations are used as sources of power to manipulate processes and procedures in the deployment and practice of EA. Technology and know-how or stock of knowledge are also used as sources of power during EA's deployment and practice.	Both IS/IT and business units' managers approve the deployment of EA, including the processes and procedures that are involved.

Clearly, it is not only the technical aspects of EA that are important. The non-technical factors are highly significant and have influential effects on the deployment of EA in organisations. This leads to why some architects think that some domains are more important than others and, as a result, use that claim as a source of dominance. Also, many organisations rely on the technical architects to provide technology-related directions. The detriment of this type of action is that it affects the domains' dependence on each other. Based on its significance, EA encompasses strategic and operational plans for the modelling, governance and management of business logics, information exchange, applications (information systems) and technology within an environment. This is an iterative process that includes relationships and connectivity amongst applications, and how agents relate and interact with each other.

The development and implementation of the domains are based on how an organisation defines the concept, which ultimately shapes the overall outcomes of EA. The consequence of the definition reveals itself as the agents form relationships and connection, which influence EA's focus and deliverables through the domains. The challenge begins, sometimes silently, when architects define EA with little or no input from business units or when a domain architect similarly does so with minimum contribution from other architects. This is a challenge of exclusivity that manifests itself as users and other stakeholders who were not involved in the gathering of the requirements are requested to participate in the implementation of the architecture. This is complex in that the relationships and connectivity have no guiding principles or formula. As a result, they are subjectively defined, based on personal interests rather than organisational goals and objectives. This situation is hugely influenced by lack of a clear definition of roles and responsibilities.

Thus, the development of the domains, which is supposed to contribute towards the development and implementation of another domain, becomes disruptive and negatively impacts the process and outcome. This happens mainly because of the ways in which roles and responsibilities are interpreted and carried out within the organisation. This type of action is enabled by the significance that is associated with the roles and legitimised by the structure of the organisation. In some organisations, policies bestow power on managers and architects, allowing them to exhibit certain functions with little or no input from other employees.

Modality: Interpretive/Facility/Norm

Many employees in some organisations see the concept of EA differently, subjectively so. This is attributable to the fact that the concept of EA is defined by small groups for the entire stakeholders. I am not suggesting that everyone needs to be involved in the definition, which is near impossible. The definition needs to be broadly communicated and training is inevitable. This is to reduce the differences in understanding, which have impacts on processes, procedures, deliverables and outcomes. Also, the different understanding which often leads to confusion and complexity is caused by insufficient and low-quality information that the stakeholders can access as they seek to equip themselves with knowledge about the concept.

The lack of common understanding among the stakeholders makes the deployment and practice of EA to be more difficult and complex than it should be. Oftentimes, the business architects struggle to understand the deliverables and how they link with the overall objectives, which is somehow caused by the ways the architecture is defined and scoped in an organisation. Thus, some of the employees employ different facilities, causing them to act in their respective ways, and creating more complexity in the deployment and practice of EA in their organisation.

Some of the facilities that are frequently employed by many of the stakeholders include stock of knowledge, roles and responsibilities, architecture standards, policies and principles. In an attempt to redefine and reposition themselves in the midst of challenging complexity, some of the employees make use of available facilities as a source of dominance through which they pursue personal interest as opposed to EA objectives. As a result, the practice of EA becomes more confusing to many of the stakeholders, in terms of understanding the goals, essentiality and values of the concept. Consequently, the more some employees try to extract and gain a better understanding of the value of EA, the more complex it becomes for them.

The trajectory that the differences in understanding the concept are ironically based on how the requirements are understood does in turn shape how requirements are gathered in an organisation. This is described in structuration as recursive. It enables and at the same time constrains but does not wholly determine how employees (or stakeholders) behave in the deployment and practice of EA in the organisation. Without a good understanding of the requirements, it is extremely difficult to develop the EA towards enabling an organisational strategy, alignment and governance. The use of unclear requirements negatively affects the strategies of an organisation by constraining the efforts, processes and events that are associated with the concept. This type of complexity can be attributed to how interactions are carried out from the point of initiating the concept in the environment.

Interaction: Communication/Power/Sanction

Interaction is fundamental to shaping the outcome of EA in an organisation. Fundamentally, there have to be relatively strong interactions between human-to-human, human-to-process, human-to-technology, process-to-process, process-to-technology and technology-to-technology in the development and implementation of EA in an organisation. This is mainly because human actions have the ability to produce and reproduce or re-engineer structure (rules and resources), such as process and technology, in the context of EA deployment and practice. Evidently, the implementation and application of IT solutions is based on how the concept of EA is defined and developed. This becomes more complex as the domains depend on each other, including their impacts.

However, some stakeholders continue to take for granted the influence and dependence the domains have on each other. The dependency is often used as a source of power by many domain architects. The elements of dependence manifest in the actors' interactions and actions that are reproduced in the development, implementation and practice of EA. Also, there is often an argument that some technical domain architects are well aware that the business units rely on them for the final products and solutions. As a result, some of the architects are cynical in taking advantage of the reliability which leads to the claim of power relationship, whereby there is a sense of superiority over employees from the business units.

The EA is intended to enable an organisation's events, procedures, processes and activities. But when it becomes complex, it is seen as a constraint to the same activities that it was meant to support and enable. This is attributed to the power exerted in the course of dependency between tasks and domains. This type of dependence is enacted by roles and responsibilities, and sanctioned according to the organisational structure, purposely to ensure and drive solution. However, it does at the same time contribute to the complexities in the deployment of the EA in some organisations, as they manifest from conscious and subconscious actions of the focal actors and other stakeholders that are involved in the EA deployment process. Some of the actions are sanctioned and therefore considered to be the norm. This influences the success or failure of EA.

Understanding EA Complexities

From the ST view of EA as presented above, it is clear that the factors that can critically and significantly influence EA complexity the most include organisational structure, technology, social context and process. Based on these factors, a framework, as shown in Figure 7.3, is developed. The framework is aimed at gaining a

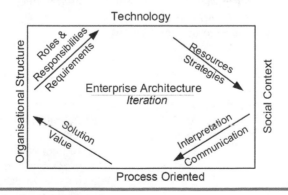

Figure 7.3   Factors of complexity in EA deployment.

better understanding of the complexity in the deployment and practice of EA in organisations. As shown in Figure 7.3, the formulation of requirements is influenced by other factors, including roles and responsibilities, strategies, resources, interpretation, communication, solution and values.

Each of the factors that lead to complexities has its own attributes of influence and implication, either during the development or implementation of EA. Table 7.2 presents a summary of the influence of the factors in the deployment of EA and their implications for both business and IT managers in an organisation. Thus, Figure 7.3 and Table 7.2 should be read in conjunction with the discussion that

Table 7.2 Implication for Managers

Factor	Influence	Implication
Organisational structure	Used as a source of power to define: (i) the relationship between employees and structures; (ii) the allocation of roles and responsibilities in the deployment of EA.	Enables and constrains activities at the same time: (i) in the gathering and interpretation of requirements; and (ii) in the allocation of tasks in the deployment of EA.
Technology	Guides how interactions are carried out among employees during the deployment of EA. Also, it determines the outcome of the goals and objectives through strategies.	How the deployment and use of various technologies manifest, derail and enable activities at different levels and organisational units, from EA perspective.
Social context	The use of rules and resources to guide the communication and interpretation of elements and components that are related to the deployment of EA.	How to apply rules and available resources in an objective manner for the benefit of strategies.
Process oriented	Processes are used to recreate through rules and regulations. It is an iterative procedure that should have a strategic approach.	Managers need to understand that (i) EA processes are not stagnant; (ii) employees will continue to subjectively interpret the processes, which then have an impact on the EA deployment.

follows in order to gain a better understanding of how each of the factors interconnect, manifest and influence EA complexity in organisations. The discussion is also intended to help business and IT managers reduce negative impacts in their roles and responsibilities in the deployment of EA.

Organisational Structure

The organisational structure (sometimes referred to as hierarchy) defines the different units and departments within which an organisation operates. Each unit or department is bestowed with certain mandates within which roles and responsibilities are defined and assigned. Also, each unit has its own requirements towards achieving the organisational mandates. Thus, in the gathering of EA requirements, some of the departments' focus seems to take priority. This causes conflicts that contribute to complexity. In the midst of such conflict, power is exerted, normally, along the organisational structure. These types of actions are consciously or unconsciously reproduced during the development, implementation and practice of EA in the organisation.

More often than not, employees are responsible for enabling processes and activities reproductively in their organisations. Thus, their attitude, behaviour and actions directly define and shape organisational events and norms, which are thereby sanctioned and legitimised over time. The organisational structure could also have embedded attributes that the people make use of to dominate and exercise of power in their organisations. These attributes partially determine the significance people ascribe to EA within their respective organisations. This becomes even more critical because it is on the basis of significance that the requirements are gathered and applied in the development and implementation of EA, which fundamentally determines the outcome, success or failure of the concept within an organisation.

Based on the mandate accorded to roles and responsibilities within the organisational structure, some employees assume power and political intent during the development and implementation of EA in their organisations. Power and politics as resources promote how individuals or groups flourish through self-enrichment, such as recognition, financial reward, job security and career development. The actions of employees, enacted by the power they consciously, unconsciously or practically possess to make a difference, add to the complexities during the development and implementation of EA in an organisation. Consequently, the organisational structure has a significant influence on the development and implementation of EA in the organisation that deploys it.

Roles and responsibilities represent some form of seniority or rank in many organisations. Within such an organisational structure, individuals' ranks are associated with authority. This results in the power to make a difference by virtue of the dominance and legitimation of mandates that are bestowed upon the roles. The act of domination could, however, essentially be used to instil order and as well reinforce the relationship of subordination through which power is manifested.

Technology

In this section, technology is discussed in the context of EA, as shown in Figure 7.3. The arrows in Figure 7.3 indicate that roles, responsibilities and requirements influence technology solutions through the organisational structure within an organisation. This is primarily because employees have the power to decide whether to use or not to use a technology solution. However, the actual selection, implementation, use and support of technologies are guided by strategies that are embedded in EA domains. Actualising this is more complex than it seems, in that it entails interaction with resources, such as processes and employees. This is one of the primary reasons some strategies are formulated but not implemented or partially implemented in many organisations. Interaction with resources is never easy or straightforward even when there are procedures to do so.

In many quarters, EA is seen as an approach that could be used to deliver both IT solutions and business strategies. This is done across the domains of EA, from business and information to technical architectures. The strategies are products of human actions, which are produced and reproduced over time to make a difference in the organisations that deploy them. The difference could be negative or positive and could benefit the organisation or be geared towards self-interest and personal gain. Such differences typically arise from the use and manipulation of processes and technologies in the course of the development and implementation of EA in an organisation.

Hence, human agents are often tasked to manage events and activities within boundaries as defined by themselves or for them by the focal actor. The outcomes from the use of technologies are based on or influenced by two main factors: (1) the interaction – how well a technology solution is understood and used; and (2) connectivity – how the technology solution is connected with other technologies and accessed. Technology interaction and connectivity are engineered through the domains of application and technical architectures. The engineering results from human recursive actions, which are often influenced by knowledge (skills) and interests. This is implicative in that the techniques and tools that are used to develop and implement EA are selected by individuals and groups in the organisation. The selection is based on the interest of individuals, the organisation or both; which is often biased if there is no controlled procedure.

Therefore, the involvement of people in the development and implementation of EA in organisations can be summarised as (1) the enablers and facilitators of EA and its processes; and (2) accountability and responsibility of the outcome of EA. The roles of people are therefore critical to the outcome, success or failure of EA. Also, human expertise is responsible for the sustainability and competitiveness that

EA is intended to advance, secure and promote for an organisation that deploys it. This is done periodically and within a social context, from the technical and non-technical perspectives.

Social Context

Typically, organisations are founded on, and within a social context which consists of rules and resources, such as employees and technologies. Employees are considered to be the main actors of properties within a social context, producing recursive action during the development and implementation of EA in an organisation. The actions are based on how information and activities relating to EA are communicated or received. This in turn influences the development, implementation and practice of the concept within an organisation.

Based on a subjective interpretation that is enacted by significance, individuals and groups make use of technologies and other available resources to advance their domination and authority and to enhance their positions and protect their interests rather than the organisation's goals and objectives. These types of actions manifest in political know-how which employees make use of to enrich their power as they influence processes and knowingly or unknowingly complicate activities within the organisation during the development and implementation of EA. Consequently, the outcome of EA is sometimes crowded by complexities.

Employees' involvement shapes and guides the processes, from the development to the implementation stages of EA; hence communication and interpretation of activities are critical. However, it is complex, in that people have different feelings, thoughts and knowledgeability, which are demonstrated through conscious and unconscious actions. The activities, including the selection of techniques and tools, are often communicated to the stakeholders and received using different channels and processes enabled by technology solutions. The stakeholders apply their own interest and understanding to interpret the significance of the activities to themselves or the organisation or both.

Stakeholders do not necessarily respond to the communication through verbal or written communiques, but through their actions, whether they agreed or did not agree to an activity. Based on employees' interpretation and the meaning that they associate with an activity, they begin to influence processes and activities consciously or unconsciously in the development, implementation and practice of EA through their actions. This makes communication and interpretation of activities very significant components in the drive to gain a common understanding of the complexities that are associated with the development and implementation of EA in an organisation. These actions are recursive, making it process-oriented.

Communication can be used to strengthen the survival or derailment of EA deployment and practice, hence its criticality in an organisation. This is mainly because architects use periodic communication as a platform to interact and share information amongst themselves and with other stakeholders. On one hand, lack of or poor interaction among architects and stakeholders can lead to the downfall of EA development or implementation. On the other hand, communication can promote positive alliances in the organisation where best practices and knowledge can be shared and incorporated into the processes and activities of EA. This increases the intellectual capacity within the organisation to formulate good approaches and techniques, and to develop and implement EA. This is primarily because individuals interpret the requirements and components that are associated with EA subjectively. Hence, continuous communication over the period of the development and implementation of EA is required.

Process-oriented

EA is also a process-oriented approach through its numerous procedures, extensive consultation with stakeholders and allocation of various technical and business tasks. Each process is intended to deliver a valuable solution. Within this premise, each process produces and reproduces results, positively or negatively, as influenced and shaped by communication and interpretation, using available resources and rules. This makes process an important component in the development and implementation of EA in any organisation. Processes are used to recreate procedures through rules and regulations within the organisational needs. However, processes by nature enable and constrain activities; legitimately so. This happens at various levels and carries different impacts, depending on the size and complexity of the organisation, as well as the phenomena concerned, such as the different domains of the EA.

Evidently, process is of key significance to EA, primarily because it is used as a guideline to identify: (1) critical tasks required in the development, implementation, as well as practice of EA; (2) the planning and management of stakeholders' requirements; and (3) different approaches required to perform the development and implementation of EA. This is purposely to provide solutions of value that enable and support the goals and objectives of an organisation.

Thus, solutions are proposed, based on results from the deployment and practice of EA, through governance. Expectedly, this is intended to add value to an organisation through organisational structure. Subsequently, IT governance is often used for decision-making, particularly for the selection, deployment, support and maintenance of information systems and technology artefacts, processes and activities. Governance is based on the value of the end product (solution) of the development and implementation of EA in organisations that deploy it. In addition, it helps to manage and monitor the scope and boundaries within which the EA is developed, implemented and practised, using the available resources over time and space.

However, each of these artefacts is encompassed by various challenges, with an impact on the EA approach, solution and value as they are recursively enacted.

Through governance, EA policies, standards and principles are formulated. The policies are used to organise the rules and regulations. The standards guide the selection of appropriate approaches and frameworks for EA solution. Activities and procedures of EA are guided by principles. Some non-technical factors, such as process and people continually have influence on EA as the process is carried out through governance. The influence is enacted through the interpretation and communication of the organisational objectives, including the stock of knowledge and resources which are of relevance to the deployment of EA in an organisation.

Summary

In the quest to examine and understand why and how EA is deployed in organisations, ST is employed to view EA complexity, from which the chapter presents the different factors that can enable and at the same time constrain the development and implementation of EA in an organisation. These are (1) how various facilities can be used to influence activities and events of EA; and (2) how various influences are legitimised and sanctioned through the enactment of power, which could have been ignored or taken for granted. Thus, this chapter should be of importance to business, and the use of ST as a lens can be of interest to academia.

Through this chapter, business managers will gain a better understanding of how some factors, including political rules, resources, people and processes can influence and impact the development and implementation of EA. Also, it will be of benefit to some organisations to understand from different perspectives the relationship that exists in a societal context when EA is problematised before the development and implementation are embarked upon. Another important factor that can be of interest to organisations is the interaction between actors, which has always been complex to understand.

References

Akaka, M. A., & Vargo, S. L. (2014). Technology as an operant resource in service (eco) systems. *Information Systems and e-Business Management*, *12*(3), 367–384.

Al-Kharusi, H., Miskon, S., & Bahari, M. (2018). Enterprise architecture development approach in the public sector. *International Journal of Enterprise Information Systems (IJEIS)*, *14*(4), 124–141.

Archer, M. S. (2010). Morphogenesis versus structuration: On combining structure and action. *The British Journal of Sociology*, *61*(s1), 225–252.

Dang, D. (2021). Institutional logics and their influence on enterprise architecture adoption. *Journal of Computer Information Systems*, *61*(1), 42–52.

Giddens, A. (1984). *The constitution of society: Outline of the theory of structuration*. Cambridge, UK: John Polity Press.

Gutierrez, A., Orozco, J., & Serrano, A. (2009). Factors affecting IT and business alignment: A comparative study in SMEs and large organisations. *Journal of Enterprise Information Management, 22*(1/2), 197–211.

Iyamu, T. (2015). *Enterprise architecture from concept to practice.* Victoria, Australia: Heidelberg Press.

Iyamu, T., & Mphahlele, L. (2010). The Role of Principles in the Deployment of Enterprise Information Architecture. *Proceedings of the 12th International Conference on Informatics and Semiotics in Organisations.* (pp. 299–307). IFIP Press.

Iyamu, T., & Roode, D. (2010). The use of structuration and actor network theory for analysis: A case study of a financial institution in South Africa. *International Journal of Actor-Network Theory and Technological Innovation, 2*(1), 1–26.

Kappelman, L. A., & Zachman, J. A. (2013). The enterprise and its architecture: Ontology & challenges. *Journal of Computer Information Systems, 53*(4), 87–95.

Lapalme, J., Gerber, A., Van der Merwe, A., Zachman, J., De Vries, M., & Hinkelmann, K. (2016). Exploring the future of enterprise architecture: A Zachman perspective. *Computers in Industry, 79*, 103–113.

MacKay, B., & Tambeau, P. (2013). A structuration approach to scenario praxis. *Technological Forecasting and Social Change, 80*(4), 673–686.

Nicholson, J., Tsagdis, D., & Brennan, R. (2013). The structuration of relational space: Implications for firm and regional competitiveness. *Industrial Marketing Management, 42*(3), 372–381.

Nyella, E. E., & Mndeme, M. (2010). Power tensions in health information system integration in developing countries: The need for distributed control. *The Electronic Journal of Information Systems in Developing Countries, 43*(4), 1–19.

Orlikowski, W. J. (1992). The duality of technology: Rethinking the concept of technology in organisations. *Organisation Science, 3*(3), 398–427.

Safari, H., Faraji, Z., & Majidian, S. (2016). Identifying and evaluating enterprise architecture risks using FMEA and fuzzy VIKOR. *Journal of Intelligent Manufacturing, 27*(2), 475–486.

Sayogo, D. S., Zhang, J., Luna-Reyes, L., Jarman, H., Tayi, G., Andersen, D. L., & Andersen, D. F. (2015). Challenges and requirements for developing data architecture supporting integration of sustainable supply chains. *Information Technology and Management, 16*(1), 5–18.

Song, H., & Song, Y. T. (2010). Enterprise Architecture Institutionalization and Assessment. In *Proceeding of the 9th IEEE International Conference on Computer and Information Science.* (pp. 870–875).

Sztompka, P. (2014). Evolving focus on human agency in contemporary social theory. *Agency and structure: Reorienting social theory, 25*–60, Londres: Routledge.

Walsham, G., & Han, C.-K. (1991). Structuration theory and information systems research. *Journal of Applied Systems Analysis, 17,* 77–85.

Woodside, A. G., & Baxter, R. (2013). Achieving accuracy, generalization-to-contexts, and complexity in theories of business-to-business decision processes. *Industrial Marketing Management, 42*(3), 382–393.

Zachman, J. A. (1996). *Concepts of the framework for enterprise architecture.* Los Angeles, CA.

Chapter 8

Readiness Assessment Model for Enterprise Business Architecture

Introduction

Enterprise business architecture (EBA) is one of the domains of Enterprise Architecture (EA) (Dang & Pekkola, 2017). Other domains of EA are information, technical and application architectures (Iyamu, 2015). The domain has distinctive deliverables. Whittle and Myrick (2016) suggest that EBA provides the blueprint for business processes, events and activities, and focuses on both the current and future views of an organisation. In the last two decades, the interest in EBA by both academic and business organisations has increased tremendously (Hadaya & Gagnon, 2017; Amit & Zott, 2015; Versteeg & Bouwman, 2006). EBA is considered to be the most dominant of the domains of EA architectures (Whittle & Myrick, 2016). Based on the interest in the concept of EBA, many projects have been carried out by both the academia and practitioners in the areas of development and implementation, as well as in practice (Wikusna, 2018; Sandkuhl, Seigerroth & Kaidalova, 2017).

EBA is used to define the critical aspects of organisational processes, its strategy, policies, monitoring methods and business organisation (Sandkuhl et al., 2017). Versteeg and Bouwman (2006) argue that EBA contributes to the governance and management of activities within the business and computing environments of an organisation. In Shaanika and Iyamu's (2018) view, EBA is used to define an enterprise from a business perspective and then leverage its formalised description to govern and manage change and transformation of environment trends. Minoli

DOI: 10.1201/9781003268420-8

(2008) explains EBA as the architectural formulation of the business function which comprises the documentation that outlines the company's most important business processes. Wikusna (2018) proposes that EBA is a domain that contributes towards clarifying the complexities within an organisation whose purpose it is to develop functional and informative process and application architectures.

Despite the benefits of the concept as highlighted above, many organisations experience various challenges with EBA implementation and practice (Hadaya & Gagnon, 2017). Some of the challenges arise from the prioritisation of the business activities that always change (Whittle & Myrick, 2016). Also, some of the challenges of EBA include an understanding of factors such as the risks involved, success factors, as well as the design and implementation of the business for enterprise purposes (Gromoff, Bilinkis & Kazantsev, 2017). The challenges are often experienced at different stages of the concept, from development to implementation and post-implementation (Iyamu, 2015). This is attributable to the lack of readiness assessment before the process is embarked upon in a specific environment.

An assessment reveals organisational strengths and weaknesses which increase the formidability of readiness in the deployment and manageability of a solution (Hedayati, Shirazi & Fazlollahtabar, 2014). Ajami et al. (2011) argue that assessment is an essential and critical stage prior to the implementation of solutions. It aims at evaluating the preparedness of all the components of an organisation, namely; application, information, technical architectures, information technology (IT) solutions and procedures. Based on the outcome of the assessment, organisations are able to make proper and well-informed decisions about whether to go ahead with the implementation or not.

Despite the fact that existing literature recognises the significance of readiness in EA and the computing environment, empirical work remains limited (Abdolvand, Albadvi & Ferdowsi, 2008). Supporting this viewpoint, Alghamdi, Goodwin and Rampersad (2011) proposed readiness assessment solutions dimensions, which include IT architecture and e-governance. Hedayati et al. (2014) proposed a model that can be used to evaluate organisational readiness in order to implement service-oriented architecture (SOA). Bakar (2014) proposes an EA assessment model for a developing country with focus on alignment between business and IT, which integrates the information systems, processes, organisational units and people in the public sector.

Among the existing assessment models, none seemed to specifically focus on readiness-assessment of EBA at the time of putting together this chapter. This is a serious challenge that has thwarted the efforts of many organisations for many years, in that it either slows the implementation of the EBA (Hussein, Mahrin & Maarop, 2017) or derails its implementation and practice (Aji & Widodo, 2019).

This chapter begins with an introduction, followed by a review of related literature and the problematisation of readiness assessment for EBA deployment. Thereafter, an intensive examination of the objectives is conducted. Next, the factors that influence readiness assessment are comprehensively discussed. Subsequently, the readiness assessment model (RAM) for EBA is presented and discussed; and the assessment model is validated and viewed from a practice point. Finally, the chapter is summarised.

Enterprise Business Architecture

EBA is a domain of EA which defines the models that represent business processes, operations, interactions and boundaries (Whelan & Meaden, 2016). Karney (2009) argues that EBA shares the artefacts of IT architecture in shaping the goals and objectives of an organisation. Iyamu, Nehemia-Maletzky and Shaanika (2016) explain how EBA is applied in an organisation to define its scope and boundaries, its design and how it can develop business process models. Some of the benefits of EBA are to improve decision-making, reduce costs and improve the alignment between business and IT units (Dang & Pekkola, 2017; Sandkuhl et al., 2017). Karney (2009) clarifies how EBA focuses on documenting organisational vision and facilitating the formulation of business requirements towards improving competitiveness.

Even though the interest in EBA has grown over the years, the concept continues to encounter challenges in practice (Hadaya & Gagnon, 2017). This hinders its maturity. According to Versteeg and Bouwman (2006), it is difficult to find an organisation that has successfully deployed EBA. Little or nothing has changed even though this conclusion was reached over a decade ago. Dang and Pekkola (2017) portray this point by arguing that the challenges that hamper the implementation and practice of EBA are documented in many studies. Whelan and Meaden (2016) suggest that, given the challenges and trends that organisations face, it is not surprising that the practice of business architecture is not on the increase. The use of complex parameters for unstructured processes during planning is one of EBA's challenges (Gromoff et al., 2017).

In addition to the slow implementation of EBA, it is difficult to find an organisation that has institutionalised the concept (Iyamu, 2015; Versteeg & Bouwman, 2006). This can be attributed to the many challenges that have been identified in literature and in practice (Hedayati et al., 2014; Ajami et al., 2011). The challenges manifest themselves because a readiness assessment has not been conducted before implementation. Adjorlolo and Ellingsen (2013) argue that readiness assessment is used to determine success factors. It is one of the ways of reducing the risk of failure in organisational projects, activities or processes. It is an official measurement of the preparedness of an organisation to undergo change or transformation, but this instrument is currently not available for EBA. As a result, the promoters of EBA struggle to convince management and stakeholders on how to mitigate risks and other challenging factors facing the concept.

Despite the increasing interest in EA from the public and private sectors, the implementation and practice of the concept in organisations remain a huge concern

(Hussein et al., 2017). The challenge is synonymous with EA domains and can be associated with lack of readiness assessment, which influences the successful implementation of the concept. Readiness assessment is helpful in reducing potential risks in the implementation of EA (Aji & Widodo, 2019). The assessment model is a useful and cost-effective method for the implementation of EA (Bakar, Harihodin & Kama, 2016). Bakar (2014) proposed an EA assessment model for the Malaysian government, with focus on the alignment between business and IT, which integrates the information systems, processes, organisational units and people in both the public and private sector.

In 2001, the Gartner group recommended five factors for measuring the value of business architecture in an organisation (Harris, Grey & Rozwell, 2001). Sixteen years later, AL-Malaise AL-Ghamdi (2017) proposed a model that could be used to measure the impact of business architecture in an organisation because the challenges persisted. Some of the existing challenges around EBA are due to the fact that organisations tend to focus on processes and services without explicitly understanding the timing factors that may make or break a business model. For example, understanding how the cycles of production are synchronised with sales cycles and cash income is critical to cash flow and inventory. A separate analysis of the two would unlikely reveal the existence or importance of the relationship (Whelan & Meaden, 2016). Some of the challenges exist primarily because EBA has not undergone a readiness assessment in the environment where it is deployed.

Readiness assessment assists with a smoother transition from the current to a future state, which is essentially needed in the deployment of the EBA in an organisation. Alshaher (2013) argues that the lack of assessment of an organisation's readiness is the primary reason for the failure of implemented projects, as has been indicated in attempts to deploy EBA in many organisations (Shaanika & Iyamu, 2018; Hendrickx, 2015). This is mainly because potential challenges are not fully identified and addressed in accordance with the processes, procedures, events, activities and structure in the course of the development and implementation of EBA. The assessment assists organisations to identify limitations and provide suitable solutions in the implementation, deployment and post-deployment phases of IT solutions. According to Alghamdi et al. (2011), a readiness assessment is purposely used to improve the effectiveness of an organisation's initiatives. Thus, the current state of an organisation's readiness can be evaluated and the desirable state can be managed to enable the transition from the current state to the desirable state (Jahani, Javadein & Jafari, 2010).

Problem and Approach

The aim of this chapter is to propose a solution through a RAM. This aim is purposely to address the problems that are summarised in Table 8.1. In the table, implications are linked to each of the problems.

Table 8.1 Problematising EBA Readiness Assessment

#	The Problem	Implication
1	The definition and identification of requirements for EBA are not guided by a model in organisations. This is a problem primarily because the content of EBA becomes not inherent property, but it is contingent on the purpose that the model is intended to serve (Gong & Janssen, 2019).	Difficult to understand the artefacts that constitute EBA. Also, the scope of the EBA becomes too broad or vague, which comes across as overly ambitious for successful implementation.
2	There is no uniformity in how EBA is defined, developed, implemented and practised in organisations. This leads to inconsistency and duplication and makes it difficult to realise the objective and value of EBA in an organisation.	The consequence is that the challenges in planning and implementing EBA will not be clear or understood (Niemi & Pekkola, 2019).
3	The pattern employed in EBA practice is either not obvious or it is unknown in many organisations. This makes it difficult to assess the value and benefits of EBA practised in organisations.	Lack of acceptance consequently results in reluctance to use the artefacts of EBA, which affects decision-making (Löhe & Legner, 2014).

In addressing the problems stated in Table 8.1, the interpretivist approach was followed in examining the factors of influence, based on which a solution is proposed in this chapter. The interpretive approach was used primarily because the approach's rules create signification or meaningful symbolic systems that provide ways for actors to see and interpret events (Iyamu, 2011). Myers and Avison (2002) explain how the interpretivist approach generally attempts to understand phenomena through the meanings that people assign to them. Chen and Hirschheim (2004) also argue that the interpretivist approach emphasises the subjective meaning of the reality that is constructed through a human and social interaction process. The overriding objective of this chapter is to propose a solution that could be used to assess the readiness to deploy EBA in an enterprise. The discussion is therefore split into three main categories: (1) identification of requirements for the Business Architecture in organisations; (2) The deployment of Business Architecture in organisations; and (3) The practice of the concept of Business Architecture in an organisation.

Interpretivism is used to focus on the objectives of the chapter, which are (1) To understand how Business Architecture requirements are defined and identified in organisations; (2) To understand how Business Architecture is deployed in organisations; and (3) To examine how the concept of Business Architecture is practised in organisations. Based on what is revealed from the discussion, the aim of the chapter is achieved; that is, the development of a RAM.

Assessing Challenges of EBA Deployment

Through the objectives of the chapter, challenges of EBA deployment are assessed, as follows: (1) to understand how the EBA requirements are identified and gathered in organisations; (2) to understand how EBA is deployed in organisations; and (3) to examine how the concept of EBA is practised in organisations.

Identification of Requirements for EBA

EBA focuses on the design and governance of processes, activities and events in an organisation (Marks, 2008). Therefore, the requirements for the development of the architecture are of utmost importance. As a result, it is critical to determine the appropriate requirements. Appropriateness refers to the requirements that are unique to the organisation's vision and specific to its goal and objectives. The process therefore necessitates the involvement of the most relevant personnel in determining the requirements. The individuals involved must have a good understanding of both the business requirements and the organisation's objectives (Hohmann, 2003).

Two factors are crucial in selecting the personnel to participate in the identification and collection of requirements for the deployment of EBA. Firstly, the participants must have a good understanding of the organisation. Secondly, the participants must be knowledgeable about the concept of EBA. The two criteria are purposely to ensure the relevance of EBA within the context of the organisation. From the organisation's perspective, there are three main focuses: (1) organisational vision; (2) business processes and events of the organisation; and (3) the organisation's relationship with its customers, partners and the environment. These must be well understood by those who identify and gather requirements for the EBA in their organisations.

The office of the Chief Information Officer (CIO) has the responsibility to communicate the identified requirements of the business architecture to the IT Department within the organisation. In many organisations, there are often no formal methods or procedures, such as a template for identifying the requirements. Also, it has habitually been the initiative of IT departments (or units) to approach the business units about their challenges. The IT unit does this as a way of sourcing for revenue for their skill sets and technology solutions. In other organisations, the approach is different. The business units initiate a contact with the IT unit. There has been a debate in recent years about whether the business architecture should be driven by the business unit or IT unit, owing to this lack of clearance (Pandit, 2012). The intention of IT representatives in some organisations is to understand how IT solutions could be used to add more value to the business goals and objectives.

Hence, in many organisations, individuals with various skill sets and roles, such as business analysts and systems analysts, are involved in identifying and gathering the requirements on behalf of the organisation for the implementation of EBA. Also, individuals' involvement in identifying requirements can be along organisational structure. In some organisations, this leads to a restructuring in order to achieve a balance of roles and responsibilities, which sometimes results in promoting some individuals over others. For example, business analysts are promoted to the position of business architects in preparation for the development and implementation of EBA. In the formulation of the requirements, factors that influenced the responses from the business units are considered. These include process fragmentation, systems' interactions and relationships. The requirements are aligned with the strategic intent of the organisation.

Business architecture focuses on business processes, activities and events. Related factors such as people and processes are also considered in identifying and gathering the requirements for the concept. This is often to help understand how these factors fit together because an organisation cannot have IT solutions if it does not understand how the business units fit together, including the processes that they underpin. Business architecture helps to understand the factors that connect the processes and IT solutions in the organisation.

The requirements for utilising EBA are customarily identified by the IT department because of two main reasons. First, the business units are considered not knowledgeable about the concept of business architecture. Generally, the business units consider the business architecture as mainly a theory rather than a concept that can be put to practice. Hence, many organisations continue to theorise the concept of business architecture. Secondly, some business units cannot precisely identify or articulate their needs. In such circumstances, the IT unit takes leadership in identifying and gathering the requirements for the implementation of the EBA in the organisation.

The Deployment of EBA

The drive is to ensure that the deployment (development and implementation) of EBA aligns with the organisation's needs as they evolve. For this reason, the deployment of EBA is governed by policies, principles and standards, which cover both business and technology requirements. In addition, deployment requires executive-level support, structured decision-making processes and a strategy that is based on an understanding of the organisation's vision.

The deployment of EBA is influenced by both business and IT factors. The business factors include process design, structure, relationships, interaction, people and management. Some of the IT factors are the integration of processes and enabling of collaboration between business units or organisations. Without an understanding and consideration of these factors, it is nearly impossible to assess the value of EBA in an organisation. Some of the challenges that are experienced with the deployment of EBA in many organisations can be associated with lack of proper preparation before the concept is embarked upon. The lack of preparation also affects the assessment of the maturity levels of the concept in organisations.

Consequently, the poor or limited preparation in the deployment of EBA leads to not following the necessary steps, lack of linear procedure, not conducting readiness assessment and not developing a template for collecting the requirements. As a result, the process is considered informal, and the promoters struggle to get buy-in from the management and some of the employees. The informal approach can work if it is solely the IT department's responsibility to make decisions about technology-related solutions and matters in the organisation. The IT department explores its mandate and imposes solutions such as EBA on the business units. This is irrespective of whether the business understands the concept or not, and whether the business units have the capability to adapt or not. This type of approach has negative implications from both technical and non-technical points of view.

In some organisations, the business units prefer to drive IT solutions that are related to their processes, events and activities. This is a challenge, as many business personnel do not have the technical expertise and know-how to translate business requirements into technical specification and to propose or evaluate IT solutions. Another challenge in some organisations is that the business units are not always in favour of process documentation and process automation, but rather prefer a legacy approach which they have operated for many years. When processes are documented properly, it aids the business to identify the gaps and opportunities. Also, automation reduces risks and mistakes, and improves efficiency.

The implementation of EBA is process-oriented. It follows sequential steps such as the documentation of the current situation; the formulation of a definition of the concept in the context of the organisation; documentation of the future shape of the organisation; formulation of structure; and upskilling of personnel (Iyamu, 2012). In some organisations, particularly the large enterprises, documentation is hard to find, which makes it difficult to track and trace business activities that are related to processes, coexisting of systems and the factors and events of alignment between units. Documented processes help to identify gaps, process duplication and opportunities.

Another challenge in the implementation of EBA comes from the human element. For example, some of the business architects do not have sufficient experience to undertake or execute some of the tasks that are allocated in the beginning of their career. Also, the main promoters of EBA have line managers who may or may not fully support the initiative of implementing EBA in the organisation. The managers' pushback can be attributed to a lack of knowledge of the concept. The fear of being exposed ignites such pushback.

The Practice of EBA

The concept of EBA is deployed in many organisations for the purpose of improving and mastering business activities, events and business processes. The deployment of the concept includes creating standardisation, structure and change management to foster competitiveness.

Standardisation is intended to ensure the unification of an organisation's documentation, processes and procedures, to enable and support a more cohesive and comprehensive collection and use of business requirements. The structure covers the hierarchy of the people involved in the practice of EBA in the organisation. In addition, it includes formalising the processes and events concerning the practice of EBA within the organisation. This is also the case with change management, where processes and the format of documents are streamlined with the purpose of unification. This helps business units to begin to understand the alignment between themselves and the IT unit.

EBA does not change the rules of an organisation but enables it to be more flexible so that it can be re-engineered. Subsequently, the process encourages a dynamic business environment. This includes regulations within which the organisation operates. An approach that allows flexibility and re-engineering of processes, rules and regulations reduces risk and improves adaptability and effectiveness. The flexibility and re-engineering of business rules and regulations increase stakeholders' confidence in the organisation and creates stability.

Challenges of fragmentation arise when there is a low or reluctant buy-in from some of the business units in the implementation of EBA. One of the consequences of such an action is that an IT solution that is deployed to serve the entire organisation will begin to encounter challenges because the requirements did not holistically cover all the units. Also, this challenge arises because the process is driven by IT. Another challenge is that during the implementation of EBA, some business units uncharacteristically make verbal requests to the IT specialists to change some services. This occurs because the business units do not like creating documentation of processes and events. The IT specialists often oblige because the requests can potentially contribute towards adding value to the business, even though they are well aware that such undocumented processes pose a huge risk to the business environment of the organisation. Through EBA, the documentation is intended to enable the tracing and tracking of incidents and events.

Communication is another key area that crucially contributes to the success or failure of EBA in an organisation. Generally, personnel from both the business and IT units need to focus and improve on the ways in which they communicate with one another in finding solutions for the organisation. The business has to understand that it is not all about systems but processes. The processes have to align. Then, the IT solutions will follow suit.

The introduction of documentation processes and formal structures sometimes makes employees think and ask questions differently. Inquisitively, the implementation of EBA creates awareness of governance signification among employees in an organisation. For this reason, there can be more buy-ins from the business units. Prior to implementation, the business units should be made to understand the consequence of late or impromptu request for change. This is because the underpinning processes had not been properly structured, and, most importantly, some employees might not be aware of whether their request had or had not made any impact on organisational activities.

One of the most significant values that the EBA can add to the business units is the ability to make informed decisions aimed at improved sustainability and competitiveness. The value addition can also be associated with a formal structure, documentation approach and flexibility, which leads to the re-engineering of processes and activities towards fulfilling the business mission, goals and objectives.

Factors Influencing EBA Readiness Assessment

Based on section four above, seven factors come across as the most prevalent in influencing the assessment of EBA readiness in an organisation. As shown in Figure 8.1, the factors are (1) requirements gathering for EBA deployment; (2) alignment between business and IT units; (3) organisational structure; (4) capability; its strength in the deployment of EBA; (5) stability; (6) re-engineering of organisational activities; and (7) flexibility of activities.

The factors as shown in Figure 8.1 are discussed in the remainder of this section. The discussion takes into consideration the significance of the connecting arrows.

Requirements

The requirements are intended to address the business initiatives and should be used as a foundation for building effective business solutions. For these reasons, requirements are identified and gathered to ensure the successful development of initiatives (Abai, Yahaya & Deraman, 2013). Based on its criticality, it is paramount that the right (skilled) people are chosen in the process to gather requirements identified by the most appropriate personnel. Thus, the requirements for the development of the business architecture are gathered from the business users, including managers, team leaders and other employees within the business units of an organisation, working towards ensuring a successful goal outcome in the organisation.

Organisations have different settings with unique objectives, goals and mission and, therefore, the process of identifying and gathering of requirements is expected to be unique from one organisation to another. Some organisations struggle to

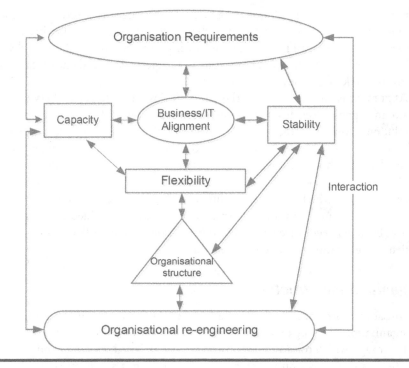

Figure 8.1   Factors influencing readiness assessment.

produce a formal approach, such as a template for identifying and gathering requirements. As a result, the requirements obtained from such a circumstance are also often not documented. Organisational requirements for EBA need to be documented for two main reasons: (1) as business changes, the requirements can be revisited; and (2) the outputs can be measured and validated against the requirements. Based on these reasons, the relationship and interaction between business and IT units are enacted and facilitated. The interaction results in alignment, which enables the sharing and use of the available capacity, including participation and common understanding of the organisation's re-engineering process. The gathering of the identified requirements and documentation is critical for assessing the readiness of EBA in an organisation.

Business/IT Alignment

Alignment between the business and IT units is significant for effectiveness and efficiency of strategic activities and operationalisation of solutions in an organisation (Silvius, 2009). Business architecture wholly relies on alignment for its development and implementation. In the absence, or low level of alignment between the business and IT units, an organisation is bound to develop challenges in understanding the factors that influence IT solutions. Also, if the alignment is weak, even if the IT solutions are architected, there would be disparity and incompatibility between the business initiatives and IT solutions. According to Connolley, Scholtz and Calitz (2013: 1), "IT is often seen not to meet business expectations and one of the reasons for this is a lack of Business-IT alignment".

Alignment is enabled through the relationships and interaction between units within an organisation. It draws upon a synergy between business processes and IT solutions. Also, alignment results in the flexible execution of events, processes and activities which, in turn, contribute to creating a stable environment. Pandit (2012) elucidates how the misalignment between IT and business is due to the fact that IT executives lack business knowledge and business leaders lack knowledge or experience of IT, which results in a stumbling block in the attempts to align both business and IT units towards the organisation's goals and objectives. The failure to meet business needs often results in information silos and affects organisational efficiency, competitiveness and sustainability.

Organisational Structure

Organisational structure refers to the hierarchical structure of the personnel in an organisation. The organisational structure creates a legal recognition of various levels through which roles and responsibilities are assigned, executed and managed. This helps an organisation to achieve its objectives, goals and mission. However, this can also be a constraining factor. The roles and responsibilities are the employees' source of power and are often employed to dictate and influence activities in an organisation. Worthily, it makes an organisational structure significantly useful for EBA implementation, in navigating through the organisation for buy-in purposes. Also, the organisational structure helps to define the ownership of tasks and activities in the development and implementation of EBA.

Alignment between the business and IT units can be established and practised through the organisational structure. In addition, it can be used to facilitate business performance. Despite this important role prior to the implementation of EBA, some organisations do not explore the usefulness of their organisational structure. This causes some IT solutions to be isolated from one another. As a result, IT solutions are not aligned with the organisation's objectives, goals and mission. The lack of the organisational structure's influence can lead to ambiguity and uncertainty of roles in the development and implementation of EBA in an organisation. Through an organisational structure, employees or stakeholders take the opportunity to interact. This enables the organisation to become more flexible in promoting the re-engineering of processes and events.

Capacity

Business capacity refers to availability of resources, both human and non-human, that are handled by an organisation's team, processes, services or tools (Suryani et al., 2010). The human capacity entails skilled personnel rather than the presence of a person. Non-human capacity includes finance and governance. The resources can be scaled up or down by adding, reallocating or removing processes and activities.

It is in this context that it is argued that the development and implementation of EBA depend wholly on capacity. This has been experienced in many organisations, as some organisations struggle in their pursuit to develop and implement the concept of EBA. It is therefore of utmost importance for an organisation to weigh up available capacity against the requirements of EBA before it proceeds to the implementation process. It is on this additional basis that interaction between business and IT units is critical in assessing the nature of the capacity that is available for the development and implementation of EBA in the organisation.

Stability

In the context of readiness assessment of EBA, stability is referred to as a situation where an environment is kept consistent with minimum challenges. It is critical to continuously assess business processes and revise business management development in relation to the environment (Vovchenko et al., 2017). The same approach of assessment applies to IT solutions, including the development and implementation of EBA. This is to detect and manage deficiencies as well as risks within the environment.

The appropriate structure of risk management enables the stability and control of business activities and IT solutions in an organisation. In some organisations, there is prioritisation of structure geared towards enablement and supporting flexibility that creates opportunities and increased innovation for the purpose of competitive advantage. Also, stability influences the requirements of the business, an alignment between business and IT units, organisational structure and flexible actioning of processes and activities in the development and implementation of EBA in an environment.

Organisational Re-engineering

Organisational re-engineering is often referred to as business process re-engineering (BPR), which focuses on the recreation of core processes and activities in an organisation (Goksoy, Ozsoy & Vayvay, 2012). The process also emphasises the analysis and design of workflows and events. The BPR aims at helping an organisation to rethink the improvement of customer service, which enhances competitiveness.

It is in the process of re-engineering that inefficiencies and ineffectiveness are identified and amended to ensure that all processes are current and relevant in helping the organisation to achieve its objectives. In deploying EBA, some organisations carry out BPR, and proper documentations of those processes are identified as gaps during the identification of requirements. If the processes are not re-engineered in an organisation for the implementation of EBA, organisational performance might not increase and this is highly likely to affect efficiency and competitiveness in a rapidly changing world. Organisational re-engineering therefore entails an interaction with the organisational structure and an understanding of the business capacity and stability.

Flexibility

Flexibility is the ability to improve on response time in a business setting. This allows changes necessary to respond effectively to the ever-changing environment as quickly as possible. Organisations need to be able to adjust easily to business initiatives with minor or no obstruction to ongoing events and activities. Bock et al. (2012) suggest that flexibility involves responsiveness to pressure and a proactive rather than a reactive approach.

In many organisations, the concept of EBA is a success due to their flexibility, which is potentially the result of restructuring, to ensure the alignment of appropriate skill sets with ongoing initiatives. Without flexibility, it becomes difficult to assess changing requirements in the light of the implementation of EBA in an organisation. As a result, deficiencies, such as risk, might be detected. The flexibility enables interactions with business/IT alignment and organisational structure.

Readiness Assessment Model for EBA

The factors discussed in Section 5 (Factors Influencing EBA Readiness Assessment) were engaged in a circle, repeatedly, in order to make sense of how they can be used for the assessment of the EBA in an organisation. The process brings out the understanding of the factors identified from the possible and potential interactions among stakeholders. The dialogic nature of the approach (Fleck, Smythe & Hitchen, 2011) helped in gaining a better understanding of the interconnectivity of the factors and how the weights influence the readiness of the EBA in an organisation. Based on the factors, a RAM is developed. The model is intended to assist in determining the success factors of the EBA in an organisation. This includes reducing the risk of failure in organisational initiatives (Adjorlolo & Ellingsen, 2013). According to Hedayati et al. (2014), readiness assessment aids organisations with gaining precision in an environment and helps gain a better understanding of the current situation.

The EBA RAM is split into two modes: Mode 1 (Table 8.2) and Mode 2 (Table 8.3). Mode 1 presents the factors of readiness, based on the findings from the data analysis. The Mode is divided in two, Y and X axes, and has a total of 40 cells. Mode 1 consists of factors and weights. In Mode 2, each of the assessment weights is defined. The outcome of Mode 1 is aligned with Mode 2. The alignment determines the current state of readiness of an organisation. The steps in the application of the RAM (Mode 1 and Mode 2) are described here.

Table 8.2 Mode 1

Factor \ Weight	1	2	3	4	5
Requirements	There are no templates or processes for collecting and formulating requirements.	There are processes, but no existing templates for collecting requirements.	Different templates and processes are used to collect or formulate requirements.	There are approved templates and processes for collecting requirements.	Templates and processes are regularly reviewed for organisational purposes.
Documentation	There are no documentations for most processes and events.	There is no uniformity in documenting processes and events.	Some processes and activities are documented. Documentations are stored sparsely.	All processes and activities are documented and stored in a central repository.	Documentations are regularly reviewed for improvement purposes.
Business/IT Alignment	Desperate silos of processes and events.	Change in the organisation is slow.	Uniform processes, activities and events.	Unified teams, melds skills and resources.	Transformation is stable and ongoing.
Ownership	Identify key performance indicators (KPI).	Define responsibilities for KPI tasks, processes and activities.	Define and assign accountability for each responsibility.	Define a role map for each responsibility and accountability.	Executive control over processes, activities and events.

(Continued)

Table 8.2 Mode 1 (Continued)

Factor \ Weight	1	2	3	4	5
Governance	Rules and regulations are not transparent.	Define authorities over rules and regulations.	Define resources, processes and value.	Standards, principles and policies are defined.	Regular review of standards, principles and policies.
Risk	Potential factors of derailment not completely identified.	Identify and understand the different types of hindering factors.	Operational plan to mitigate against potential factors of derailment.	Strategic plan to mitigate against potential factors of derailment.	Regular review of operational and strategic plans.
Skill-set	Personnel are trained. Basic knowledge acquired.	Qualified personnel are in accordance with job description.	Defined growth paths for the available qualified personnel.	Highly skilled personnel are in all areas of responsibility.	Implement strategy for skill retention.
Funding	Resources and rationale have yet to be identified.	Identify and understand the resources and benefits.	Able to quantify and identify benefits and value.	Able to compare the cost of IT services to the next best alternatives.	Able to associate value with the identified benefits.

The weight associated with the assessment model as shown in Mode 1 was grouped into four categories (1–4): 1 = Foundation; 2 = Intermediary; 3 = Good; and 4 = Excellent. Each of the categories is defined and presented in Model 2.

Mode 1 consists of a total of forty (40) cells: eight (8) rows and five (5) columns. Each of the rows has a maximum weight of five (5) points, which is a total of forty (40) points. There are three steps in the application of the RAM:

- Step #1: From each of the rows, mandatorily select a cell, not more than one.
- Step #2: Add up the weights of the selected cells. The total cannot be less than 5 points; and cannot be more than 40 points. Otherwise, step #1 has not been adhered to.
- Step #3: Align the total score with Mode 2.

Table 8.3 Mode 2

Weight	Description
5–13	Foundation – The process has been initiated. Little has been done to kick-start the processes that have been established. There are potentials in the processes or activities are on the right tract and have potential to improve.
14–22	Intermediary – The processes, activities or events are sufficient for the operation, but do require more work. The current state is desirable, manageable and ready for transition from the current state to a future state (Jahani et al., 2010).
23–31	Good (in operation) – The activities are generally acceptable but require continuous review. The review process identifies areas of improvement. The organisation has the capacity to undergo a change (Adjorlolo & Ellingsen, 2013).
32–40	Excellent (stable) – All processes and activities are seemingly accepted in an excellent form. It is a stage of institutionalisation in an organisation. Iyamu (2011: 28) refers to "institutionalisation as the process where a practice is assimilated into the norm and is not easily disassociated, dismantled or re-designed".

Validation of the Assessment Model

To validate the assessment model, there was no existing model that focused on EBA. The focus was therefore expanded to EA, which covers information, business, technical and application domains (Iyamu, 2015). As shown in Table 8.4, in recent years (less than 10 years), only four studies were found to have proposed an assessment model for the implementation of the EA in organisations.

In general, the lack of readiness assessment is one of the main factors that particularly affect the deployment of EA in enterprises. (Bakar, 2014). Even though the domains have general principles, each domain is distinct (Sandkuhl et al., 2017). As such, the business architecture requires a specific model to assess its readiness in an

Table 8.4   Validation

Scope	Description
Readiness Assessment Model	EA readiness' critical successful factors include Governance, Cognition, Planning, Documentation, Communication, Participation and Commitment, Organisation Culture and Information Technology.
	Enterprise Environment, Process, People and Technology are the four main factors that influence the readiness of EA in an organisation.
	The EA assessment factors include Internal Process, Learning and Growth, Authority Support, Cost, Technology and Talent Management.
	The primary factors of the EA assessment model are financial, customer, internal, innovation and learning.

organisation. Thus, it was difficult to validate the RAM proposed in this chapter against existing models, because no model that specifically focused on business architecture seemed to exist.

As shown in Tables 8.2 and 8.4, some of the influencing factors, such as alignment, people (skill set, ownership), process and cost (funding) collaborate. However, the EA factors cannot be used to measure or assess the readiness of the EBA because of their distinctive coverage and deliverables. The EBA focuses on process model (Iyamu et al., 2016), while the EA holistically covers the organisation (Sandkuhl et al., 2017).

The Assessment Model in Practice

In an organisation, the points should be balanced across the assessment factors. It is therefore recommended that the weight be at the levels of acceptability, which are between three and five points. The assessment model is used for an organisation that plans to implement or has implemented Business Architecture. Each of the factors listed in Table 8.2 has its objectives and requirements and must be defined by the organisation within its context. The model can be used to achieve the following:

i. Assist an organisation to identify limitations which can possibly hamper the objectives of the business and its return on investment.
ii. Gain a better understanding of the gaps that might exist in moving towards a formidable deployment of the concept (Jahani et al., 2010).
iii. Create the opportunity for an organisation to conduct an assessment even though it has started with the deployment of Business Architecture.
iv. Shape and define the development and implementation of EBA. Business Architecture is an essential domain of EA (Versteeg & Bouwman, 2006).

In practice, the model can be used to identify the factors and as a reference point to determine the readiness of EBA in an organisation (Aji & Widodo, 2019).

Summary

The lack of a RAM has slowed down the implementation of Business Architecture in organisations and affects its advancement. This chapter proposes a solution in the form of a readiness-assessment model to be used specifically for Business Architecture and which can be used by an organisation that is interested in deploying the concept. Figure 8.1 can be used to assist organisations and managers in their quest to gain a better understanding of the factors that influence readiness assessment. The model (Table 8.2) can be used to guide business architects and managers in developing templates and criteria for assessing the EBA readiness in their organisations. By means of the model, an organisation is able to justify the deployment of the concept, which has been a challenge for many individuals and organisations for many years. The chapter adds to literature from both business and IT perspectives. Thus, the chapter contributes to both business advancement and academic development.

References

Abai, N. H. Z., Yahaya, J. H., & Deraman, A. (2013). User requirement analysis in data warehouse design: A review. *Procedia Technology, 11*, 801–806.

Abdolvand, N., Albadvi, A., & Ferdowsi, Z. (2008). Assessing readiness for business process reengineering. *Business Process Management Journal, 14*(4), 497–511.

Adjorlolo, S., & Ellingsen, G. (2013). Readiness assessment for implementation of electronic patient record in Ghana: A case of university of Ghana hospital. *Journal of Health Informatics in Developing Countries, 7*(2), 128–140.

Ajami, S., Ketabi, S., Isfahani, S. S., & Heidari, A. (2011). Readiness assessment of electronic health records implementation. *Acta Informatica Medica, 19*(4), 224–227.

Aji, A. S., & Widodo, T. (2019). Measuring enterprise architecture readiness at higher education institutions. *International Journal of Applied Business and Information Systems, 3*(1), 14–20.

AL-Malaise AL-Ghamdi, A. S. (2017). A proposed model to measure the impact of business architecture. *Cogent Business & Management, 4*(1), 1–8.

Alghamdi, I. A., Goodwin, R., & Rampersad, G. (2011). E-government readiness assessment for government organizations in developing countries. *Computer and Information Science, 4*(3), 3–17.

Alshaher, A. A. F. (2013). The McKinsey 7S model framework for e-learning system readiness assessment. *International Journal of Advances in Engineering & Technology, 6*(5), 1948–1966.

Amit, R., & Zott, C. (2015). Crafting business architecture: The antecedents of business model design. *Strategic Entrepreneurship Journal, 9*(4), 331–350.

Bakar, N. A. (2014). An assessment model for government enterprise architecture establishment phase. *Journal of Computational and Theoretical Nanoscience, 20*(10), 1987–1991.

Bakar, N. A. A., Harihodin, S., & Kama, N. (2016). Assessment of enterprise architecture implementation capability and priority in public sector agency. *Procedia Computer Science, 100*, 198–206.

Bock, A. J., Opsahl, T., George, G., & Gann, D. M. (2012). The effects of culture and structure on strategic flexibility during business model innovation. *Journal of Management Studies, 49*(2), 279–305.

Chen, W., & Hirschheim, R. (2004). A paradigmatic and methodological examination of information systems research from 1991 to 2001. *Information Systems Journal, 14*(3), 197–235.

Connolley, A., Scholtz, B., & Calitz, A. (2013). Achieving the Benefits of Business-IT Alignment Supported by Enterprise Architecture. In *Presentado en 7th International Business Conference.* Seychelles.

Dang, D. D., & Pekkola, S. (2017). Systematic literature review on enterprise architecture in the public sector. *Electronic Journal of e-Government, 15*(2), 130–154.

Fleck, K., Smythe, E. A., & Hitchen, J. M. (2011). Hermeneutics of self as a research approach. *International Journal of Qualitative Methods, 10*(1), 14–29.

Goksoy, A., Ozsoy, B., & Vayvay, O. (2012). Business process reengineering: Strategic tool for managing organizational change an application in a multinational company. *International Journal of Business and Management, 7*(2), 89–112.

Gong, Y., & Janssen, M. (2019). The value of and myths about enterprise architecture. *International Journal of Information Management, 46*, 1–9.

Gromoff, A., Bilinkis, Y., & Kazantsev, N. (2017). Business architecture flexibility as a result of knowledge-intensive process management. *Global Journal of Flexible Systems Management, 18*(1), 73–86.

Hadaya, P., & Gagnon, B. (2017). *Business architecture: The missing link in strategy formulation, implementation and execution*, 1–254, Montreal: ASATE Publishing.

Harris, K., Grey, M. C., & Rozwell, C. (2001). Changing the View of ROI to VOI—Value on Investment. *Gartner Research Note, SPA-14-7250.*

Hedayati, A., Shirazi, B., & Fazlollahtabar, H. (2014). An assessment model for the state of organizational readiness inservice oriented architecture implementation based on fuzzy logic. *Computer Science and Information Technology, 2*(1), 1–9.

Hendrickx, H. H. (2015). Business architect: A critical role in enterprise transformation. *Journal of Enterprise Transformation, 5*(1), 1–29.

Hohmann, L. (2003). *Beyond software architecture: Creating and sustaining winning solutions.* Boston, MA: Addison-Wesley Longman Publishing Co., Inc.

Hussein, S. S., Mahrin, M. N. R., & Maarop, N. (2017). Preliminary study of Malaysian Public Sector (MPS) transformation readiness through Enterprise Architecture (EA) establishment. In *Proceedings of Pacific Asia Conference on Information Systems (PACIS).* 16-20 July, Langkawi Island, Malaysia.

Iyamu, T. (2011). Institutionalisation of the enterprise architecture: The actor-network perspective. *International Journal of Actor-Network Theory and Technological Innovation (IJANTTI), 3*(1), 27–38.

Iyamu, T. (2012). A framework for developing and implementing the enterprise technical architecture. *Computer Science Information Systems, 9*(1), 189–206.

Iyamu, T. (2015). *Enterprise architecture: From concept to practice.* (2nd ed.). Australia: Heidelberg Press.

Iyamu, T., Nehemia-Maletzky, M., & Shaanika, I. (2016). The overlapping nature of business analysis and business architecture: What we need to know. *Electronic Journal of Information Systems Evaluation, 19*(3), 169–179.

Jahani, B., Javadein, S. R. S., & Jafari, H. A. (2010). Measurement of enterprise architecture readiness within organizations. *Business Strategy Series, 11*(3), 177–191.

Karney, J. (2009). *Introduction to business architecture*, 1–225, Cengage Learning.

Löhe, J., & Legner, C. (2014). Overcoming implementation challenges in enterprise architecture management: A design theory for architecture-driven IT management (ADRIMA). *Information Systems and e-Business Management, 12*(1), 101–137.

Marks, E. A. (2008). *Service-oriented architecture governance for the services driven enterprise.* John Wiley & Sons.

Minoli, D. (2008). *Enterprise architecture a to z: Frameworks, business process modelling, SOA, and infrastructure technology.* New York, NY: Auerbach Publications.

Myers, M., & Avison, D. (2002), An introduction to qualitative research in information systems, in *Qualitative research in information systems, Introducing Qualitative Methods,* 2–12, London: SAGE Publications, Ltd.

Niemi, E., & Pekkola, S. (2019). The benefits of enterprise architecture in organizational transformation. *Business & Information Systems Engineering, 62*(6), 585–597.

Pandit, V. (2012). Challenges in business and IT alignment: Business and IT consulting project report. http://www.slideshare.net/panditvidur/challenges-in-business-and-it-alignment [28 August 2019].

Sandkuhl, K., Seigerroth, U., & Kaidalova, J. (2017). Towards Integration Methods of Product-IT into Enterprise Architectures. In *the Proceedings of the 21st International Workshop on Enterprise Distributed Object Computing (EDOCW).* 10-13 October, Quebec City. IEEE.

Shaanika, I., & Iyamu, T. (2018). Developing the enterprise architecture for the Namibian government. *The Electronic Journal of Information Systems in Developing Countries, 84*(3), 1–11.

Silvius, A. G. (2009). Business and IT Alignment. *International conference on information management and engineering (ICIME '09).* 3-5 April, Kuala Lumpur, Malaysia.

Suryani, E., Chou, S. Y., Hartono, R., & Chen, C. H. (2010). Demand scenario analysis and planned capacity expansion: A system dynamics framework. *Simulation Modelling Practice and Theory, 18*(6), 732–751.

Versteeg, G., & Bouwman, H. (2006). Business architecture: A new paradigm to relate business strategy to ICT. *Information Systems Frontiers, 8*(2), 91–102.

Vovchenko, N. G., Holina, M. G., Orobinskiy, A. S., & Sichev, R. A. (2017). Ensuring financial stability of companies on the basis of international experience in construction of risks maps, internal control and audit. *European Research Studies Journal, 20*(1), 350–368.

Whelan, J., & Meaden, G. (2016). *Business architecture: A practical guide*, (1), 1–304.

Whittle, R., & Myrick, C. B. (2016). *Enterprise business architecture: The formal link between strategy and results.* London: CRC Press.

Wikusna, W. (2018). Enterprise architecture model for vocational high school. *IJAIT (International Journal of Applied Information Technology), 2*(01), 22–28.

Chapter 9

Enterprise Architecture as Agent of Change for Enterprises

Introduction

The concept of enterprise architecture (EA) is not new; it has been adopted and practised in many private organisations and government institutions and agencies for many years. The concept is an approach that enables and supports an organisation's competitive edge through its governance of information technology (IT) solutions, business design and information management to significantly fulfil consumers' needs. Organisations' reliance on IT solutions to deliver services continues to increase, owing to the need to have a better and seamless service delivery and remain competitive.

Many organisations employ EA to facilitate the design of core services and functions and to transition into desired states. Other benefits of EA that have been extensively discussed are the alignment and bridging of gaps between business and IT units (Gong & Janssen, 2019). Some of the benefits are intended to foster sustainability and competitiveness through efficiency and efficacy. Johnson, Ekstedt and Lagerstrom (2016) argued that irrespective of the level of reliance, the complexity of business logic and processes, as well as IT solutions, continues to increase in organisations. According to Shaanika and Iyamu (2018), some of the challenges of IT solutions include incompatibilities, lack of integration and lack of scalability. In attempts to address these challenges, organisations invest in EA as a remedial approach.

Since John Zachman introduced the concept of EA over three decades ago, other frameworks have been developed (Tamm et al., 2011). This includes META Group Inc., Forester, Department of Defence Architecture Framework (DoDAF), the Federal EA Framework (FEAF), the Treasury EA Framework (TEAF), the Open Group Architecture Forum (TOGAF) and the Zachman Framework (Lapalme et al., 2016; Urbaczewski & Mrdalj, 2006). The existence of different frameworks has helped to drive various viewpoints from multiple angles about the concept of EA in many organisations and government enterprises. This includes academic discourses, research and curriculum development. One of the focuses is how to employ EA to provide governance for change, from IT solutions' perspectives.

The role of EA is to guide an organisation's strategic goals and facilitate change within which the activities of IT are governed and managed. Another significant area of EA is it helps to maintain uniformity and consistency when building, deploying and managing complexities of both business and IT, which are constantly evolving. Thus, to both private organisations and government enterprises, EA facilitates change, based on how it is defined, scoped, deployed and managed, which manifests into its signification in an environment. It is within this context that Iyamu (2015) describes EA as an agent of change.

EA promises a different approach through which both private organisations and government institutions and agencies can transform activities from a current state to a desired state to improve service delivery (Hjort-Madsen & Pries-Heje, 2009). As many enterprises strive to employ EA as an agent of change, and exhume the benefits, so come risks and challenges (Safari, Faraji & Majidian, 2016). Some of the challenges were highlighted by Buckle et al. (2011) as follows: the gap between requirements and product; unclear time of product delivery; and uncertainty around committed parties. The challenges could be caused by factors such as: how EA was problematised by the promoters among the various stakeholders known as networks, which attracts different types of interest and shapes participation (Bui & Levy, 2017).

Also, many enterprises do not understand how they can employ EA as an agent of change in their environments if they cannot measure the value, which is the most significant aspect to majority of stakeholders. The most common critique of EA is the difficulty of measuring its value, which manifests from the following: the uncertainty around the definition of value, which is subjective to the stakeholders (Rodrigues & Amaral, 2010). The complexities of EA value come from both technical and non-technical perspectives, which require a deeper understanding of the sociotechnical viewpoints. Thus, the actor-network theory (ANT) is applied herein to examine how EA can be employed as an agent of change in an organisation. The theory brings fresh perspectives in examining and understanding the sociotechnical factors in the deployment of EA within the computing environments of organisations.

An actor-network consists of actors linked together through various interests to form a network consciously or unconsciously. The theory emphasises the heterogeneous nature of actor-networks consisting of and linking together both human and non-human elements (Callon, 1986). A core assumption in ANT is that no actor is different in kind from another. Instead, how size, power or organisation is generated should be studied in an unprejudiced manner.

Works and developments on EA by academics and IT practitioners have over the years transformed the concept into a field of discipline. However, there are still more questions than answers, particularly in practising EA in organisations. In Shaanika and Iyamu (2018), the question was, what is the purpose of EA to organisations? Hjort-Madsen and Pries-Heje (2009) asked, what has driven the use and adoption of the EA concept in organisations? In this chapter, I pose a question: how do actors and their networks influence EA as an agent of change in both private and public institutions towards a successful implementation and practice? These are some of the questions that shape many organisations' decisions about EA, and which this chapter examines from the point of theorising the concepts towards developing a conceptual framework that can be used to guide implementation and practice.

This chapter began with the introduction. Thereafter, a review of related literature, covering EA and ANT, is presented. This is followed by more emphasis on EA in enterprises. Next, is the conceptualisation of the concept of agent of change. The discussion about EA as an agent of change is expanded and comprehensively presented. The implication of practice is covered and the chapter is summarised.

Literature Review

A review of literature relating to this subject covers EA from organisations' perspective and ANT. The review is presented in two subsections as follows.

Enterprise Architecture in Organisations

Through principles, standards and governance, EA provides guidance to organisations towards solving the complexities that reside in their environments (Lapalme et al., 2016). At some points, EA's strengths of covering multiple units in an organisation become a challenge as it gets harder to employ and articulate its value, which leads to its criticisms (Roth et al., 2013). Löhe and Legner (2014) state that some of the criticisms of EA include the effort it takes to deploy and manage the activities of the concept; the difficulty in measuring its success; and how the benefits often come at a later time than anticipated by the stakeholders. Some of the challenges of EA are ultimately costly to organisations, including government institutions and agencies.

Some organisations lack an understanding of EA, leading to failure in justifying their investment in the approach and how they benefit from it (Tamm et al., 2011). This relates to Shaanika and Iyamu's (2018) argument where they stated that the shortage of skill set remains a challenge in the deployment of EA. The shortage of skill set can be attributed to lack of, or hesitant investment in EA by enterprises. However, it is difficult to invest in an area where knowledgeability is lacking. Chapter 12 of this book dwells extensively on EA skill set as a key capability to make the concept successful.

Organisations seek to implement the concept of EA for strategic and operational purposes. This includes the planning, execution and management of business activities and IT solutions. However, the development, implementation and practice of EA are challenging to many organisations and could be attributed to both technical and non-technical factors, including know-how. Shaanika and Iyamu (2018) discussed some of the factors that influence the deployment of EA. In a study of EA deployment, Paul and Paul (2012) found structure and people as key challenges. Lee et al. (2013) explained that the challenge is how to integrate EA practices into the entire views and mission of an organisation.

Despite the challenges, private and public organisations continue to show interest in the concept of EA. According to Olsen and Trelsgård (2016), organisations' challenges in the implementation of EA are caused by numerous factors, such as lack of understanding by practitioners and top management's failure to commit to the approach. Lnenicka and Komarkova (2019) propose the use of EA to address new information and communication technology's challenges. Gong and Janssen (2019) suggest that organisations employ EA purposely to increase the value of IT solutions.

EA in itself does not provide benefits and value or competitiveness. However, it can be used for the enablement of competitiveness, creation of value and as a bridge for communication gaps between units in an organisation. EA's usefulness, as mentioned above, depends on how it is defined and shaped in an organisation. In Chapter 3 of this book, definitions and their relevance and consequences are discussed. The concept of EA is intended to improve business and IT alignment, which is weak in many organisations. Another potential benefit of EA is in its premise to support decision-making that can fortify return on IT investment in an organisation. However, extracting the benefits and value of EA has been challenging to demonstrate in many organisations.

Even though each organisation is unique, as shaped by rules, culture and resources, there is a common critical challenge, which is integration. Many organisations are challenged by the integration of processes and IT solutions. EA facilitates the integration of activities, processes and governance within a unit and across an organisation. The integration effort is across the domains of EA and is aimed at coherence and eradication of duplications and redundancies. Integration is an additional motivating factor for many promoters of EA and organisations in general.

Actor-network Theory

ANT is a sociotechnical theory that is embedded within science and technology (Dwiartama & Rosin, 2014). The main tenets of ANT are actor, network and moments of translation. Actors are entities that have the ability to make a difference. By implication, actors can alter one another through their action. Callon

(1986) clarifies that an actor can be human or non-human. Network in ANT is a group of actors with allied or common interest, through which they consciously or unconsciously form or create a link. In ANT, neither the actor nor the network can be independent of each other due to the ramification in their existence. Networks exist because there are actors, and actors exist within networks.

The theory therefore focuses on shifting and negation from one point to another, which entails the interaction and relationship between actors within a network. Consequentially, human and non-human actors are inseparable. The inseparability circumstance between actors and networks enables them to establish negotiations through translation. Through translation, the interest of human and non-human actors is linked in stable heterogeneous networks. There are different moments in the process of translation, which Callon (1986) split into four: problematisation; interessement; enrolment; and mobilisation, as shown in Figure 9.1. In the context of ANT, translation is a state or process in which actors form a relationship, interact and negotiate to transform an activity from one stage to another.

The first moment of translation is problematisation. It refers to the presentation of an issue which requires a solution. A focal actor problematises an issue. In addition, the focal actor lures or convinces other actors to partake in providing a solution. During problematisation, roles and responsibilities are assigned. This is subsequently followed by interessement. Interessement entails the conveyance of actors to a network whose goal is already problematised. At this stage, actors declare interest in the problem and accept the roles or tasks that have been assigned to them by the focal actor. The interest is either voluntary, contractual or imposed on the actors. Actors' interest in an activity does not automatically translate into participation.

The third moment of ANT is enrolment, which refers to actors' commitment and actual participation in an activity that has been problematised by a focal actor. It goes beyond interest; meaning, not all interested actors participate. At this stage, actors execute the tasks that have been assigned to them. As long as actors execute

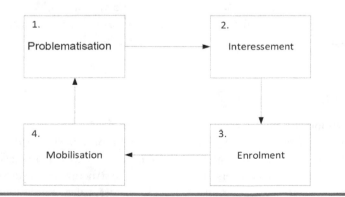

Figure 9.1   Moments of translation. (Callon, 1986)

their tasks, they remain part of the network. Finally, is the moment of mobilisation; a stage where actors are appointed or voluntarily take the role of spokespersons. At this stage, the spokesperson demonstrates allegiance to the course being pursued by the network. This is the stage that affirms the stability of the network and actors are in a state of unison.

Moments of translation can assist in the formulation and conceptualisation of EA in an organisation, and the unpacking of processes, including the complexities that are involved in the development, implementation and practice of EA in an organisation. Translation significantly finds the success factors in the deployment of EA, and gradually strengthens into institutionalisation over time.

Its human and non-human focus makes ANT useful to social sciences and found its relevance in EA and IS studies. Significantly, this is attributable to its focus on the various meanings, which humans associate with things from sociotechnical viewpoints. Hence, the theory is suitable for studying technological innovation, and its adoption and implementation in the field of information systems. It is from this angle that the theory helps to gain knowledgeability and understanding of complex phenomena, such as EA. Also, the translation aspect of the theory can assist to comprehend the process which takes place in the development, implementation and practice of EA in an organisation.

Enterprise Architecture for Enterprises

The moments of translation from ANT are applied as a lens to examine how EA acts as an agent to facilitate business and IT activities towards change and transformation in organisations. The theory, with specific focus on moments of translation, is discussed in the succeeding section. Table 9.1 provides a summary of how EA can be employed as an agent of change, using the moments of translation. Thus, the discussion that follows should be read with the table in order to gain a better understanding of the discourse.

The discourse begins by establishing the actors and networks that partake in the development, implementation and practice of EA in organisations. Thereafter, the moments of translation are explored to unpack how EA can act as an agent of change in an organisation.

Actor-network

In the development, implementation and practice of EA, there are two main entities: (1) human actors, including the chief information officer (CIO), usually the head of IT department, chief architect (CA), architects, IT managers, business managers and other stakeholders, depending on the structure of the organisations; and (2) non-human actors, comprised of technologies, rules, regulations and processes. These two groups need each other for an activity to be performed.

Table 9.1   EA's Moments of Translation

Problematisation (1)	Interessement (2)
The concept of EA is problematised (initiated) within an environment by the Chief Architect (Architecture manager) or senior management. Also, consultants can initiate the concept with or without invitation from the organisation to do so. The initiation is done based on signification, a meaning which was at the time associated with the concept by the initiator. The basis for problematising the concept may not necessarily be understood by all the stakeholders at the time of such an action.	Human actors (stakeholders) show a common interest in EA to deploy the concept in the organisation. Although, the interest may vary, depending on how and why each actor is interested in the deployment of EA in the organisation. Individuals or groups' interest is drawn from the premise that is based on how EA was communicated and how it influences actors' opinions and views. The interest is not the end but a means to the next stage, which is whether or not to participate in the activities of EA.
Mobilisation (4)	*Enrolment (3)*
Actors such as IT managers, architects and consultants can be officially appointed staff or volunteers (self-appointed) as representatives who act as spokespersons on behalf of the EA team (or organisation). The spokespersons exist within the networks that were consciously (within the organisational structure) or unconsciously formed. The spokespersons portray EA in an attractive manner, purposely to draw interest and appreciation from the entire organisation or public.	The interest of individuals and groups inform actors' actual participation in the development, implementation and practice of EA in an organisation. The participants, consisting of employees and consultants, consciously or unconsciously form participatory networks. The participations are influenced by various factors, such as self-development, know-how, contractual obligations (such as employment contract) and finance incentive (bonuses). Consultants' interest is mainly in the financial returns.

Within an organisation's rules and regulations, actors consciously or unconsciously form groups (networks), based on their interest in the activities of the EA. Through the networks, the human actors carry out constant interactions with each other and with the non-human actors in performing tasks. This makes the relationship and interaction between the actors to be the ultimate influence in the success or failure of EA in an environment. There is a bigger challenge that comes with lack of knowledge or understanding of the concept, which often influences stakeholders' interactions and affirms their stance in the tasks ahead.

Furthermore, the formation of some networks is unconsciously influenced by personal interest rather than organisational aspirations. This increases the difficulty in the negotiation among stakeholders within or between networks. Ultimately, such unpleasant negotiations affect processes and activities in the development, implementation and practice of EA in an environment. The complexity in negotiation emanates from the fact that each actor has the ability to make a difference through their intended and unintended actions.

Moments of Translation: Problematisation

In many organisations, the concept of EA is problematised often by the focal actor, who is customarily the CIO. The problematisation defines the purpose and rationales, including the deliverables of EA in the organisation. It is a process that is carried out through a committee (network) of senior management. Thereafter, it filters down to various groups with allied interest, such as the architects and other domains. The interest is centred on EA objectives and deliverables towards improving service delivery. Such improvement can only come from different types of approach. Thus, the concept is problematised to engineer change and transformative drive to a desired state. Some organisations are more complex than others. A more complex environment requires two different levels of problematisation: introduction and definition of the concept.

At the first level, EA is introduced to the stakeholders, using various mediums of communication and interaction. The concept might be new to many of the stakeholders in some organisations. In such environments, many stakeholders consider EA to be another theoretical exercise rather than an applied concept. Hence, preparatory work towards problematisation of the concept is crucial, in that it is a point where failure or success is initially brewed.

The second level of problematisation entails the definition of EA in the context of the enterprise. This is irrespective of the fact that the concept has been defined in various quarters, organisations and academic studies. It is a holistic classification of events, processes and activities of business and IT solutions into domains' architectures, which provides fundamental governance that can be used iteratively to manage and bridge the gap between strategic planning and operations. This involves relevance and context, based on the fulfilment of goals and objectives.

An organisation's definition should be aligned with the EA framework that is selected. This helps to refine the scope of the EA within the organisation in terms of context and relevance. Most importantly, it helps the promoters to have a good understanding of the concept, and therefore prepares them to solicit buy-in and interest from other stakeholders through interaction and negotiation. Also, problematisation happens at domain level mainly for distinct purposes.

Moments of Translation: Interessement

By default, employees (IS/IT specialists and managers) are stakeholders in the deployment of EA in organisations. The stakeholders are assigned to networks by virtue of their teams' work or expertise in executing the various activities of EA. Within the networks, the stakeholders (human actors) establish relationships and interaction. This type of relationship involves inseparable interaction between the human actors and the EA processes and activities. Interests that are shown in the deployment and practice of EA within organisations come from two main perspectives; personal agenda and organisational goals and objectives. Notwithstanding, the interest geared towards organisational goals is influenced by both technical and non-technical factors and aligns with EA in order to effect change from one state to another.

Personal interest is often based on the human actors' interaction with the processes, which manifests into know-how, hunger for ambition, self-development, voluntarism and contractual obligations. Employees make use of their technical know-how as a source of power to make a difference in the deployment and practice of EA. This type of behaviour and actions dictate how EA is scoped, developed, implemented and practised within an environment (Bui & Levy, 2017), and affects its alignment with the enterprise's goals and objectives. Voluntarism manifests from personal interests, such as job security, financial incentive and loyalty to the line managers. Although these circumstances have influence on the deployment and practice of EA, the challenge is that it is not easy to detect or foresee how and why personal interests are expressed and applied in the processes and activities.

Contractual obligations have several implications in the deployment and practice of EA, in that employees are forced to be interested in the subject that they ordinarily would not like to associate with. Primarily, service providers (consultants) have the best interest of their organisations through the EA framework that they problematise to an organisation. Some of the consultants show fallacious interest to the clients in order to maintain a presence in the environment. Also, some employees rely on consultants due to lack of, or limited capacity in their environments. This is caused by the desperate need to extract the value and contribution of EA to the organisation's growth.

The significance of EA is drawn from the various interests that are founded on its primary aim and strengths, intended to bridge the gap between business and IT units, and to enforce change from the current to the desired states. In the context of this chapter, 'change' means strategy or a new way of working in an organisation. In applying this new approach within an environment, the plan is to improve the chances of success through the practice of EA *as an Agent of Change*. Mythologically, EA is intended to consistently address gaps and deficiencies and many other related concerns of IT solutions that support and enable service delivery through business processes and activities. On this basis, it is critical to understand how and why EA is: (1) problematised in an environment; (2) problematised in the way that it was; and (3) received in the way that it was, by the stakeholders. Without clarifications and understanding of these rhetorical inquiries, the purpose of the concept in the organisation is defeated.

Moments of Translation: Enrolment

The deployment and practice of EA requires participatory efforts by the stakeholders, beginning with the identification of individuals and groups. However, not every person or stakeholder that shows interest in EA participates (enrols) in the execution of tasks, activities and processes in an environment, for various reasons. Enrolment is shaped by personal and contractual obligations which are influenced by both internal and external factors. Through negotiation, actors accept responsibilities that have been assigned to them by the focal actor, CIO, Chief Architect or any other IT manager.

The internal factors include both human and non-human actors. The human actors consist of technical (IT specialists) and non-technical employees in business units. The technical personnel include managers, IT architects and others, such as software developers, network administrators and systems analysts. These specialists focus on the application and technical domains for the planning and deployment of IT solutions to enable and support the services of the organisation.

The external factors consist of consultants and government policies, which concern organisations' existence and operations. The consultants are hired for the development and implementation of EA. The aim is to deploy and operationalise an organisation's goals and objectives through strategies that cover information management, software services and network administration. The policies influence how EA is defined, developed, implemented and practised within an organisation. For example, the policies guide how information is categorised, used and exchanged for interaction purposes. It is therefore mandatory for IT specialists, including the managers, to have a good understanding of the policies as they develop and implement the information architecture of the organisation's EA.

Moments of Translation: Mobilisation

As mentioned several times earlier, the concept of EA is a process that is iterative in nature. By implication, the deployment of EA is not a traditional project that starts and ends within a period of time. The process is considered iterative only when the network becomes stable; a state where the implementation of EA repeatedly completes a circle. By virtue of mobilising other actors within and outside of the network to partake in the plans and operations, problematisation is in itself taking place. This means that at the point of mobilisation, a new beginning and a fresh negotiation take place.

Through the iterative process, the EA is theoretically problematised, and via mobilisation, the concept is translated into practice. The results from both the current and future states are the outcomes of human and IT solutions' actions and interactions, produced and reproduced through the domains of EA within a space (organisational platform) and over a period. Giddens (1984) describes such a process of reproduction as a duality of structure. In the reproduction of actions, both human and technology act within heterogeneous networks in an organisation to develop, implement and manage EA. It is difficult or near impossible to separate the human and IT aspects in transforming the concept of EA into a significant approach within an environment. This is mainly because neither human nor IT operates in a vacuum.

Conceptualise EA as an Agent of Change

From the discourse above, four factors that can significantly influence how EA is defined, developed, implemented and practised in an organisation are revealed. The factors are (1) criticality of actor-network; (2) structural collaboration; (3) transformative process; and (4) iterative approach. The disclosure comes from the interactions that happen between actors: human-to-human; human-to-non-human; and non-human-to-non-human. As discussed below, the factors affect how organisations employ EA to enable and support their strategies and operations for growth and sustainability. Based on the factors, a conceptual framework is developed, as shown in Figure 9.2. It illustrates how EA can be used to facilitate change from organisational level to divisional levels and further down to departmental levels.

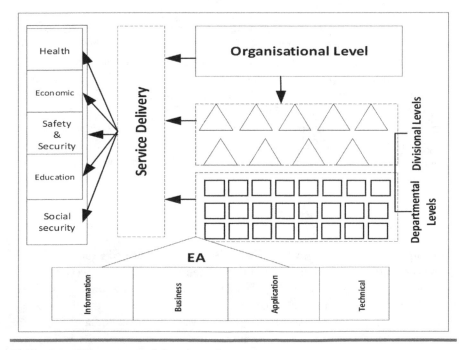

Figure 9.2 EA conceptual framework.

As a change agent, EA is neither static nor restricted to specific sectors. It can be applied in sectors such as health, economic (e.g., financial institutions), safety and security, education and social security as shown in Figure 9.2. Change in the organisation is facilitated through the domains of EA, which are information, business, application and technical architectures. Thus, the discussion that follows should be read with Figure 9.2 in order to comprehend how EA acts as an agent of change.

Criticality of Actor-network

In ANT, a network consists of a group of actors with common interest, based on which they are connected and have a relationship. Services and organisational structures are the two main networks within an organisation. The structures influence the deployment and practice of EA from different viewpoints. Based on services, there exist networks comprising clients' needs, customer relationship and collaboration with partners. Similarly, there are networks within an organisational structure, at the divisional and departmental levels. The existence of these networks makes it inevitable to have silo processes and deployment of IT solutions. A silo state ignites inconsistencies, duplication and redundancy of processes and IT solutions, resulting in lack of uniformity and standardisation, and increased complexities and disparities within the environment.

During the period of application and infrastructure deployment, requirements often change and, sometimes, they change so rapidly due to shifts in business or IT strategies. Through the various networks, IT solutions and business processes are employed to respond to changing needs. This is critical for organisational pursuit, service delivery and competitiveness, which are deterministic factors for EA success or failure. Through the networks, IT architects and other delegated IT specialists trace and manage how the entire activities within the organisation change from problematisation, assembling, disassembling and reassembling to make a difference and circumstantially improve service delivery for competitiveness.

Structural Collaboration

Many organisations, especially large enterprises, are multifaceted structures engaging with clients through divisions and departments and providing services to the customers. As shown in Figure 9.2, services in many organisations are at different divisional and departmental levels. The EA is fundamental to enabling change from strategic planning, systems design, software development and hardware deployment, to the reproduction of multiple processes and activities to improve the organisation's services and clients' attractiveness. Thus, collaborations between divisions and departments are vital in enhancing synergy and synchronisation, including strategic and operational governance of processes, and deployment of IT solutions. This approach enables reuse, reduces cost and improves the effectiveness and efficiency of organisations' service delivery.

One of the challenging factors in collaboration is that EA is not well understood among employees within many organisational structures. As a result, some employees from the different divisions or departments may not be in sync or have the same level of knowledge about the tasks that are supposed to be collaboratively performed. Implicatively, some processes and IT solutions are not integrated, which leads to duplication and support vacuum. The EA facilitates change through collaboration between the units and structures within an organisation.

Transformative Process

The EA is the agent that facilitates the transformation of strategy into operation through its processes and deployment of IT solutions to enable and support organisation-driven initiatives for growth and sustainability purposes. The EA approach provides the flexibility to enable long-term and short-term views of an organisation's needs and pursuits from both business and technology perspectives. Hence, EA is seen or considered as a roadmap that promotes knowledge and information sharing across an organisation, through which change happens in delivering and receiving services.

Transformation is a process that starts from the point of problematisation (initiation) to practice (mobilisation) through which changes are engineered to provide services to clients and foster a competitive edge. In each step of transformation, there are agents who effect change or are affected by change, such as business artefacts, information components and IT solutions. Thus, EA enables transformation through the planning, deployment and operationalisation of business processes and IT activities towards service delivery. Transformation brings about stability within networks only when it is iterative, which is tantamount to institutionalisation.

Iterative Approach

Each domain of EA has its distinctive objectives, but they do depend on each other to effect change. Similarly, the structures that exist within organisations are dependent on each other in delivering services and achieving organisational vision and mission. This form of dependency is not project-like, but an iterative process that happens over a period of business-cycle or end-of-life of an IT solution.

Iteratively, EA is used to manage and govern business design, processes and the deployment and use of IT solutions in an organisation. The iterative approach aims to improve effectiveness, efficiency and reduction of risk in service delivery via a new set of governance and operating models. This includes the rationalisation, consolidation and integration of existing and future solutions in fulfilling organisational needs.

Nothing is static; designs, processes and IT solutions continue to evolve, and sometimes very rapidly. As an agent of change, EA is flexible enough to employ the iterative approach in responding to changing business needs and emerging IT solutions. The iterative approach aids the continuity of relationships and connectivity among human actors (employees, clients and others) and non-human actors (business designs, processes and IT solutions), including how the actors interact with each other in facilitating change in an organisation.

EA as Change Agent for Enterprises

Architects, through the deployment of EA as an agent of change, provide guidelines and frameworks to design and structure an organisation's components and their relationships from business processes to IT solutions. Through its ability to facilitate change, many organisations have been able to improve their governing principles and policies, reference models and standardisation of design and processes and deployment of IT solutions.

In addition, the deployment of EA engineers changes between business and IT strategies and processes (Löhe & Legner, 2014). As shown in Figure 9.3, EA

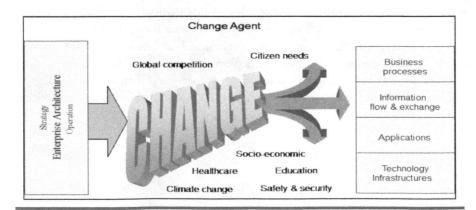

Figure 9.3   EA as agent of change.

facilitates change from both strategic and operational perspectives in service delivery in any area of socioeconomic services, such as healthcare, education, climate change and safety. The change happens via the business processes, information flow, application systems and technology infrastructures.

The activities and services offered by organisations enabled and supported by IT solutions are influenced by technical and non-technical factors. In delivering services to clients and maintaining sustainability, organisations rely on enablement and support from IT solutions that are defined, designed and deployed according to architecture and governance. This is an edifying structural approach that improves efficiency, effectiveness and quicker response time. Iyamu (2015) explains that technologies are selected, developed and implemented by people through processes, in accordance with structures, rules and processes.

The deployment of EA supports the integration and dependency between technical and non-technical factors through its domains: business, information, application and technology in facilitating change. The linkages and dependency between the domains significantly provide traceability to the relevant stakeholders of EA at the organisational, divisional and departmental levels. Thus, EA aids and acts as an agent in addressing complexity, integration challenges, lack of collaboration and enabling business processes and guiding the deployment of IT solutions in organisations. This allows change from the current to future states in the areas of organisational needs for competitive advantage.

Implication of Practice

It is clear that the factors of signification in the deployment of EA as an agent of change include criticality of networks, structural collaboration, transformative process and iterative approach. The factors have implications for the activities that the architects, other IT specialists and the general stakeholders and managers carry out. The primary implications are described in Table 9.2.

Table 9.2 provides a summary of the implications of practice in the deployment of EA as an agent of change within organisations. This includes the fact that many employees and their managers find themselves struggling and challenged with problems such as the integration and consolidation of processes and IT solutions across different levels of the organisational structure. The challenges remain significant as they determine the success or failure of an IT department within an organisation.

Table 9.2 Implication of Practice

Factor	Information Technology	Organisation
Criticality of networks	IT specialists, consciously or unconsciously, sometimes confine themselves to their individual networks. Within such confinement, some IT specialists carry out their tasks implicitly and execute their activities in silos, which affect the deployment of the EA. This can be traced to why IT personnel know little or nothing about the domains of EA, outside areas of their immediate responsibilities, which negatively influences EA deployment.	Some actors and networks are heterogeneous across the structures of some organisations. This makes negotiations difficult in many areas, such as the allocation of tasks in the development and implementation of EA in an organisation.
Organisational structure	Interactions between the business and IT units are often misconstrued through different interpretations due to limited knowledge about each other's activities. Also, this is primarily because such interaction is not guided by the objectives of EA. In addition, this results from the power associated with individual structures.	This requires continuous synergy and training of employees on the concept of EA, which helps to enable an alignment between the activities of the organisation. Otherwise, actors will continue to determine the direction of EA towards agenda opposed to organisational needs.
Transformative process	The transformative process must be understood in the context of IT to avoid challenges which can obstruct change within IT solutions. Through the connectedness of the EA domains, the transformation of IT solutions can be negatively affected if not controlled and managed.	This can create parallel activities between EA and the organisation's goals and objectives. The primary implication is that it affects the stability of the environment towards achieving the organisational needs.
Iterative approach	The iterative process fosters the institutionalisation of the EA, through which the benefits of the concept are gained (Iyamu, 2015). The iterative nature of the EA can be challenging and constraining for its deployment if IT solutions are not aligned with the business needs of an organisation.	The iteration approach influences the change that happens from current to future states. Thus, the approach must be consistent in order to ensure systems' availability, improved performance, scalability and interoperability.

Summary

This chapter discusses how EA can be employed as an agent of change, which many organisations continue to struggle with. The chapter fills this aspect of EA that has been lacking in the academic front for many years. The use of moments of translation of ANT does not only bring a fresh perspective into how EA is viewed, but it also makes a strong case for rigour, to the interest of both academics and practitioners. The theory therefore enhances the advancement of EA in organisations.

The implementation of EA does not really mean the actualisation of the end in achieving its objectives within organisations' environments. It does require institutionalisation of the practice. Only then can the culture be imbibed, from which the benefits begin to manifest over a period of time. This is a critical area of study because it can help to build reference models for both enterprises and academic domains.

References

Buckle, S., Matthes, F., Monahov, I., Roth, S., Schulz, C., & Schweda, C. M. (2011). Towards an Agile Design of the Enterprise Architecture Management Function. In *Enterprise Distributed Object Computing Conference Workshops (EDOCW), 15th IEEE International.* (pp. 322–329). 29 August-2 September, Helsinki, Finland. IEEE.

Bui, Q., & Levy, M. (2017). Institutionalization of Contested Practices: A Case of Enterprise Architecture Implementation in a US State Government. In *Proceedings of the 50th Hawaii International Conference on System Sciences.* 4-7 January, Waikoloa, Hawaii. IEEE.

Callon, M. (1986). Some elements of a sociology of translation: Domestication of the scallops and the fishermen of st brieuc bay. In J. Law (ed). *Power, action & belief: A new sociology of knowledge?*, 196–229, London: Routledge & Kegan Paul.

Dwiartama, A., & Rosin, C. (2014). Exploring agency beyond humans: The compatibility of actor-network Theory (ANT) and resilience thinking. *Ecology and Society, 19*(3), 28–38.

Giddens, A. (1984). *The constitution of society: Outline of the theory of structuration.* Cambridge, UK: John Polity Press.

Gong, Y., & Janssen, M. (2019). The value of and myths about enterprise architecture. *International Journal of Information Management, 46*, 1–9.

Hjort-Madsen, K., & Pries-Heje, J. (2009). Enterprise Architecture in Government: Fad or Future?. In *System Sciences. In the Proceedings of the 42nd Hawaii International Conference.* (pp. 1–10). 5-8 January, Waikoloa, Hawaii. IEEE.

Iyamu, T. (2015). *Enterprise architecture from concept to practice.* Victoria, Australia: Heidelberg Press.

Johnson, P., Ekstedt, M., & Lagerstrom, R. (2016). Automatic Probabilistic Enterprise IT Architecture Modeling: A Dynamic Bayesian Networks Approach. In the Proceedings of the 20th International Workshop on Enterprise Distributed Object Computing Workshop (EDOCW). (pp. 1–8). 5-9 September, Vienna, Austria. IEEE.

Lapalme, J., Gerber, A., Van der Merwe, A., Zachman, J., De Vries, M., & Hinkelmann, K. (2016). Exploring the future of enterprise architecture: A zachman perspective. *Computers in Industry, 79*, 103–113.

Lee, Y.-J., Kwon, Y.-I., Shin, S., & Kim, E.-J. (2013). Advancing Government-wide Enterprise Architecture – A Meta-model Approach. In the Proceedings of the 15th International Conference on Advanced Communication Technology (ICACT). (pp. 886–892). 27-30 January, PyeongChang, South Korea. IEEE.

Lnenicka, M., & Komarkova, J. (2019). Developing a government enterprise architecture framework to support the requirements of big and open linked data with the use of cloud computing. *International Journal of Information Management, 46*, 124–141.

Löhe, J., & Legner, C. (2014). Overcoming implementation challenges in enterprise architecture management: A design theory for architecture-driven IT management (ADRIMA). *Information Systems and e-Business Management, 12*(1), 101–137.

Olsen, D. H., & Trelsgård, K. (2016). Enterprise architecture adoption challenges: An exploratory case study of the Norwegian higher education sector. *Procedia Computer Science, 100*, 804–811.

Paul, A., & Paul, V. (2012). The e-Government Interoperability through Enterprise Architecture in Indian Perspective. In the Proceedings of World Congress on Information and Communication Technologies. (pp. 646–650). 30 October-2 November, Trivandrum, India. IEEE.

Rodrigues, L. S., & Amaral, L. (2010). Issues in enterprise architecture value. *Journal of Enterprise Architecture, 6*(4), 27–32.

Roth, S., Hauder, M., Farwick, M., Breu, R., & Matthes, F. (2013). Enterprise architecture documentation: Current practices and future directions. In *Wirtschaftsinformatik* (p. 58).

Safari, H., Faraji, Z., & Majidian, S. (2016). Identifying and evaluating enterprise architecture risks using FMEA and fuzzy VIKOR. *Journal of Intelligent Manufacturing, 27*(2), 475–486.

Shaanika, I., & Iyamu, T. (2018). Developing the enterprise architecture for the Namibian government. *The Electronic Journal of Information Systems in Developing Countries, 84*(3), e12028.

Tamm, T., Seddon, P. B., Shanks, G. G., & Reynolds, P. (2011). How does enterprise architecture add value to organisations? *Communication of the Association for Information Systems, 28*(1), 141–168.

Urbaczewski, L., & Mrdalj, S. (2006). A comparison of enterprise architecture frameworks. *Issues in Information Systems, 7*(2), 18–23.

Chapter 10

Unified Architecture Framework for Enterprises

Introduction

Modern businesses across industries continue to grapple with the growing challenges in providing essential services to clients and communities, staying sustainable and gaining competitive edge. These contraptions can be better served by less complexity in accessing big data, the engine room of the 'organised chaos'. Despite the numerous attempts that have been made by both practitioners and the academia, the challenges persist in many organisations. This invigorates the need for a different type of solution that addresses secure means and ease of access to big data, such as a unified data architecture. The remainder of this section introduces the concept of big data and the potential benefits of architecture.

Big data refers to datasets with identifiable characteristics of unprecedented volume, variety and velocity (three Vs). This ascription to big data is not new; many studies such as Cervone (2016) also referred to it as three Vs. One of the differences with typical or popular types of data is that big data cannot be captured, managed or processed by traditional software tools, and therefore requires a more sophisticated information technology (IT) solution (Zhang et al., 2016). Primarily, this is where the differentiation essentially comes from; volume, velocity and variety of its data. Owing to its vast characteristics, big data can be difficult to access or manage. It is worse in large and complex organisations.

The state of big data in many organisations is overwhelming. Some employees are not aware of how much big data is under their guardianship and some of

DOI: 10.1201/9781003268420-10

those who seem to be aware are unwitting of its potential significance. This raises the fundamental interest of, or on behalf of organisations: (1) an awareness of big data's usefulness in an organisation; and (2) the factors that influence accessing big data for business purposes. In addressing awareness and its consequence, one more thing comes to mind; that awareness of the factors is not a solution by itself to the challenge of using mobile systems to access organisations' big data. The use of technology is evidently critical. However, the challenge gets unhealthier due to fragmented IT solutions that are used to enable and support the big data in some environments.

There is hardly any modern organisation that does not interact or make use of big data for its business. The extent at which big data is gathered at district and national levels is boggling. Financial institutions accumulate big data. Government institutions and agencies amass it. Yet, it is difficult to find organisations that have the tenacity to make use of their big data near its potential. Some of the organisations dispense of their big data sets owing to the complexity in accessing it in the rightful ways.

In the context of enterprise architecture (EA), architecture provides guidelines which define processes, standards and selection criteria for designing, developing and implementing IT solutions in an organisation. The guidelines include standards, principles and policies for the governance and management of IT solutions in an environment. Thus, reaping the potential benefits of big data is vitally based on an understanding of its architecture and the different functionalities of the components. The components of architecture can be viewed from different angles, including logical linkage, internal format of datasets and structure of the systems. An architecture is required and employed to ease flexibility, scalability and integration of IT solutions, which essentially helps to create the security and ease of access to big data. However, the architecture cannot be generic due to the uniqueness of some enterprises, systems or environments. For example, there is heterogeneity in datasets, as well as high level sensitivity (Iyamu & Mgudlwa, 2017).

This chapter focuses on the challenges that hinder the use of mobile systems in accessing big data for service delivery by enterprises. The chapter proposes the Unified Architecture Framework (UAF) as a solution to guide and enable flexibility, scalability and integration between mobile systems and big data. This is primarily to ease manageability, promote governance and ultimately improve the quality of service delivery and enhance competitive advantage.

The remainder of this chapter is divided into five sections organised in the following order: The introduction and the problem being investigated are first presented, followed by a review of literature which focuses on big data, and architecture. How mobile systems are used to access big data is discussed next. Thereafter, a unified architecture framework is presented and discussed. Lastly, the chapter is summarised.

The Problem

Currently, many enterprises are struggling with how they access their big data to yield useful prospects for business purposes. This challenge is caused by many factors. Three are profound: know-how; human interaction with technologies; and complexities of IT solutions. The challenges are to the detriment of services which some organisations offer and their determination to remain sustainable, over the years. Although some studies have been conducted in the areas of management and access to big data, the challenges persist. This is primarily because the contributions of these studies were however limited in the area of architecture framework. Thus, the focus of this chapter is presented twofold, as shown in Table 10.1.

The consequence of the disjoints between components in the attempts to access big data within an organisation or from different locations manifests from lack

Table 10.1   The Problem

#	Description of Problem	Implication
1	The technical and non-technical factors that enable and support the use of mobile systems in accessing big data are either not empirically known or not employed appropriately in many enterprises (Iyamu & Shaanika, 2020). This makes it difficult or impossible to integrate or enable connectivity between mobile systems and other technologies in accessing datasets (Katal, Wazid & Goudar, 2013).	1. Technologies' integration and interaction in accessing big data lack governance in many enterprises (Shaanika & Iyamu, 2019). 2. Allows a porous process in using mobile systems to access datasets in some organisations. 3. This leads to or keeps the status quo of poor service delivery.
2	There is no unified architecture framework that can be used to govern the selection of mobile systems and technologies for managing databases by some organisations. This affects the interaction between mobile systems and big data in enterprises (Shaanika & Iyamu, 2019). Sabooniha, Toohey and Lee (2012) argue that some of the challenges in the use of IT solutions for services are caused by uncollaborated design and development of the solutions. Integration of components improves services.	1. Mobile systems and other technologies are randomly selected and used. 2. Mobile systems and other technologies become incompatible and lack governance (Iyamu & Shaanika, 2020). 3. As a result, datasets are either compromised or cannot be accessed in some organisations.

of an architecture framework. This constrains the useful intentions of big data in many organisations. An architecture framework is required largely because access to organisations' databases is becoming more complex than ever before, for two main reasons: (1) the datasets are shared simultaneously between numerous internal and external actors, and (2) the need for confidentiality and privacy is increasing as organisations embark on a competitive trail. This therefore requires an architecture design that integrates mobile systems in accessing organisational big data. This chapter presents a *unified architecture framework that guides, governs and manages.*

The problem being addressed in this chapter arises from two studies, Shaanika and Iyamu (2019) and Iyamu and Shaanika (2020), which were combined to construct an architecture framework to fill the voids that were limitations in the two studies. Table 10.2 presents the findings from the studies. The construction is

Table 10.2 Source of Data

Source	Description	Findings
Shaanika and Iyamu (2019).	The factors that influence the interaction between mobile systems and organisations' big data in the delivery of services are not clear because of the confidentiality and privacy policies that are involved. This includes an understanding of the interaction which exists between humans and technologies in both public and private organisations.	Primarily, the deterministic factors for interaction between humans and IT solutions include: (1) communicative tools; (2) network of people; (3) policy compliance; (4) technology monopoly; (5) governance of IT solutions; (6) big data management system; and (7) lack of interactive systems.
Iyamu and Shaanika (2020).	Stakeholders in many organisations are considered to be missing out on the potential benefits of using mobile systems to access clients' big data towards improving service delivery. The high or intensive level of control is associated with lack of secure or fear of weak access to the datasets.	Eight factors: (1) mobile systems' ease of use; (2) system user training: (3) online consultation; (4) medical history traceability; (5) access to external facilities; (6) practitioner's collaboration; (7) systems decentralisation; and (8) technology infrastructure flexibility were found to have some influence on how big data is accessed, used and managed for service delivery.

possible only because of humans' ability to associate meanings with the findings from the two studies. This chapter consists of many realities of human actions, which required an understanding in developing an architecture framework that can guide the use of mobile systems in accessing big data in organisations.

The hermeneutics approach was used to examine and understand the findings from the two studies; #1 and #2, to gain a better understanding of their collaboration, influence and implication in the use of mobile systems to access big data for services to clients. Although these studies were conducted in a healthcare environment, the results can apply to any type of organisation. The objective of this chapter is to develop a UAF that can guide, govern and manage the use of mobile systems in accessing big data in organisations to enhance processes and improve services that are provided to clients and partners. In achieving the objective, the following were the primary focus:

i. Collaboration between technical and non-technical factors to ease the use of mobile systems in accessing big data to improve services;
ii. Integration of IT solutions (or their components) in enabling and supporting services through the use of mobile systems; and
iii. Management of mobile system, including process and activities towards enabling and supporting the accessing of persons' big data for organisation's big data.

A Review of Related Literature

In addition to the three Vs, other characteristics of big data include veracity and value (Chen, Kazman & Haziyev, 2016). Zhang et al. (2016) argue that processing big data by traditional methods is not only too complicated but it is also far more time consuming. This is mainly because there are rapid increases in volumes, speeds and complexities of various dataset types, which are challenging in many ways, including the integration and use of mobile systems (Kohli & Tan, 2016). Within this context, it is arguable that the management of big data is one of the challenges affecting many organisations in providing services online or electronically.

This discussion begins by pointing out that big data is not only about collecting or generating massive amounts of data, but also about making sense and use of it (Mousannif et al., 2016). From various perspectives, organisations are inspired and are rather more concerned with how to make sense of the big data they have acquired. Howard, Michael and Betram (2016) explained that the use of big data technologies is at different stages in various organisations. This means that efforts in advancing the use of IT solutions, such as mobile systems, are ongoing. This requires the integration of both non-technical and technical factors to capture the value and usefulness of big data.

Some organisations, such as education, healthcare and finance store a huge stock of various sensitive datasets of individuals and groups. In the struggle to be useful, some organisations are more fragile than others, especially as it involves humans and their expertise. Also, some environments are more sensitive than others in terms of the data that they have in store. The sensitive and fragile nature of organisations' ability to handle big data makes it critical to ensure appropriate management and prevent erroneous processes that could compromise the integrity of the data. Shaanika (2016) acknowledges that due to the sensitivity of big data, service providers require adequate and reliable tools and approaches, such as an architecture framework, to ensure the integration and stability of IT solutions that enable and support big data. There is also a need to provide governance and regulation in the use of mobile systems to access organisational big data.

In addition to their general complexity and challenges, structures differ from one organisation to another. This influences the management of clients' datasets (Sarkis & Mwanri, 2013). For example, there are dual systems in many organisations that consist of both private and public big data (Katuu, 2016). These structures or approaches influence interoperability of systems that enable and support the activities of organisations' practices. An architecture framework is essentially required to guide the use of IT solutions (mobile systems) in accessing big data within organisations that have various structures and approaches. In addition, the framework enables a back-up plan, which is crucial to systems' unpredictability, and the management of systems' failure, and can be detrimental in some organisations (Shaanika & Iyamu, 2019).

An architecture framework can be employed to guide the management and support of the current, and design of future systems, including their big data (Ramesh, 2015). Thus, it is important to view architectures as living products that are dynamic in their growth, according to the changes in the environment (Tupper, 2011). An architecture framework is therefore an ongoing process that must be regarded as a vehicle through which organisations can accommodate changing needs and evolve processes and activities. Lankhorst (2017) explains how architecture changes as new technological opportunities arise. Ideally, an architecture framework should be viewed as a change agent (see Chapter 9) supporting organisations' agility (Shaanika & Iyamu, 2015). According to Ahsan, Shah and Kingston (2009), the architecture is the description of the set of components, their interactions and their relationships in a given domain. This can help to address the complexities that are associated with the use of mobile systems in accessing and managing an organisation's big data for service delivery.

Accessing Big Data Using Mobile Systems

Two phases were combined. The phases are outcomes from previous studies. The purpose is to fill the gaps uncovered in the studies, which is an architecture that enables and supports scalability and integration between mobile systems and big data. This is to promote the governance of mobile systems, the ease of its manageability and ultimately improve the quality of service delivery an organisation provides to her clients and remain competitive.

In phase one, the factors that influence the interaction between mobile systems and big data in the delivery of services were examined. This includes an understanding of the interaction existing between humans and technologies in public or private organisations. From the study of Shaanika and Iyamu (2019), seven factors were found to have significant influence on how big data is accessed, used and managed for service delivery: (1) communicative tools; (2) a network of people; (3) policy compliance; (4) technology monopoly; (5) governance; (6) big data management system; and (7) lack of interactive systems.

In phase two, the factors that can be used to guide and enable the integration between mobile systems and an organisation's big data to improve service delivery and competitiveness were examined. From the study by Iyamu and Shaanika (2020), eight factors were found to have a significant influence on how big data is accessed, used and managed for service delivery: (1) mobile systems' ease of use; (2) system user training: (3) online consultation; (4) medical history traceability; (5) access to external facilities; (6) practitioner's collaboration; (7) systems' decentralisation; and (8) technology infrastructure. This includes the impact the factors can have on the implementation, management and use of mobile systems in accessing big data.

Following the hermeneutics subjectivist approach, the two sets of findings were mapped against each other as shown in Figure 10.1. The factors that appeared to be

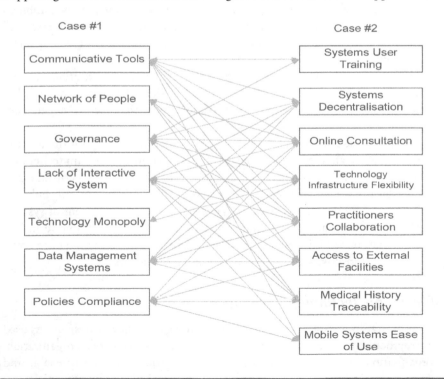

Figure 10.1 Factors influencing accessing big data.

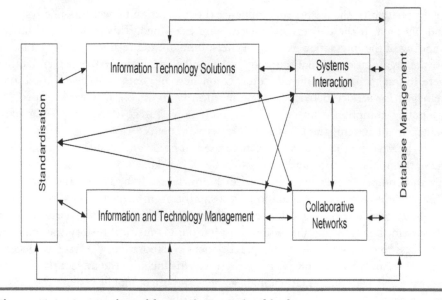

Figure 10.2   Integration of factors in accessing big data.

similar or closely related were connected with arrows and subsequently combined into six categories as follows: (1) IT solutions, (2) standardisation of processes and solutions, (3) systems' interaction, (4) collaborative networks, (5) IT management and (6) database management.

A diagram (Figure 10.2) is used to show the connection and relationship that exist among the six factors. The arrows in the figure show the existing relationship among the factors. Also, the arrows help to understand that there is dependence and influence among the factors.

The use of some specific technologies by many users increases performance and productivity. From another angle, some users think that using a certain technology eliminates difficulties and challenges. Ease of use of technologies is a critical deterministic factor in the use of systems. The use of mobile systems can only enhance the ease of use through the integration, governance and management of systems (IT solutions), which are ultimately defined by an architecture framework. The discussion that follows is intended to help gain a better understanding of the relationship, interconnectivity and dependence among the factors.

Information Technology Solutions

IT includes hardware, software and network and together they form solutions used to store, process, manage and support the processes and activities of an organisation. In organisations, various IT solutions are used in varieties of ways to enable and support the storing and transferring of big data for services. In some organisations, paper-based systems or processes have been replaced with IT solutions, such as mobile applications. This reduces potential errors in sharing information and promotes a high (or higher) level of data accuracy and integrity.

Consequently, to enrich the quality of service and improve competitiveness, the selection and deployment of IT solutions must be appropriate and specific to the needs of the organisation. The appropriateness is engineered by an architecture framework, which provides guidelines and standards for the selection, deployment and management of the mobile systems. This helps to address the technology monopoly situation that currently exists in many organisations. In addition, the architecture framework enables the scalability, compatibility and flexibility of mobile systems, which facilitates and supports its centralisation or decentralisation, while achieving the aim and objectives. Moreover, an architecture framework makes possible the integration of decentralised or standalone systems and facilitates better service delivery through improved human collaboration.

Also, an architecture framework enables the documentation of mobile systems' attributes, including the appropriateness of scalability, integration and flexibility. The documentation approach enables ease of trace, assessment, governance and manageability, and potentially influences users' and stakeholders' attitude towards the usefulness or ease of use of mobile systems for services towards sustainability and effectiveness. The increasing popularity of mobile systems makes a strong case for its usefulness in many organisations, including connecting with clients at all levels. Users that adopt positive behaviours towards the use of mobile systems consider the technology useful in delivering and receiving services. However, to employ the use of mobile systems requires integrated IT solutions that will enable and support the ease of use. This is attributable to the fact that many IT solutions are not compatible and scalable. Also, security challenges are increasing in the use of mobile systems or management of big data.

Standardisation

Standardisation brings cohesion and leads to a routine of well-defined activities, alignment of artefacts and appropriateness in the selection of IT solutions. However, standardisation does not operate in a vacuum. Thus, standardisation of processes and the technologies (such as communicative tools) that are used to support organisations' services must be enforced through policies. Additionally, without standardisation, it is difficult to integrate the many mobile systems that exist for a similar function. Another critical point is that standardisation helps to control the security and privacy of information in the use of mobile systems for services and the management of data. The policies guide both mobile systems and stakeholders' interactions. However, the policies are often understood and interpreted differently, based on the user's skill, experience, interest or knowledge.

Standardisation facilitates uniformity and compatibility; therefore, enabling connectivity in the use of mobile systems. Thus, the standardisation of processes and activities promotes consistencies and uniformity in IT solutions' processes and activities. This is important in promoting the usefulness of mobile systems as a communicative tool among the users and stakeholders in accessing big data. However, it depends on how standards are enforced to influence both users' and stakeholders' behaviour towards communicative tools within the environment. According to Shaanika and Iyamu (2019), some employees perceive the use of mobile systems as not productive. As a result, some of the employees' negative attitudes towards mobile systems result in the actual use of both paper-based and automated communicative tools in many organisations.

Systems Interaction

Through systems interactions, clients and stakeholders' physical presence is not always required at the point of care service (Shaanika & Iyamu, 2019). As such, clients can request for some of the services offered through online interactive systems. The use of interactive systems offers potential benefits to both organisations and their clients through cost savings and improved service delivery. The use of online systems for interaction between organisations and clients reduces the inconvenience of travelling back and forth to locations. Also, clients get an immediate response, which eradicates delays in providing and receiving services.

Interaction through systems allows for better and improved collaboration in improvising services: person-to-person; system-to-system; and person-to-system. The thought of this possibility influences the stakeholders on the usefulness and ease of use of systems for services (Iyamu & Shaanika, 2020). However, the usefulness can be reconsidered based on other factors, such as eligibility, security and privacy, which influence their intention to use, and the actual use of the systems when interacting for business purposes.

Online consultation is a service that can be embedded in mobile systems, such as emails (instant messaging) and video conferencing; thereby improving services and competitiveness. This does not guarantee the identity and security of a user's profile. In many organisations, information relating to some services are considered to be highly confidential; the interactive systems need to take security and privacy seriously to promote its usefulness. Lack of secured IT solutions (mobile systems) reduces the level of confidence which clients and stakeholders have in an organisation's businesses and processes. In a submission, Shaanika and Iyamu (2019) explained how users are likely to grow resistance towards such systems due to potential vulnerability to hackers and virus attacks. Mobile systems that have sophisticated levels of security enable authorised users to access big data using measures such as authentication, username and passwords (Jahan, Chowdhury & Islam, 2018).

Collaborative Networks

On behalf of organisations, employees offer services and interact with individuals or groups of people, thus consciously or unconsciously forming a network. Furthermore, the employees of the same or different specialist fields in the same organisation or division collaborate by drawing on each other's experience and sharing information and resources. A network refers to a group of actors with an allied interest. Each area of service that brings employees and clients together constitutes a network. This type of collaboration contributes to improving the quality of service delivery.

For effective collaborative networks, employees need access to external facilities, facilitated through the engineering of databases. External facilities include both local and international resources where stakeholders can interconnect. Access to external facilities can be achieved through integrated systems that enable a seamless interaction. When mobile systems are integrated, the perception is that employees, clients and stakeholders are able to collaborate with ease, sharing real-time data via secure networks.

Based on the interest, other persons gather their intention to enrol in a group or groups. Collaborative networks require mobile systems' connectivity. Connected mobile systems enable the efficient flow of information, prompting fast decision-making across the networks of people. This influences stakeholders to perceive the system to be useful.

Information and Technology Management

The implementation of mobile systems (IT solutions) in organisations necessitates management, which requires both IT specialists and other stakeholders (users and managers). This is primarily to ensure the continuity of operations and services. The management of IT solutions entails governance and users' capability and includes skill and knowledge gathered from various sources, such as training. The management, therefore, creates stability of the solutions that are critical in an environment. The stability guarantees increased technology connectivity.

Based on the stability and connectivity of IT solutions for organisations' services, employees and stakeholders form their perceptions on their usefulness and/or ease of use. Furthermore, intentions are created on the actual usability of the solutions. In the justification of perception, some stakeholders believe that IT management enables the selection, development and implementation of mobile systems that are flexible and compatible. As revealed in Shaanika and Iyamu (2019), an organisation that lacks flexible infrastructures, which are supposed to enable systems compatibility and modification in order to support constantly changing needs and processes, suffers competitiveness. This promotes the ease of mobile systems' connectivity and integration with other systems that employees use for their operations. IT management in an organisation is influenced by the employees' skills and knowledge (Iyamu & Shaanika, 2020). Employees are able to manage systems they are knowledgeable about, making the selection of mobile systems easier.

Database Management

Organisations rely heavily on clients and stakeholders' big data for decision-making in business operations and strategic intent. In addition, big data from business operations, clients' profile and records influence the selection and deployment of mobile systems. Hence, accuracy, security and reliability of big data are critical. Thus, engineering a database through an architecture framework increases the quality of management and improves service delivery at the business locations.

In many organisations, big data is managed through the use of manual and electronic systems (Iyamu & Shaanika, 2020). Both systems are used in parallel to meet an organisation's needs and requirements. These have caused various challenges, such as big data inconstancies and duplication of efforts that endanger operations. Such challenges helped to form stakeholders' perceptions that the hospital's usefulness is limited.

Many organisations continue to struggle with transforming clients' big data into usefulness. This includes the traceability of clients' big data and linking of the data sets. Traceability can be optimised by having integrated database systems across business divisions and departments. Integrated databases enable systematic data entry, storage, retrieval and management. Through integrated database management, security measures, such as data backups, can be implemented. This will create a perception of better management towards improved service delivery, which increases the actual enrolment (participation) of employees, clients and stakeholders in organisational operations and services.

A Unified Architecture Framework for Enterprises

As discussed in previous section, the hermeneutics approach from the interpretivist perspective was used in the analysis, which helps to provide a fresh viewpoint of the results from the two studies (Iyamu & Shaanika, 2020; Shaanika & Iyamu, 2019). From the analysis and discussion, a solution can be used to address organisations' challenges, including privacy, systems' integration and governance in accessing organisational big data. The solution is proposed through the UAF as shown in Figure 10.3. The framework aims to guide stakeholders in the design, development and implementation of flexible and scalable mobile systems with specific focus on systems' connectivity and process integrations.

The UAF provides a guide for the development, implementation, technical support, governance and management of mobile systems in accessing organisational big data for service delivery. The framework is uniquely important in that it boosts both organisations and clients' confidence through secure information from big

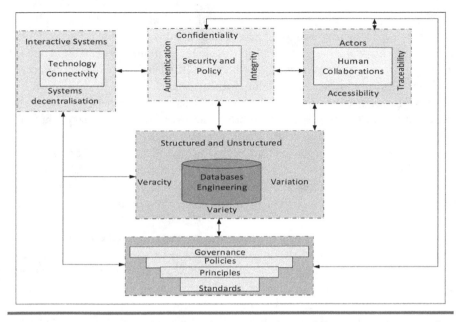

Figure 10.3 Unified architecture framework for mobile system in accessing big data.

data, timely access and swift response time. It therefore improves efficiency in services that clients and stakeholders can rely upon with a degree of sureness. As depicted in the framework, the main factors of the architecture are governance, databases engineering, security and privacy, technology connectivity and human collaborations. The factors are discussed as follows.

Governance

IT governance provides the mechanism and endorses the power to control and manage resources and artefacts within an environment. The governance approach instils discipline and uniformity in the selection (or development), implementation and use of IT solutions in an organisation. This can also be expanded to patterns of interaction, which covers how mobile systems can be used to connect and access information from clients' big data. The approach can therefore be used to provide consistence for both technology (e.g., software, database and server) and nontechnical (e.g., processes and procedure) operations and activities. Governance comprises three main components: policies, standards and principles. Operations and activities are strictly compelled to comply with these components of governance. It therefore guides the appropriate design and engineering of systems and databases that consist of unprecedented high volume, variety, veracity and variation.

The quest to improve efficiency and effectiveness are enacted by compliance with policies, standards and principles which ensure appropriateness and best practices in the deployment, use and management of mobile systems in accessing clients' information from big data. Furthermore, there are rules that guide access to clients' information and interaction with organisations' big data in providing services. However, enforcing policies and standards can be challenging due to the complexity from varying levels of structured access to sets of big data. Thus, IT governance is a crucial aspect of architecture framework for privacy, flexibility, scalability and uniformity purposes. Strategically, an architecture framework is needed to coordinate human-to-technology interactions that happen at the different levels and provide a guide to actors in the development and implementation of policies, standards and principles to ensure an alignment with various business units and stakeholders' needs.

The use and integration of mobile systems to access big data in organisations necessitates policies, standards and principles. Mobile systems, if not governed, can be vulnerable to mismanagement; which has the potential of endangering clients' information and privacy. Thus, the selection, development and implementation of mobile systems need to be guided by an architecture framework to enable technology flexibility and scalability. The flexibility and scalability of mobile systems are critical for systems and processes' integration. Systems are considered to be flexible if they can be re-engineered to accommodate changes in business processes. Potentially, an architecture framework is used as a change agent governing the transition from the current to desired states of the use of mobile systems to access big data in organisations.

Database Engineering

Database technologies enable and support the management of big data through the storage, retrieval and structuring of the data sets. Thus, the quality of data sets is influenced by the data management approaches employed by the organisation. Database technologies and governance of big data are some of the factors that influence the quality of services in which big data are used. It begins with the quality of data sets' structure. The compromise of the integrity of data sets and availability have detrimental effects on the organisation's decision-making.

The engineering of databases through an architecture framework guides the design and development of database technologies that enable and support an organisation's current and future big data management and use. Also, the engineering of database technologies is required to manage a variety of an organisation's big data types; such as images, videos and text. This is crucial in that organisations gather their data from various sources; thus, they are of different structures and formats. In affirmation, the data of many organisations are in both structured and unstructured formats. In addition, an architecture framework guides the design and development of data management approaches such as back-ups and data recovery that are needed to minimise data loss. Moreover, big data security mechanisms are engineered into the database systems to promote data privacy through enabling secure access to clients' big data.

Security and Privacy

Sensitivity in accessing clients' data is increasingly high. As a result, organisations are investing in the security and protection of clients' privacy more than ever before. This includes the authentication and validation of access to big data to ensure integrity and confidentiality. The security and privacy of clients' information for services are attained through the enforcement of governance and architecture frameworks, primarily because they guide technologies' deployment and users' access and interactions. Marcella and Stucki (2014) recommend policies and procedures for protecting information.

The development and implementation of policies and standards are also challenging activities in themselves. The complexity of the environments of some organisations makes it more challenging to develop comprehensive policies. Thus, there is the need for an architecture framework to guide management and stakeholders in the development of policies and standards that align with organisations' mission and vision. In addition, the architecture framework can be used to define the types of communication that occur between various stakeholders and to describe attributes' overview of mobile systems and IT solutions in general. Security and privacy mechanisms must be integrated into mobile systems in their use for accessing organisations' big data. Otherwise, mobile systems are perceived as communicative tools endangering clients' information. In the use of mobile systems to access clients' big data, collaborative tools rely on technology connectivity for enablement and support.

Technology Connectivity

In this chapter, technology connectivity refers to the interface and interaction between computer application systems. In other words, it is the linkage between computer systems and individuals who make use of the systems. Through technology connectivity, communication and information sharing are enabled, supported and, at the same time, controlled and managed. When technologies, such as mobile systems are connected, employees can have access to big data for providing services to the clients. In terms of collaboration or linkage, if a system fails to connect, information about clients cannot be shared or transmitted to the system of another user who needs to provide a service to a client or stakeholder. This challenge contributes to the ineffective flow of information within and across organisations and hinders timely decision-making.

Technology connectivity needs to be guided and achieved through an architecture framework to ensure scalability and governance. An architecture framework drives the organisation's technical direction by defining the criteria for its selection and mechanism of operation. This promotes technology standards for the selection and development of technologies needed to support access to organisations' databases. Additionally, through architecture frameworks, systems' flexibility and compatibility are assessed accordingly (Zhao, Zheng & Litvinov, 2016). Due to the dynamic nature of emerging businesses, the flexibility of mobile systems is vital for effective systems' integrations and operations. It is worth noting that there are however rapid changes in modern business which affect competitive positioning and developing flexible and adaptable mobile systems.

Challenges such as lack of flexibility and incompatibility hinder connectivity and lead to systems' isolation or stand-alone. That aside, the use of stand-alone systems leads to human collaboration inefficiency; as such, access to big data cannot be readily available to the collaborators.

Human Collaboration

Human collaboration refers to business-to-client and business-to-business relationship and interaction. The collaboration is used to facilitate the sharing of information and knowledge required to provide integrated services to clients or stakeholders. In collaboration, employees share information, resources and other capabilities that are needed to achieve an outcome that cannot be achieved individually. Collaboration between employees and business is essential for promoting best practices and continuity of services. Collaboration without governance can invoke huge challenges and disruption in providing services by accessing big data using mobile systems. Hence, an architecture framework plays a critical role in fostering successful collaboration by establishing rules and structures that govern the collaborators.

Collaboration is attained through various tools, such as emails, video conferencing and mobile systems. The use of mobile systems for collaboration promotes fast access to information, creating an effective flow of information across the collaborators. Mobile systems enable effective responses to commercialisation that rely on frequent updated or real-time information to provide services. Consequently, effective collaboration depends on technology connectivity to enable instant messaging and sharing of information. Thus, by having an architecture framework, information vital for collaboration is made available by designing and implementing interconnected systems.

Summary

First, the chapter presented the factors that influence the use of mobile systems in accessing big data in organisations. Based on the interpretation, the factors were revealed, which led to the second phase. Secondly, the chapter presented a UAF.

From an enablement and support angle, the UAF can be used to guide the development and implementation of IT solutions that are flexible and scalable according to an organisation's needs and requirements. The integration and connectivity of the solutions allow for ease of access to big data, which enables effective collaboration among the different actors. This will potentially ease some operations and activities of organisations, partners and clients, including how information from clients' big data can be better managed and securely accessed through the integration of mobile systems.

References

Ahsan, K., Shah, H., & Kingston, P. (2009). The Role of Enterprise Architecture in Healthcare-IT. In *Proceedings of the 2009, Sixth International Conference on In Information Technology: New Generations*. (pp. 1462–1467), IEEE.

Cervone, H. (2016). Organizational considerations initiating a big data and analytics implementation. *Digital Library Perspective, 32*(3), 137–141.

Chen, H.-M., Kazman, R., & Haziyev, S. (2016). Agile big data analytics for web-based systems: An architecture-centric approach. *IEEE Transactions on Big Data, 2*(3), 234–248.

Howard, K., Michael, R., & Betram, R. (2016). Priming the pump for big data at sentara healthcare. *Frontiers of Health Services Management, 32*(4), 15–26.

Iyamu, T., & Mgudlwa, S. (2017). Transformation of healthcare big data through the lens of actor network theory. *International Journal of Healthcare Management, 11*(3), 182–192.

Iyamu, T., & Shaanika, I. (2020). Factors influencing the use of mobile systems to access healthcare big data in a Namibian public hospital. *Information Resources Management Journal (IRMJ), 33*(3), 81–99.

Jahan, S., Chowdhury, M., & Islam, R. (2018). Robust user authentication model for securing electronic healthcare system using fingerprint biometrics. *International Journal of Computers and Applications, 41*(3), 233–242.

Katal, A., Wazid, M., & Goudar, R. (2013). Big Data: Issues, Challenges, Tools and Good Practices. In *Sixth International Conference on Contemporary Computing (IC3)*. (pp. 404–409). 8-10 August, Noida, India. IEEE.

Katuu, S. (2016). Transforming South Africa's health sector: The eHealth strategy, the implementation of electronic document and records management systems (EDRMS) and the utility of maturity models. *Journal of Science and Technology Policy Management, 7*(3), 330–345.

Kohli, R., & Tan, S. L. (2016). Electronic health records: How can IS researchers contribute to transforming. *MIS Quarterly, 40*(3), 553–574.

Lankhorst, M. (2017). *Enterprise architecture at work: Modelling, communication and analysis.* (4th ed.). London: Springer.

Marcella, A., & Stucki, C. (2014). Privacy and security part III: Worlds in collision. *EDPACS, 50*(3), 1–20.

Mousannif, H., Sabah, H., Douiji, Y., & Sayad, Y. (2016). Big data projects: Just jump right in! *International Journal of Pervasive Computing and Communications, 12*(2), 260–288.

Ramesh, B. (2015). Big data architecture. In: H. Mohanty, P. Bhuyan & D. Chenthati (eds). *Big data. Studies in big data*, 11, 29–59. New Delhi: Springer.

Sabooniha, N., Toohey, D., & Lee, K. (2012). An Evaluation of Hospital Information Systems Integration Approaches. In *Proceedings of the International Conference on Advances in Computing, Communications and Informatics*. (pp. 498–504). 3-5 August, Chennai, India, ACM.

Sarkis, N., & Mwanri, L. (2013). The role of information technology in strengthening human resources for health: The case of the pacific open learning health network. *Health Education, 114*(1), 67–79.

Shaanika, I. (2016). Human interaction in the use of health information systems: A case of a developing country. In: T. Iyamu & A. Tatnall (eds). *Maximizing healthcare delivery and management through technology integration*, 257–269, IGI Global.

Shaanika, I., & Iyamu, T. (2015). Deployment of enterprise architecture in the Namibian government: The use of activity theory to examine the influencing factors. *The Electronic Journal of Information Systems in Developing Countries, 71*(6), 1–21.

Shaanika, I., & Iyamu, T. (2019). The use of mobile systems to access health care big data in the Namibian environment. *The Electronic Journal of Information Systems in Developing Countries, 86*(2), e12120.

Tupper, C. (2011). *Data architecture: From zen to reality*. San Francisco, CA: Morgan Kaufmann Publication.

Zhang, Y., Guo, S. L., Han, L. N., & Li, T. L. (2016). Application and exploration of big data mining in clinical medicine. *Chinese Medical Journal, 129*(6), 731.

Zhao, J., Zheng, T., & Litvinov, E. (2016). A unified framework for defining and measuring flexibility in power system. *IEEE Transactions on Power Systems, 31*(1), 339–347.

Chapter 11

Assessing the Value of Enterprise Architecture in Organisations

Introduction

In many quarters, the concept of enterprise architecture (EA) is defined as an approach used by organisations to holistically view business design and processes, and information technology (IT) solutions. This includes interrelationships of processes and artefacts, and the alignment between business and IT units in an organisation (Tamm et al., 2011). Without contrast, Ross, Weill and Robertson (2006) viewed EA as an approach that organises the logic of business processes and IT solutions into an integrated and standardised format for an operating model. Hence, the development and implementation of EA is sought as a solution for managing the activities of both business and IT units (Niemi & Pekkola, 2017). Van den Berg et al. (2019) explain how EA artefacts are used for IT investment decisions where it has been deployed.

EA is considered as an important component of business process design, information value chain, application and technology strategic management (Safari, Faraji & Majidian, 2016). Urbaczewski and Mrdalj (2006) explain that EA and its corresponding documentation allow for IS/IT maintenance in order to ensure that systems do not become obsolete before they are even built, deployed or used. One of the primary aims of EA is to bridge the gap between business and IS/IT units and enable organisations to plan and manage change periodically and iteratively. For many years, EA has been developed, implemented and practised in organisations using different frameworks, such as the Open Group Architecture Framework

DOI: 10.1201/9781003268420-11

(TOGAF), the Zachman Framework and Gartner Inc. (Kappelman & Zachman, 2013). The enticement and interest about EA could be drawn from the promise of its potential benefits and value.

However, the potential value from EA is neither easy to achieve nor articulate, given the advancements and complexities of business processes and activities, including technological artefacts. Lehong, Dube and Angelopoulos (2013) explain that the value and benefits provided by EA include assisting senior managers and other stakeholders to make certain critical business and IT decisions at both strategic and operational levels. In practice, this is a difficult realisation primarily because without an understanding of the value of EA, it is hard to determine its contributions. This has been debated by practitioners and academics for many years. The discourse is increasing, and it is being extended to aspiring researchers and postgraduates who frequently inquire why they need to focus on EA if organisations are not boastful about the outcome.

Instead of increasing the interest of applied researchers, the discourse is slowing down the evolvement. Bradley et al. (2012) argue that studies that empirically focus on the assessment and maturity of EA are lacking. The reason can be ascribed to the void in systematically assessing and measuring the value of EA. The goal of this chapter is to present a model that can be used to assess the value of EA in an organisation. To accomplish this goal, two objectives were drawn: (1) identify the key factors which influence the value of EA in organisations; and (2) examine these factors in detail to gain a better understanding of their deterministic effect on EA practice.

After so many years of existence, EA continues to be engulfed in credibility challenge because return on investment (ROI) is not as visible as many organisations had wanted (Niemi & Pekkola, 2019). Some of the challenges of EA are not always clear or obvious, as the agents of complexity include both technical and non-technical factors, such as inconsistency of procedures, principles and standards. This is an effect of EA not being well understood in many organisations and, as a result, senior management are not keen in investing in the concept (Ajer & Olsen, 2019).

The remainder of this chapter is divided into five main sections. It begins by presenting a review of literature, which focuses on EA, and the assessment of EA value in organisations. This is followed by discussion about the factors that influence the value of EA in organisations. Next, is the interpretation of the influencing factors, which include the business process, value chain, documentation and consolidation. Thereafter, the assessment model is presented and comprehensively discussed. The weights and criteria of EA value are presented. Lastly, the chapter is summarised.

Review of Related Literature

The review of literature focuses on two key areas: (1) the discussion covers challenges and benefits of EA in organisations; and (2) factors influencing assessing and the implications of not assessing the value of EA in organisations.

Enterprise Architecture

EA is typically used to manage an organisation's activities from strategic to operational levels. Lagerström et al. (2011) suggest that some organisations employ EA for IS/IT concerns alone, while others make use of the approach for both business and IT activities. Regardless of the purpose for which the EA is developed and implemented, there exist common convictions amongst organisations and researchers that EA can facilitate efforts and activities which are required to transform an organisation from its current state to a future state (Tamm et al., 2011). Hence, the development and implementation of EA requires an in-depth understanding of the activities and operations of both business and IT units (Shaanika & Iyamu, 2018). Iyamu (2015) demonstrates that the development and implementation of an appropriate EA depends on people, technology and process.

For an organisation to benefit from EA, it must have a clear understanding of its structure, products, operations and IT artefacts (Azevedo et al., 2015). The development and implementation of EA enables an organisation to achieve significant benefits from IT and business activities (Bradley et al., 2012). Also, EA facilitates the integration of rules, principles and guidelines for projects and business operations in order to assure efficient improvements and changes to the IT environment (Ullah & Lai, 2011), and enables improved information sharing (Safari et al., 2016; Abraham, Aier & Winter, 2015). Lagerström et al. (2011) and Tamm et al. (2011) focused on EA from the perspectives of risk management and resources portfolio optimisation in organisations. However, it is important to note that the potential benefits from EA do not necessarily or automatically transform to value for an organisation. Therefore, the efforts and objectives and benefits of EA need to be assessed to ascertain its value in the context of an organisation (Fritscher & Pigneur, 2015).

Many organisations embrace the concept of EA due to its potential benefits without having a good understanding of the implicit challenges (Nygård & Olsen, 2016). Debates about the EA value often become intensified among diverse stakeholders (Iyamu, 2019). Such debates are justified since many EA projects fail, owing to lack of clearly defined goals and objectives (Lapalme et al., 2016). For some organisations, EA is a challenging and confusing concept (Kappelman & Zachman, 2013). In the view of Lagerström et al. (2011), EA is a 'heavy approach' which requires the implementation of several activities in accordance with frameworks and models. Some of the frameworks include Zachman, Gartner Inc. and TOGAF. There are no frameworks or models that are specifically tailored to an organisation's needs. Each organisation is required to customise an EA framework of their choice to fit its business environment and characteristics. Bijarchian and Ali (2013) explain that there is lack of well-defined criteria to assess the EA frameworks' (EAFs') usability in providing value to an organisation. The EAFs give a comprehensive description of relevant elements, principal structure and classification schema about an organisation (Vargas et al., 2016; Chalmeta & Pazos, 2015).

Even though EA supports both business and IS/IT strategies, more focus is usually on technical domains (Chuang & Loggerenberg, 2010). Many of the challenges encountered in developing and implementing an appropriate EA for an organisation are largely of non-technical nature (Safari et al., 2016). In Nygård and Olsen (2016) and Chuang and Loggerenberg (2010), some of the challenging factors are named as (1) lack of role clarity; (2) management knowledge and commitment; (3) communication inefficiency; (4) buy-in from the stakeholders; and (5) ownership of activities. Some of the non-technical factors that influence EA challenges include people and processes (Fritscher & Pigneur, 2015).

Despite such longevity of interest and the benefits that are associated with EA concept, there are many challenges. According to Iyamu (2011), it is difficult to find organisations that have institutionalised the concept in the country. Chuang and Loggerenberg (2010) explained that some of the challenges are caused by the emphasis that is given to the technical aspects while neglecting other aspects, such as people and process that are as equally important. Nygård and Olsen (2016) stated that only about five per cent of EA efforts succeed in organisations. The challenges are influenced by several complexities, such as lack of uniformity and integration of IT solutions in the deployment and practice of EA in organisations (Iyamu, 2019).

Both technical and non-technical factors together determine the success of the implementation and practice towards value realisation of EA in an organisation (Gilliland, Kotzé & van der Merwe, 2015). Another crucial challenge faced in embracing the concept of EA is lack of buy-in from the stakeholders who question how truly effective the concept can be for the organisation (Lehong et al., 2013). In Lapalme's (2012) study, the EA challenges were linked to a lack of understanding of an organisation's dynamics. These challenges will continue to affect the deployment and institutionalisation of the EA, if formal metrics are not utilised to measure the real value of EA to an organisation.

Assessing the Value of EA

Assessment can be defined as a process of calculating and quantifying components that ensure the realisation of a concept. Such metrics include the key performance indicator (KPI), ROI, net present value (NPV), internal rate of return (IRR), Benefit/Cost ratio and Break-Even point. An assessment is often conducted to ascertain and understand the value of an activity and components, such as IS/IT. According to Sedera and Dey (2013), an assessment is purposely done to understand the fundamental characteristics of value.

Potential benefits of EA in an organisation are many. What is missing is how to transform or translate the potential benefits of EA into value for an organisation. Tamm et al. (2011) stated that numerous benefits that are claimed in the literature are often not explained or supported by empirical evidence. For many organisations, the resources spent or invested in EA must be justified with a demonstration or proof of positive effects of the concept (Akaka & Vargo, 2014; Morganwalp & Sage, 2004).

In essence, the effects of the EA should be assessed by how it contributes to the business value of an organisation (Fallmyr & Bygstad, 2014). Value can be defined as a measure of concrete difference that an object can contribute to an environment.

Value is created through the efficient production of goods and services based on a variety of resources (Gottschalk, 2006: 1061). Yuan and Dong (2006) suggest that the establishment, maintenance and proper operation of an organisation hugely depend on its employees' interest and enrolment in the concept of value. A common understanding of value contributes to the efficiency of an organisation's productivity. However, several employees and senior managers who are aware of EA do not understand or cannot agree on how the concept can contribute to value creation in their organisations. An organisation's concept of value is influenced by its culture. As pointed out by Fallmyr and Bygstad (2014), business value is achieved through management practices and culture across an organisation. This is because culture defines the acceptable norms, behaviours and processes through which activities are carried out in an organisation.

However, extracting the value of EA is a complex process, which makes it far-reaching for some managers (Gong & Janssen, 2019). Also, EA is more prevalent in large organisations (Van den Berg et al. (2019), limiting the diversity in looking for organisations that have successfully had ROI.

Factors Influencing EA Value

Based on the aim, which is to provide a model for assessing the value of EA in organisations, the question is: *What are the factors that influence EA value in organisations?* In order to go beyond abstraction and connect with actual events and precise substances, the main question was split into three, as follows: (1) How does EA influence the business and IT processes and activities in organisations? (2) What are the benefits of EA to the organisation? (3) Why are benefits of EA assessed or measured in organisations? The following helps in providing answers to the questions, towards achieving the aim of the chapter: (1) the value of EA in organisations – what an organisation defines as value in the context of the EA; and (2) the factors that influence the value of EA in an organisation – how the factors manifest themselves to influence or impact EA development, implementation and practice. The most common factors of EA desirability in organisations are alignment, communication, evolution, governance and ownership. My 15 years as an EA expert, and literature affirm this conclusion.

Alignment of Activities

Alignment – bridging processes, requirements and strategies between business and IT units of an organisation. Many managers rely on the EA process in understanding how to address the disparities that exist between the business and IT units, which are often complicated, especially in large organisations. However, it is not always easy to find managers who excitedly take the responsibility of ensuring that an alignment between the business and IT units is achieved.

Various activities exist at both strategic and operational levels within the business and IT units in organisations. Majority of the activities are usually far apart from each other even though they are meant to achieve common goals for the organisations. This challenge is worse in government institutions and agencies. More than others, some organisations struggle for many years to align the activities of business and IT solutions in a holistic manner. This means that it does not completely work for all the units of the organisations.

EA facilitates alignment between organisational units, based on the synergy and interdependence that exist between technical and business architecture domains. Lack of alignment between teams, units and divisions is usually cited as a major concern by employees and management in many organisations. Also, there is a high expectation from the concept of EA by the management, particularly in the area of ROI. When some employees are trained to understand that EA will be used to bridge the gap between the units, they wonder how that can be actualised. Instead, some employees look forward to a tangible software. This concern could be attributed to the fact that there has always been more focus on the technical aspects of EA.

Communication

Communication enables shared vision, requirements gathering, information flow and business events management within an organisation. Also, communication is employed to facilitate operations and strategies in both the business and IT units in an organisation. It is therefore critical to understand how actors communicate the activities of the organisation to the stakeholders. In addition, communication can be used to facilitate the alignment between business and IT units in an organisation. This, in turn, fosters synergy and adds value to the organisations' activities. Subsequently, the inconsistencies, discrepancies and lack of uniformity between business and IT units can be better governed to improve the productivity and competitiveness of the organisation.

Communication and interactions amongst employees and units help to facilitate the implementation and practice of EA. These types of interactions are carried out through the EA domains primarily to bring value to an organisation that employs it. Although communication improves teamwork and access to resource and expertise, it is not as easy in practice as proclaimed in theory. Communication requires clear guidelines and structures, as defined by EA. As the interactions between the business and IT units get stronger through the process of EA, a common understanding is reached and value can be assessed.

The value of EA in organisations needs to be assessed and measured continually. Through a formal process, organisations need to understand the impact and assess the value and contribution that EA brings to the formulation and operationalisation of their strategies. An effective organisational structure is needed for assessing EA value, which can be gained from defining communication channel, alignment between business and IT units and the hierarchy of employees' roles and responsibilities at the operations and strategy levels. The structure directly or indirectly influences the communication of policy, implementation of standards and principles, as well as the allocation of tasks in the development and implementation of EA in organisations.

Evolution of Artefacts

Evolution is the change that happens over a period of time in the areas of processes, business events, strategies and IT solutions. In some quarters, EA is considered an agent of change, which Chapter 9 covers extensively.

EA enables and supports the evolution of activities such as processes, business events, information flow, strategies operationalisation and application portfolio in an organisation where it is deployed. However, there has been little or no acceptable approach for assessing how EA can enable and support the evolution of operations in an organisation. This void is a catalyst hindrance or makes it challenging to embark on some important activities in many organisations. It is in this vein that some significant initiatives end in the form of 'white elephants' primarily because the promoters (or initiators) could not prove the value, and therefore the activities could not be measured against investment as theoretically promised by EA.

EA is also used to maintain and manage how an organisation can approach the evolution of events, artefacts and activities that happen within its environment. EA guides evolution by assessing potential activities through its standards, principles and policies. Some organisations rely on organisational catalogues which consist of services, products and events to guide the evolution of their strategy and operations. Managing by evolution requires EA specialists to be able to identify the benefits or value in the events and activities as they evolve.

EA is a distinct field that requires special scarce skills that are scarce for various reasons. The next chapter deals with the subject of skill and capacity. The retention of employees that have EA skill is critical. Such skilled personnel help to build the maturity of EA, thus add to its value in an organisation. Having mature and experienced EA experts promotes the effective management of the evolution of new relevant events and activities in an organisation.

Governance

Governance – although governance is covered in many chapters of this book, in this section it refers to the control and management of activities, such as design, information flow, integration, standards and technology selection in an organisation.

Governance is primarily to guide, monitor and improve processes and activities such as the control and management of people and IT solutions. This includes the design of business logics and processes, information exchange and flow and integration of IT solutions. Also, governance provides a guide for standardisation in the selection, implementation and use of IT solutions in an organisation. Due to the complexity of some organisations, governance gets more critical. If implemented appropriately, the organisation begins to realise the value of EA as complexities are reduced. This saves time and cost and improves time to market. Another example is, through governance, policies and principles are formulated as dictated by both business and IT solutions' requirements. Also, IT solutions are configured and deployed based on standards provided by governance.

The potential value from governance includes improved competitiveness, sustainability and productivity. In addition, governance through EA enables and facilitates flexibility, efficiency and effectiveness, thereby reducing the cost and resource to maintain and manage complexities and inefficiency. The value that EA brings to an organisation is often hard to assess and measure. One of the reasons is that some employees' expectation of tangibility makes it difficult for factors such as flexibility and effectiveness to show value in organisations.

The development and implementation of EA is an iterative process and the ensuing value to the organisation can be detected and assessed to show gaps and differences between previous and current states. Such value is influenced by both business and IT perspectives. Some organisations operate within dynamic environments requiring continuous changes to operations and strategies of business and IT solutions. The iterative process is facilitated by people through an organisational structure to effect change on business artefacts and IT solutions. The iterative process is meant to gain an understanding of how the factors manifest and affect the value of EA in an organisation, and how to achieve an acceptable ROI. This iterative process is intended to have a positive impact on the organisational structure, such as placing certain skilled employees in strategic positions to protect the investment in EA.

Ownership

Ownership refers to the component through which roles, responsibilities and accountability are defined and assessed, thereby fostering buy-in, organisational structure and skill set (training) in an organisation.

Similar to other factors, ownership also contributes to the value of EA in an organisation. It defines and clarifies roles and responsibilities, particularly those that are complex to understand, such as the overlapping nature of business analyst and business architecture; see Chapter 5 of this book. The clarification makes for ease of accountability through which quicker response time is gained. In the context of EA, accountability also ensures the buy-in of new investments by relevant management authorities within the organisational structure, and acceptable implementation and use of best practices by diverse stakeholders in an organisation. The roles and responsibilities are associated and aligned with skill set, which requires training and development as operations and strategies evolve within various units in the organisation.

Training and skills development are essential for ownership. This is to prepare those who take ownership of the maintenance and management of EA process in organisations. Individual skills manifest in their performances, and therefore determine further training and development. Boh and Yellin (2006) emphasise the criticality of skills and specialisation of EA domains. In essence, an assessment of the impact of EA in an organisation requires a skilled workforce with a good understanding of the concept.

Interpretation of the Influencing Factors

The five factors; alignment, communication, evolution, governance and ownership, presented in the preceding section are interpreted, towards knowing how EA value can be assessed or measured in organisations. The process of interpretation was divided into two steps to ensure an attainable differentiation between influencing factors and business indicators:

Step # One – the first step was to understand how the factors manifest themselves in the practice of EA. This helps to understand how the factors influence activities and add value to an organisation:

i. **Alignment** – organisations are often challenged when units or divisions are not in alignment in their operations. The operations and outcome become prohibitive. Also, competitiveness is affected. It is for this reason that EA is meant to enable the alignment between units and divisions of an organisation and should be seen as value. In addition, alignment helps to facilitate the consolidation of efforts and processes through documentation.

ii. **Communication** – business processes and activities which form the value chain are communicated through a communication strategy. Many employees and stakeholders find it difficult to understand the strategies of business or IT, or both. This can be costly to the sustainability of an organisation. Also, roles and responsibilities are confused for one another, and loosely used, affect structural accountability. These are effects of poor communication, particularly where technology tools are used. EA adds value from this perspective by streamlining the use of the tools through governance.

iii. **Evolution** – in order to realise the value of the evolution of business processes that happen over a period of time, they need to be documented. Also, evolution comes from different aspects of an organisation and requires consolidation for reuse purposes. Without such documentations, humans remain the organisational memory, which some employees use as a source of power to dominate and negotiate their undeserved positions.

iv. **Governance** – business processes and the consolidation of processes and documentation format are defined and streamlined through governance. This is in order to achieve transparency, reduce complication, ensure track and trace and promote clean audit. Without EA, this is a huge challenge as evident in many organisations.

v. **Ownership** – roles and responsibilities require ownership to ensure accountability towards the actualisation of value. Ownership clarifies the complexities that are associated with the growth trajectory of an organisation. The complexities can also be prohibitive if not addressed.

Step #Two – from the first step, the most common elements that can serve as stimuli to an organisation's activities or operations were extracted. The elements are referred to as business indicators. The elements include business process, value chain, documentation and consolidation. As shown in Table 11.1, the business indicators are linked to the domains of EA, which are business, information, application and technical architectures. The link means that the business indicators are enabled and supported by EA domains within an organisation. The business indicators are discussed here.

Table 11.1   Factors of Influence

Business Indicator ╲ EA Domain	Business	Information	Application	Technical
Business Process	X	X	X	X
Value Chain	X	X	X	X
Documentation	X	X	X	X
Consolidation	X	X	X	X

Business Process

Processes are used to guide the strategies and operations of an organisation. Business process can be defined as procedural through which an organisation carries out its operations, to create or fortify value for its customers and stakeholders. The business processes of EA are interlinked and cannot be separated from one another towards accomplishing specific goals and objectives in an organisation.

The information architecture defines the flow, usage and governance of information artefacts within an organisation. Thereafter, the application and technical architectures are employed to enable and support information flow of the business processes and operations. This enables employees to carry out business processes for competitiveness and sustainability. Without the flow of information, processes and activities are often disconnected and disjointed within an organisation, as well as between customers and partners. Chen et al. (2014) assert that the link between the business and IT processes is critical to organisational performance because it enhances practitioners' capability to make effective decisions about the development, acquisition and implementation of various solutions and services within an environment.

Value Chain

Value chain in an organisation refers to networks of activities and processes, which include networks of information and catalogues of events. The value chain is enabled and supported by EA in an environment. Walters and Lancaster (2010) explain how value chains convert inputs via organisational processes in order to create strategic outcomes. The network of information shows how information is managed and used in an organisation. English (2009) argues that it is impossible to achieve business excellence if the information that the organisation depends upon is defective in its presentation. Thus, value chain contributes to the growth, competitiveness and sustainability of an organisation. Value chain is mainly gained from strategic and operational outcomes as supported and enabled by business processes, information flow, applications (software) and technologies (server and other hardware), as defined and governed, and standardised and managed through EA domains.

Documentation

Documentation is an EA mechanism for storing documents and artefacts in an organisation. It is enforced into inventory. The mechanism promotes transparency, track and trace and reduces complexity. Based on the criticality of these activities in many organisations, documentation can be considered as a strength of EA. Also, because documentation enables access to the stock of knowledge, it enhances business continuity and organisational sustainability and competitiveness. The stock of knowledge often covers information about organisational structure, process flow, historical events, applications' logics and technologies' know-how to which stakeholders frequently request access for decision-making. To enhance the usefulness of the documentation process, EA documents are stored in a central repository. This helps with the manageability of business operations and activities for improved effectiveness and efficiency. In addition, the documentation process increases the level of security to sustainability. Through the domains of the EA, templates are provided to guide the documentation of historical events, legacy systems and other activities.

Consolidation

One of the benefits of EA is consolidation. Through the domains of EA, business operations and IT solutions within organisations can be consolidated. The consolidation of business processes and IT artefacts is required in order to reduce complexity and eradicate duplications and redundancies in an environment. Through such consolidation, an organisation's competitiveness and sustainability can be improved. Consolidation therefore necessitates the integration and linkage of both business processes and activities within an organisation. Through consolidation, an organisation is able to supply its customers, employees, stakeholders and partners with real-time information and integrate processes, systems and media beyond organisational boundaries (Lapalme et al., 2016). Also, through consolidation, business processes and information activities are instantaneously synchronised and enabled by information systems and technologies. In addition, the consolidation of business processes helps to eradicate redundant data and the repetition of efforts which often thwart competitiveness in an organisation.

Assessment Model of EA Value

Based on the influencing factors and business indicators, a model (Figure 11.1) was developed. The model is intended for assessing EA value in an organisation. As shown in Figure 11.1, the model consists of three main sets: (1) the factors that influence EA value and its assessment, as stated in Table 11.2; (2) the criteria that weigh the value of the factors towards assessment; and (3) the value itself. Figure 11.1 also illustrates the links and interconnection between the sets of factors, so as to gain a better understanding of the assessment model.

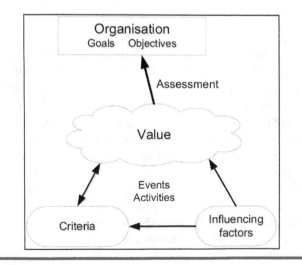

Figure 11.1   Assessing the EA value.

Weight of EA Value

The weights that are associated with EA value are presented in Table 11.2. Each component in Table 11.2 is briefly described to guide users in employing the model to assess the actual value of EA in an organisation. The components, as shown in Table 11.1, were derived from Section 4. Subsequently, Table 11.3 was derived from Section 5. The weights range from 1 to 5. The value components are put in an ascending order of relevance; which means: 1 as the lowest, and 5 as the highest unit. The columns in the table present the criteria for assessment, which are alignment, communication, evolutionary, governance and ownership. In the table, middle management and senior management refer to divisional and organisational levels, respectively.

As shown in Table 11.2, the rows and columns are inseparable if the value of EA is to be appropriately assessed for an organisation's benefits and purposes. The rows consist of the numeric weights of the components, which are explained and discussed as follows.

Business and IT Alignment

Alignment is the dependency between business and IT units in an organisation, which entails the internalisation of partnership. It therefore facilitates the delivery of excellence in an organisation. By implication, both units should at all times work together to avoid a compromise in achieving the organisation's aim and objectives. In Ullah and Lai's (2011) words, alignment is the process through which business and IT units become interrelated. The business unit focuses on the organisation's activities, such as finance, human resource, sales and marketing, while the IT unit enables the automation of various business operations, activities and processes through its solutions.

It is therefore logical that the architecture domains that support and enable those activities and processes are of critical importance to the organisation that deploys it. Zarvić and Wieringa (2014) discuss EAFs as a conceptual framework for business and IT alignment, in which authors highlight some of the implications, such as the decomposition of alignment problems into domains. The goal of EA is to ensure the alignment of a holistic view between business and IT units. Also, the alignment of both units supports and enables effective communication across an organisation.

Communication

This is primarily to foster the interaction of aligned interests of enterprise architects and other stakeholders. Communication contributes to bridging the gap that exists towards an understanding of a common goal between individuals and groups in both business and IT units. Simon, Fischbach and Schoder (2014) identify

Table 11.2 Value Weights and Criteria

#	Alignment	Communication	Evolutionary	Governance	Ownership
1	There is no alignment of operations at units, divisional or organisational level.	There is informal communication between business and IT units at management level.	There are no changes to the processes, operations and ways in which the activities are run.	There is neither a governance structure nor uniformity in the processes and activities.	There are no defined or assigned ownerships of processes and activities.
2	Alignment is initiated at both divisional and organisational levels.	There is a formal tool used for communication between business and IT units in random circumstances.	There is minimal progression in the processes, operation and activities.	There are policies, standards and principles, but there is lack of compliance.	Roles and responsibilities are defined, but not the ownership.
3	There is alignment at both the divisional and organisational levels.	There is a formal tool used for communication between business and IT units at divisional level.	The changes that happen in the processes and activities are random; they are not iterative.	Policies, standards and principles are not always used to guide the operations, processes and activities.	There exist conflicts between roles, responsibilities and ownership.
4	Alignment exists in the operations carried out at both divisional and organisational levels.	There is a formal tool used for communication between business and IT units in strategic and daily operations.	Some of the processes and activities are iterative. Others are static.	Processes and activities are guided by the policies, standards and principles, but they are not being monitored and evaluated.	Not all the processes and activities are assigned ownership.
5	Tools are used for the alignment of processes and activities at all levels in the organisation.	At all times, a formal tool is available and used for communication in all processes and activities between the business and IT units at all levels in the organisation.	Change remains constant at advancement positions in all the processes and activities of the organisation.	All processes and activities are guided by standards and principles and they are frequently monitored and evaluated.	Ownership in all the processes and activities is well defined and aligned with the organisational structure.

weaknesses in communication between employees in senior and lower levels within an organisational structure as one of the most critical obstacles to a successful strategy implementation. Communication enables a link and alignment between business and IT units' operations, processes and activities. Routine communication amongst the interested actors fosters and ensures cooperation and collaboration at a near-guaranteed level. Kang et al. (2010) argue that lack of, or limited communication among stakeholders hinders the integration of processes and activities in collaborative work. Also, methods of communication must be flexibly evolutional to avoid rigidity, which has the potential of creating gaps in the tasks that are undertaken by employees for organisational purposes.

Evolutionary

Evolution is a type of progression or advancement of an artefact that is beyond maintenance. As a result, processes and activities of IT solutions must be evolutionary in practice in order for change and transformation to happen within an organisation. In continued support and enablement of an organisation's competitiveness, IT solutions should be engineered to undergo a substantial degree of evolution (Breivold, Crnkovic & Larsson, 2012). Technology evolution can be ambiguous and can make the solutions more complex than ever before. As a result, the IT solutions require governance in order to improve on the quality of services they provide to an organisation and its partners.

Governance

Through policies, principles and standards, governance provides guidance in the selection, development, implementation, use and management of IT solutions, as well as business design processes and activities within an organisation. Governance is used to set boundaries at operational and strategic levels for both technical and non-technical domains. The increasing complexities of IT solutions and processes promote the need for governance and allow the alignment of business and architectures within an organisation to take place (Simon et al., 2014). Also, governance creates a culture of uniformity. In addition, the use of governance helps to eradicate inconsistencies, duplications and obsolete artefacts. The adequacy of an organisation's capabilities and capacity to operate efficiently is compellingly associated with effective governance.

Ownership

Through the concept of ownership, the capacity of units and capabilities of artefacts within the context of EA are defined in an organisation. Also, the ownership concept facilitates managerial, operational and strategic roles and responsibilities in the development, implementation and practice of EA in an organisation.

Ownership helps to conduct the assessment of value chain in an organisation. Through an ownership approach, conflicts that manifest from power relationships can be minimised. Also, through ownership, accountability can be more transparent and improvement on service delivery can be gained (Maglio & Spohrer, 2013).

Weight of the Criteria

The numeric values of 1–5, as presented in the rows of Table 11.3, were used to develop the assessment metrics. The numeric value is ascribed with contents as follows: 1 = Foundation; 2 = Inadequate; 3 = Sufficient; 4 = Good; and 5 = Very Good. The value is linked to a set of business/IT influencing factors, which were discussed in Section 4. The factors include business process, value chain, business/IT alignment, retention and consolidation. These sets of critical factors are variables that can be replaced, depending on the unique or critical needs and focus of the organisation that deploys them.

Table 11.3   EA Assessment Metrics

Criteria	5	4	3	2	1	Weight
Business Process						
Value Chain						
Business/IT Alignments						
Retention						
Consolidation						

Assessment Model

Figure 11.2 depicts the model that can be used to assess the value of EA in an organisation. The model contains five value types, in the categories of: (1) Very Good; (2) Good; (3) Sufficient; (4) Inadequate; and (5) Foundation. The categorisation is based on the assessment that is presented in Table 11.3. The value of EA in an organisation should therefore be assessed in categories. Also, each of the categories should be represented by a level of maturity. Through the categories, an organisation can weight how its EA contributes to operations, growth, processes and activities towards profitability, competitiveness and sustainability. Through this approach, an organisation can detect the areas where there are deficiencies and gaps. The metrics is an approach which organisations can employ to assess the value of EA from the perspectives of: Very Good = 21–25; Good = 16–20; Sufficient = 12–15; Inadequate = 8–11; and Foundation = 0–7.

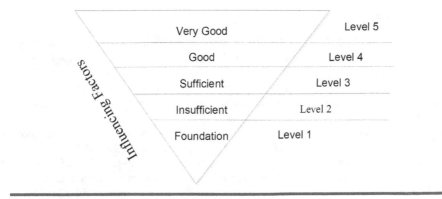

Figure 11.2   EA value assessment model.

In the context of the model, 'Very Good' is the fifth and highest level of value associated with the assessment categories, as shown in Table 11.3. It is a level at which an organisation can attain the institutionalisation of EA. At the level of 'Very Good', there should be more frequent and regular assessments of EA value. The fourth level requires minimal work but must attain an iterative process. Owing to the fact that only minimum work is required, it means that the institutionalisation of EA can also happen at this level. The third level requires more work in all fronts, if it is to begin to realise the value and return from investment in EA. The first and second levels are basics, which mean a major engineering of operations, processes and activities, towards the realisation of the EA goals and objectives.

In order to attain the highest level, which is 'Very Good', all components that are discussed above must be strongly evident and used as the primary criteria in the assessment of EA value in an organisation. Levels 4, 3, 2 and 1 mean that there are gaps, and some degree of improvement is needed as the practice progresses.

Summary

Persistently, organisations increasingly continue to show interest in the concept of EA. Academics too have progressively embraced the concept and EA has been included in the curriculum of many higher institutions of learning. Thus, an understanding of how to measure the value of EA in organisations is critically important. This is to ascertain the levels of its maturity and contribution to an organisation, which requires a formal and iterative process. This chapter is therefore of benefit to both practitioners and academics. The chapter can assist enterprise architects and other EA stakeholders to gain a better understanding of how to assess the value that EA brings to their organisations through creating awareness and categorising the influencing factors. Continually, these factors have been consciously or unconsciously missed or dismissed by enterprise architects and other stakeholders for many years. This affects management buy-in as well as ROI.

References

Abraham, R., Aier, S., & Winter, R. (2015). Crossing the line: Overcoming knowledge boundaries in enterprise transformation. *Business & Information Systems Engineering, 57*(1), 3–13.

Ajer, A. K. S., & Olsen, D. H. (2019). Enterprise architecture implementation is a bumpy ride: A case study in the Norwegian public sector. *Electronic Journal of e-Government, 17*(2), 79–94.

Akaka, M. A., & Vargo, S. L. (2014). Technology as an operant resource in service (eco) systems. *Information Systems and e-Business Management, 12*(3), 367–384.

Azevedo, C. L., Iacob, M. E., Almeida, J. P. A., van Sinderen, M., Pires, L. F., & Guizzardi, G. (2015), Modeling resources and capabilities in enterprise architecture: A well-founded ontology-based proposal for ArchiMate. *Information Systems, 54*, 235–262.

Bijarchian, A., & Ali, R. (2013). A Model to Assess the Usability of Enterprise Architecture Frameworks. In *the Proceedings of the International Conference on Informatics and Creative Multimedia (ICICM)*. (pp. 33–37). 4-6 September, Kuala Lumpur, Malaysia. IEEE.

Boh, W. F., & Yellin, D. (2006). Using enterprise architecture standards in managing information technology. *Journal of Management Information Systems, 23*(3), 163–207.

Bradley, R. V., Pratt, R. M., Byrd, T. A., Outlay, C. N., & Wynn, D. E. Jr (2012). Enterprise architecture, IT effectiveness and the mediating role of IT alignment in US hospitals. *Information Systems Journal, 22*(2), 97–127.

Breivold, H. P., Crnkovic, I., & Larsson, M. (2012). A systematic review of software architecture evolution research. *Information and Software Technology, 54*(1), 16–40.

Chalmeta, R., & Pazos, V. (2015). A step-by-step methodology for enterprise interoperability projects. *Enterprise Information Systems, 9*(4), 436–464.

Chen, Y., Wang, Y., Nevo, S., Jin, J., Wang, L., & Chow, W. S. (2014). IT capability and organisational performance: The roles of business process agility and environmental factors. *European Journal of Information Systems, 23*(3), 326–342.

Chuang, C. H., & Loggerenberg, J. V. (2010). Challenges Facing Enterprise Architects: A South African Perspective. In *the Proceedings of the 43rd Hawaii International Conference on System Sciences (HICSS)*. 5-8 January, Honolulu, Hawaii. IEEE.

English, L. (2009). *Information quality applied*. London, UK: John Wiley & Sons.

Fallmyr, T., & Bygstad, B. (2014). Enterprise Architecture Practice and Organisational Agility: An Exploratory Study. In *the Proceedings of the 47th International Conference on System Sciences (HICSS)*. (pp. 3788–3797). 6-9 January, Waikoloa, Hawaii. IEEE.

Fritscher, B., & Pigneur, Y. (2015). A visual approach to business IT alignment between business model and enterprise architecture. *International Journal of Information System Modelling and Design, 6*(1), 1–23.

Gilliland, S., Kotzé, P., & van der Merwe, A. (2015). Work Level Related Human Factors for Enterprise Architecture as Organisational Strategy. In *the Proceedings of the International Conference on Enterprise Systems (ES), 2015*. (pp. 43–54). 14-15 October, Basel Switzerland. IEEE.

Gong, Y., & Janssen, M. (2019). The value of and myths about enterprise architecture. *International Journal of Information Management, 46*, 1–9.

Gottschalk, P. (2006). Information systems in value configurations. *Industrial Management & Data Systems, 106*(7), 1060–1070.

Iyamu, T. (2011). The architecture of information in organisations. *South African Journal of Information Management, 13*(1), 1–9.

Iyamu, T. (2015). *Enterprise architecture: From concept to practise.* Australia: Heidelberg Press.

Iyamu, T. (2019). Understanding the complexities of enterprise architecture through structuration theory. *Journal of Computer Information Systems, 59*(3), 287–295.

Kang, D., Lee, J., Choi, S., & Kim, K. (2010). An ontology-based enterprise architecture. *Expert Systems with Applications, 37*(2), 1456–1464.

Kappelman, L. A., & Zachman, J. A. (2013). The enterprise and its architecture: Ontology & challenges. *Journal of Computer Information Systems, 53*(4), 87–95.

Lagerström, R., Sommestad, T., Buschle, M., & Ekstedt, M. (2011). Enterprise Architecture Management's Impact on Information Technology Success. In *the Proceedings of the 44th International Conference on System Sciences (HICSS).* (pp. 1–10). 4-7 January, Kauai, Hawaii. IEEE.

Lapalme, J. (2012). Three schools of thought on enterprise architecture. *IT Professional, 14*(6), 37–43.

Lapalme, J., Gerber, A., Van der Merwe, A., Zachman, J., De Vries, M., & Hinkelmann, K. (2016). Exploring the future of enterprise architecture: A Zachman perspective. *Computers in Industry, 79*, 103–113.

Lehong, S. M., Dube, E., & Angelopoulos, G. (2013). An investigation into the perceptions of business stakeholders on the benefits of enterprise architecture: The case of telkom SA. *South African Journal of Business Management, 44*(2), 45–56.

Maglio, P. P., & Spohrer, J. (2013). A service science perspective on business model innovation. *Industrial Marketing Management, 42*(5), 665–670.

Morganwalp, J. M., & Sage, A. P. (2004). Enterprise architecture measures of effectiveness. *International Journal of Technology, Policy and Management, 4*(1), 81–94.

Niemi, E., & Pekkola, S. (2017). Using enterprise architecture artefacts in an organisation. *Enterprise Information Systems, 11*(3), 313–338.

Niemi, E., & Pekkola, S. (2019). The benefits of enterprise architecture in organizational transformation. *Business & Information Systems Engineering, 62*(6), 585–597.

Nygård, M., & Olsen, D. H. (2016). Enterprise architecture implementation challenges: An exploratory study of the Norwegian health sector. *NOKOBIT, 24*(1), 1–9.

Ross, J., Weill, P., & Robertson, D. (2006). *Enterprise architecture as a strategy: Creating a foundation for business execution.* United States of America: Harvard Business Press.

Safari, H., Faraji, Z., & Majidian, S. (2016). Identifying and evaluating enterprise architecture risks using FMEA and fuzzy VIKOR. *Journal of Intelligent Manufacturing, 27*(2), 475–486.

Sedera, D., & Dey, S. (2013). User expertise in contemporary information systems: Conceptualization, measurement and application. *Information & Management, 50*(8), 621–637.

Shaanika, I., & Iyamu, T. (2018). Developing the enterprise architecture for the Namibian government. The Electronic Journal of Information Systems in Developing Countries, 84(3), e12028.

Simon, D., Fischbach, K., & Schoder, D. (2014). Enterprise architecture management and its role in corporate strategic management. *Information Systems and e-Business Management, 12*(1), 5–42.

Tamm, T., Seddon, P., Shanks, G., & Reynolds, P. (2011). How does enterprise architecture add value to organisations? *Communications of the Association of Information Systems, 28*(10), 141–168.

Ullah, A., & Lai, R. (2011). Modelling business goal for business/IT alignment using requirements engineering. *Journal of Computer Information Systems, 51*(3), 21–28.

Urbaczewski, L., & Mrdalj, S. (2006). A comparison of enterprise architecture frameworks. *Issues in Information Systems, 7*(2), 18–23.

Van den Berg, M., Slot, R., van Steenbergen, M., Faasse, P., & van Vliet, H. (2019). How enterprise architecture improves the quality of IT investment decisions. *Journal of Systems and Software, 152*, 134–150.

Vargas, A., Cuenca, L., Boza, A., Sacala, I., & Moisescu, M. (2016). Towards the development of the framework for inter sensing enterprise architecture. *Journal of Intelligent Manufacturing, 27*(1), 55–72.

Walters, D., & Lancaster, G. (2010). Implementing value strategy through the value chain. *Management Decision, 38*(3), 160–178.

Yuan, G., & Dong, L. (2006). On value and culture. *Frontiers of Philosophy in China, 1*(2), 237–244.

Zarvić, N., & Wieringa, R. (2014). An integrated enterprise architecture framework for business-IT alignment. *Designing Enterprise Architecture Frameworks: Integrating Business Processes with IT Infrastructure, 63.*

Chapter 12

A Capacity Maturity Model for Enterprise Architecture

Introduction

Enterprise architecture (EA) is an approach that is used to provide guidelines for the development, implementation, management and governance of business design and processes, information flows and exchanges and information technology (IT) solutions. The approach can also be considered as an instrument for managing enterprises' strategy and daily operations towards sustainability and competitiveness. Another important aspect is that EA can be used to assess and evaluate the benefits and impacts of IT solutions, particularly emerging technologies, on organisations' goal and objectives. In addition to other bases, EA is commonly used to facilitate the alignment between the business and IT units, which is critical in many organisations (Lapalme et al., 2016). Consequentially, because alignment promotes effective and efficient operationalisation of strategies, goals and objectives, this leads to improved performances in organisations.

Based on the promises it so far presents, it is of paramount importance and benefit for organisations to employ EA (Lange, Mendling & Recker, 2016). Some of the benefits of EA are that it helps to create opportunities, and improve process effectiveness and efficiency of automation and the operationalisation of activities in organisations. These are potential benefits which can only be achieved by organisations through persons with an EA skill set. Aier and Schelp (2010) suggest that organisations struggle to achieve its EA goals because of the shortage of skills. EA is a highly specialised discipline; hence its skill sets are scarce.

DOI: 10.1201/9781003268420-12

The challenges of skill shortage spread across technical and non-technical aspects of EA, which are evidently reflective in the development, implementation and management of the concept in organisations that attempt to deploy it. The challenges are crucial in that they significantly affect an understanding of EA, particularly when, where and how decisions are made in organisations about the concept. The different stages in the development, implementation and practice of EA require decisions of high knowledgeability. The allocation of EA activities is therefore critical and should be in accordance with knowledge and skill set. However, that is not always the case in some organisations. This is a challenge that has often been attributed to shortage of EA skills in many organisations (Shaanika & Iyamu, 2014). What is even more important is the retention of available skill sets towards maturity levels where the specialists are able to deliver effective and efficient operations and services. Tamm et al. (2011) argue that managing the already scarce EA skill sets is a challenge on its own in many organisations. Thus, a model is needed to guide the development and retention of EA skill sets towards various levels of maturity. As of the time this book was written, such a model was not in existence. This is the primary motivation for this chapter.

Maturity models are not new; this expands to the field of computing (information systems, IT and computer science). Some models have been proposed and used in many areas, including software development (Paulk et al., 1993). Tiku, Azarian and Pecht (2007) developed and proposed a matrix model which electronics manufacturers can make use of to evaluate the maturity of their practices for quality and improvement purposes. Considering the significance, strong cases have in the past been made for a capacity model; hence it is needless to invigorate another motivation. For example, Paulk et al. (1993) argue that maturity implies a potential for growth in capability and indicates richness of process and consistency within an environment.

Capability Maturity Model (CMM) defines key performance areas from an initial level of maturity to a level of optimisation of software (Curtis, Hefley & Miller, 2009). However, specialised skill set is instrumental in managing and making use of the capacity maturity model, which is acute to growth and development in an organisation. It is therefore important to understand the types of skills that are needed; assess the type of skill sets that are available, as determinants to the development of capacity. The fore step is critical within the ambit that EA is broad, considering the fact that it has four main domains that have distinct objectives and deliverables.

The Hershey and Blanchard (1993) model was thus employed in helping to determine the areas of capacity development. Although the model is not specific to EA, it helped to place the different skill sets into categories. The model has been used in various studies relating to skill sets, competency and management. Sluss and Ashforth (2007) employed the Hershey and Blanchard (1993) model to analyse the meaning and significance of role-relationship in an organisation. They argued that roles associated with identities are arranged in a cognitive hierarchy that ranges from generalised to particularised schemas. Müller and Turner (2010) applied the model to examine employees' competency profiles against different types of projects. Spillane, Halverson and Diamond (2004) followed the Hershey and Blanchard (1993) model to gain an understanding of how new organisational structures and new roles matter to innovation and development.

The aim of this chapter is to develop a capacity maturity model through which EA skill capacity can be built and retention can be managed, to improve maturity level within an organisation. The remainder of the chapter is organised into four main sections. The literature review covering EA and skill set is first presented. Next, knowledge of practitioners is examined and discussed. The capacity maturity model is presented and discussed. A summary of the chapter is presented.

Enterprise Architecture and Skill Set

EA enables and supports business processes and IT solutions through the integration and standardisation of activities. As has repeatedly been highlighted in other chapters of this book, there are different domains of EA; business, information, application and technical architectures. Each of the domains requires a specialised set of skills for their respective activities and distinct deliverables.

The enterprise business architecture (EBA) identifies and defines elements and connections to ensure that the strategic intents of an organisation are effectively executed. This is completely different from the focus of other domains. The enterprise information architecture (EIA) is undertaken to create accessibility and the eradication of inconsistencies and duplication of information flows and exchanges across an organisation and between organisations. Based on the EBA and EIA, the enterprise application architecture (EAA) is engineered to focus on the development, implementation and use of enterprise systems. The EAA focuses on applications and their components, such as specifications, requirements, modules and databases, including the procedures that produce, distribute and support information in accordance with business requirements and logics. Enterprise technical architecture (ETA) is concerned with the deployment and governance of infrastructure (hardware and platform) aspects of IT solutions to support and enable organisational needs. In achieving these objectives, different sets of skills become critical for organisations that deploy EA, thus requiring the development and retention of capacity.

One of the challenges in developing capacity in this discipline is that only few institutions of higher learning offer EA as a course or subject. It is long established that the shortage of EA skills is attributed to lack of education or training, or both. EA cannot be developed based on experience alone (Shaanika & Iyamu, 2014). The nature of the EA discipline requires its practitioners to have both theoretical grounding and experience. Thus, institutions of higher learning, being the cradle of knowledge, have a crucial role in the theorisation of concepts and should lead in the foundation, development of capacity and acquisition of skills.

However, many organisations that are interested in the concept of EA have only one option, which is to engage with consultants in the field. The consultants have different content or curriculum that are not customised or specific to an organisation. As a result, some organisations employ the services of multiple consultants who provide various EA frameworks (EAFs) for the same purpose. The reliance on various content or curriculum makes it even more difficult for some professionals or specialists to measure their individual or group maturity levels. This has a huge impact on the development of the skill sets that are required by organisations.

It is critical to note that organisations rely on EA to define their operating models and technological needs, and how both components complement each other. Such efforts and responsibility require employees with specialised skills to execute in order to align the strategies with the business and IT units in an organisation. Also, different aspects of business designs, operations and processes are expressed in unique ways in order to enhance competitiveness through EA implementation and practice. The EA approach helps to align resources and strategies from both business and IT units in an organisation. Additionally, organisations can confine the alignment between business and IT units into fundamental principles and common methodologies that govern the operationalisation of activities. Thus, EA is often employed to assist in facilitating consistency, uniformity of solutions, processes and artefacts while continuously adapting to change and transforming the organisation.

The competitiveness and sustainability of many organisations depend on the identification and participation of rightful people (skill set) in order to effectively and efficiently make use of their available resources, such as IT solutions for organisations' purposes. However, the use, governance and management of IT solutions in an organisation are carried out by people, based on their skills and know-how, through the domains of business, information, application and technical architectures (Iyamu, 2015). For efficiency and effectiveness purposes, a model is needed to guide and assess the skill levels of individuals for development, growth and retention purposes. The maturity model can be used as a means to support incremental capacity development at different levels in various domains (areas of EA), including deliverables and training of specific competences. Meyer, Helfert and O'Brien (2011) argue that EA maturity approaches are still a scarce resource in literature, with implication for practice, as organisations and managers search for guidelines or terms of reference.

Interest in maturity models continues to grow and has resulted in a range of models that have so far been proposed in the last three decades. This includes business intelligence (Brooks, El-Gayar & Sarnikar, 2015); business/IT alignment (Khaiata & Zualkernan, 2009); digital government (Gottschalk, 2009); project management (Crawford, 2006); knowledge management (Lin, Wu & Yen, 2012); and enterprise resource planning systems (Holland & Light, 2001). These models

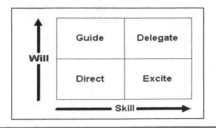

Figure 12.1 Hershey and Blanchard (1993).

are used as evaluative and comparative bases for process improvement and/or assessment, assuming that higher process capability or organisational maturity is associated with better performance. None of these models focuses on EA or EA skill set.

In various disciplines, models are used for capacity building and retention. It is within this context that Hershey and Blanchard (1993) developed a matrix, as shown in Figure 12.1, which can be used to assess employees' skills and willingness to carry out specific tasks. The result of the assessment is intended to guide employers and managers on how best to manage employees towards capacity building and retention (Sluss & Ashforth, 2007).

As shown in Figure 12.1, Hershey and Blanchard (1993) describe two main components, namely Skill and Will as: Skill – experience that comes from task, training, knowledge and natural talents; and Will – the desire to carry out a task, confidence in abilities and feelings about a task. From Figure 12.1, it is clear that employees are rarely static in a quadrant; there are movements. The direction of the movement is always known, but the rationale for such movements is also often not known. Many employees often fall into one quadrant or another, depending on skills and the stages in individuals' career. Based on the aim of this chapter, which was to develop an EA skill set capacity maturity model, questions were formulated, following the Hershey and Blanchard (1993) model, to gain an understanding from four different angles about what is known or unknown of EA by potential experts.

Knowledgeability of Enterprise Architecture

A careful assessment was conducted about the type of EA skill set that is available or could be needed. This entails gaining an understanding of individuals' knowledge (known or unknown) of the discipline. As shown in the quadrant; Figure 12.2, there are four categories: *(1) I do Know what I do know; (2) I do Know what I do not know; (3) I do Not know what I do know; and (4) I do not know what I do not know.*

In the context of this chapter, the word 'know' is used on the basis of its meaning from the Oxford dictionary, as well as the field of EA, and is therefore defined as the awareness that is gained through knowledge, experience, observation, inquiry

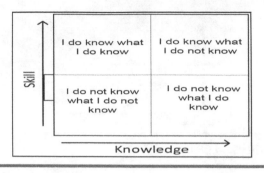

Figure 12.2   Knowledge of EA.

or information. The explanation extends further to say that, in order for an individual or group to truly affirm their knowledge of a specific subject or object, there exists a level of understanding, comprehension, proficiency, certainty or surety without hesitation. This means or indicates known; unknown; known unknown; and unknown unknown.

I Do Know What I Do Know About EA

This is a statement of the holistic coverage of both the concept and the environment. Knowing what you do know is a level of knowledge certainty. Thus, the IT architects need to be able to predict futuristic states of IT, as well as business and environmental trends, on behalf of an organisation. Some employees are well aware of what they do or do not know during the development, implementation or practice of EA in their organisations. The IT architects who are at this level of certainty have the capacity to plan mitigations for risks or potential risks that may be associated with operations, processes, requirements and activities within the business and IT units of their organisations. The experts are therefore expected to be clear and concise about their knowledge and skills in the field, industry and environment. This is often not clear to many employees, until after attaining a certain level of training or education. The assumptions of what they thought they knew begin to diminish and practice, rather than theory, starts to settle in.

Also, it requires extensive familiarity and awareness to authoritatively position, defend an understanding and exercise knowledgeability through actions and duties. Knowing what you do know entails a level at which a professional has a thorough understanding of the concept, as well as other factors which directly or indirectly impact the execution of their roles and responsibilities. With continuous training and capability development through formal learning and experiences, an individual gets better than their former self. Only then is an individual able to assert what they know or do not know. It is a level of expertise and authority in the field of specialisation. It is a gradual progression to reach this level, particularly because EA is broad and wider than many aspiring architects had thought in the beginning.

I Do Know What I Do Not Know About EA

Circumstantially, not all IT architects are able to define the boundaries of EA in every unit of their organisations. This is irrespective of their knowledge and experience. The cumbersome nature comes from the fact that there are different layers of definition, development and implementation of business, information and technical architectures. At some stages, some IT architects affirm that they do know what they do know, as well as what they do not know. It is at such stages that the architects reveal their challenges. Also, it is at this stage that some architects begin to understand and differentiate between the theory and practice of the concept. Another known aspect some architects struggle with is not knowing how to guide software developers in developing systems with poorly defined user requirements and architectural principles.

Also, some IT architects begin to realise that they do not know when and how to formulate principles from business and IT requirements and apply governance to guide IT solutions, including the development and implementation of business design and processes. The complexities of EA make some employees come to the realisation of how much they actually do or do not know in the holistic process. This is primarily because, as the standards are aligned with business requirements, the computing environment increases in complexity. As a result, some IT architects lose track of the link between their roles and responsibilities and the application of their know-how. In the course of this, processes and procedures are sometimes compromised. In addition, this is primarily because some of the architects do struggle when governance issues become too complex. As a result, some of the rules breakers are likely to be the best software developers in the organisation.

It is critical that IT architects are aware of what is required of them to understand and measure systems' life cycle and technologies' life span. This includes two fundamental factors: how the measurement should be carried out; and an understanding of the factors that constitute the measurement criteria. It entails a certain level of skill to carry out such a technical function of responsibility. Some of the things that seem clear are: (1) many of the IT architects do know that there are goals for the iterative process; (2) some of the IT architects do not know how those goals were formulated and engineered towards organisational objectives. During the iterative process of the EA, gaps are identified which are often caused by factors such as lack of skill and knowledge. It could also be informed by lack of awareness arising from practical unconsciousness, as described by Giddens (1984). Thus, some IT architects do not know what they do in fact know.

I Do Not Know What I Do Know About EA

IT architects require technical and business knowledge and experience of each EA domain. This is in order to assess and fulfil their roles and responsibilities, as mandated by the organisation. Also, IT architects should be well-informed to the extent of decision-making and be conversant and knowledgeable about the subject (EA) and object (IT and business operations). This is central to knowing what an IT architect should know in the deployment and practice of EA in an organisation. The level of knowledge and awareness can only be assessed through a management formal method, such as the capacity maturity model, which gives managers a different kind of responsibility to monitor and detect gaps. The model provides scientific evidence and credibility to the assessment.

EA is an iterative process that involves both business and IT units. Nonetheless, how the iterative process is carried out is not clear or known to every IT architect, particularly those who were appointed on the basis of their seniority in the organisation rather than qualification, training and experience. This could be attributed to unknown know; for example, some employees have driven the IT as well as the business operations for many years in achieving organisational objectives for the purposes of sustainability and competitiveness.

However, what they do not seem to know is the extent of correctness of their processes and activities in the quest to enable and support the organisation to achieve its goals and competitiveness. It is in such instances you hear employees say, "we have always done it this way and it works". However, where and when these guidelines are applied remains challenging to some architects, particularly junior IT architects in the organisation. Logically, this means that some architects do not really know how much they do know in carrying out their duties.

I Do Not Know What I Do Not Know About EA

I do not know what I do not know means '*unknown unknowns*' about architecture domains and their value and deliverables in an organisation by the IT architects and other employees. This makes it difficult for some IT architects, especially aspiring IT architects, to be specific in distinguishing between their roles and responsibilities in their organisations. Ironically, it does imply that those groups of IT architects are unaware that they do in actual sense know something about EA. This can be paradoxical in nature; an act of knowing that there are certain things that you do not know, to some degree, means that you in fact know about it. Thus, Giddens (1984) describes practical unconsciousness as an act in which people carry out activities in their everyday life but may not be able to put them into words.

The use of the word "architect" in the field of IT is on its own confusing for many people, especially those outside of the computing field. Hence, even some IT specialists argue that the concept of EA is academic and too theoretical. It is also considered difficult to distinguish between some existing roles and responsibilities, such as business architect (or architecture) and business analyst (or analysis), which Iyamu, Nehemia-Maletzky and Shaanika (2016) tried to clarify. This could be attributed to the fact that some of the architects or aspiring architects do not know what they do not know. Thus, many of the personnel who are promoted to the ranks of architects based on their levels of seniority in the organisation struggle or find it difficult to differentiate their former roles from the new architectural responsibilities. This includes the definitions of the scope and boundaries of EA within their organisations. As a result, many of them do not know what they do not know.

In summary, the 'known' are vital: (1) in the selection of EAFs; and (2) in the development, implementation, maintenance and manageability of EA within an organisation. The IT architects at any level will possibly not know what they actually do know, until their skills are continuously assessed, validated and measured. Thus, the maturity model becomes critical. From EA perspective, it is intended to enhance and promote capacity building and continuity for organisational sustainability and competitiveness.

Maturity Model for Enterprise Architecture Skill Set

For the purpose of capacity building, some organisations do employ personnel without the necessary EA skills from different sources, such as academic institutions and other organisations, including their competitors. The employees are categorised for the purpose of further training and development, in lieu of expected values and return on investments. The categorisation of individuals with certain skill set is based on assessments performed through different formal methods. Based on Section 3, three factors: (1) categorisation; (2) assessment; and (3) measurement come across as the main influencers of EA skill sets towards maturity. Also, the factors are interrelated and iterative. Based on the iterative nature of the factors, a model was developed as shown in Figure 12.3.

The successful development, implementation and practice of the EA concept require an understanding of business requirements, information flow, applications' profiling and technology engineering. Some of the main challenges in the development, implementation and management of EA in organisations include: (1) lack of thorough understanding of the concept; (2) lack of available skilled personnel;

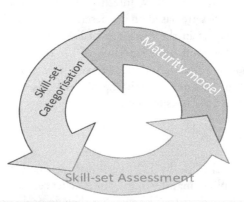

Figure 12.3 Developing EA skill in organisation.

(3) lack of commitment from management; (4) lack of skill development programmes; and (5) the implementation of organisational structure. It is therefore of critical importance to categorise and assess available EA skill set in an organisation. This is intended to detect gaps at both EA domains and managerial levels through which the concept is employed in an organisation. Also, it guides the development of a capacity programme, as well as the alignment of skill set within organisational structures.

Categorisation of EA Skill Set Levels

The concept of EA is aimed at supporting and providing guidelines for decision-making in organisations as business objectives continue to change and IT solutions evolve rapidly. The change and evolution are part of the external environmental factors which influence EA. As a response, the EA needs to be constantly maintained in order to support changes from both internal and external perspectives. To achieve this, the available skill set must be known and classified in contexts and perspectives. Consequently, EA skill sets are categorised into four levels, from 1 to 4, as shown in Table 12.1. This is to help get a better understanding of the current state towards building a future state.

The categorisation of skills levels as summarised in Table 12.1 is in relation to both business and architectural requirements for assessment purposes and towards capacity building. Also, it helps with understanding and documenting what is known and unknown for continuity purposes. The capacity maturity model, as presented in Figure 12.4, is developed based on the interpretation of the discussion of Section 3. It is explicitly to measure EA skill set in an organisation. The model indicates actual availability of resource, as well as capacity building in the areas of EA. In addition, it is intended to help in skill retention and continuity and in aiding business sustainability and competitiveness.

Towards building a stable organisational capacity, skill set levels can be grouped into categories of expert, proficiency, intermediate and foundation, as shown in Figure 12.4. The categories are based on the description of the skill sets as presented above. Level 4 is an expert in the discipline of EA. Proficiency is at level 3, with high competency and a good understanding of the concept. Levels 2 and 1 are aligned with intermediate and foundation, respectively. Both levels are beginners and aspiring stages in the capacity building of EA skills. The four categories are discussed in the context of EA as follows.

Level 4: Expert

This is the highest level of skill set. Professionals at this level have some sort of authority in the discipline, manifesting from excellence, stock of knowledge and awareness. This is why experts that know what they do or do not know are considered as highly skilled professionals. It requires an expert to be able to establish their

Table 12.1   EA Skill Set Level Classification

Category	Description
Level 1	Undertake formal training in EA and gain an understanding of the EA concept from a theoretical perspective within an organisational context. Able to gather a business unit's requirements in relation to EA. Should be able to lead in the definition and development, at least from a domain architecture perspective.
Level 2	Understand and be able to define EA at organisational (enterprise) level. Able to articulate the organisational vision and the business requirements towards the development, implementation and practice of EA. Able to examine and translate the business requirements into architectural requirements. Understand the implementation of EA in an organisational context.
Level 3	Understand and be able to link the business requirements with the different domains, from business to technical architectures. Able to document the contents as well as the processes that are involved in the iterative process of EA. Provide leadership, through technical guidance, training and mentorship for the junior IT architects in the organisation. Able to communicate the values and returns on EA investment to senior management and executives. Liaise with vendors and consultants on behalf of the organisation.
Level 4	Understand the implementation and practice processes, including the politics involved in the development and implementation of EA in the organisation. Transform EA as an IT strategy and align it with the business strategy. Develop a strategy and provide leadership in the development and management of the iterative processes. Manage the resources and the influencing factors that are associated with EA in the organisation. This includes technology, politics, financial, budget, contracts and relationship with partners.

individual level of knowledgeability, specialisation, and competence. The skill is acquired over a period of time from a combination of academic training and industry experience. It requires at least a 4-year university degree and as many as 10 years of practical hands-on experience. This includes the development, implementation and management of EA. Also, an expert focuses on EA, as opposed to specialisation and concentration on a specific domain.

Expertise is not (or should not be) based on seniority or based on the organisational structure. It requires specialised and high skill set. This is particularly

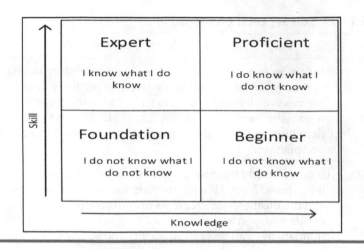

Figure 12.4 EA skill assessment model.

so because an EA expert undertakes complex roles in the form of technical, governance and management at the enterprise level, which horizontally covers the domains of business, information, application and technical architectures. Also, an expert has a holistic view and an understanding of the enterprise from business to IT units' perspectives. The experts are considered leaders in the discipline and are therefore involved in critical decision-making processes. The experts can lead as technical resource, as well as project managers, which includes the development, implementation, policy and governance stages. The expert should be well aware of the roles and significance of IT governance and policy in the practice of EA. Also, the expert should be skilful enough to drive the compliance of both IT governance and policy in the development, implementation and practice of EA in an organisation. This helps in decision-making and as a management mechanism for mitigating risks and for return on investment purposes in an organisation.

Level 3: Proficiency

Proficiency is a level at which professionals have enough stock of knowledge to decisively know what they do or do not know in their areas of discipline and specialisation. Similar to the level of an expert, complex tasks can be undertaken at this level. Thus, proficient is at skill set maturity level 3. It is a level of mastering the field from concept to practice stages and being able to adapt to responsibilities between the domains of EA.

A mix of good technical and leadership skills is a core component of the proficiency level. At the proficiency level, an architect should be able to lead both technical and non-technical personnel at the organisational level. This includes the capability to coach others within the architectural space. An enterprise architect should have a good understanding and can discuss terminologies, concepts, principles and standards with the relevant parties, including vendors. Another major aspect at the proficiency level is the skill to communicate complex technical information to the stakeholders from business and IT units, at both senior and junior levels within the organisational structure.

Level 2: Intermediate

Intermediate is a level before proficiency at which IT architects have enough stock of knowledge and an understanding of basic techniques to engage in EA processes and activities. Therefore, the IT architects can discuss the application and implications of changes to both business and technology processes, policies and procedures across the architecture domains. Another competence aspect that is crucial at this level is an understanding of the structure of the different components, their inter-relationships and the principles that govern their design and evolution over time and space. The intermediate level requires an architect to have a good understanding of the descriptions of necessary functions to build different types of IT solutions, such as distributed systems. This includes the documentation of the relationship that exists between the systems and other technology components.

Thus, an IT architect at the intermediate level can guide the creation and selection of products and services within the frame of business and architectural requirements. The architect also guides the development of business products and services that are enabled and supported by IT solutions. Also, the IT architect should be skilled enough to develop templates that can be used for the selection and deployment of IT solutions in an organisation.

Level 1: Foundation

This is the entry level into the EA discipline or profession. It is a foundation for EA skill capacity building in an organisation. Foundation is a stage where the IT architects or aspiring IT architects do not know what they do not know, based on their limited knowledge and awareness in the EA discipline. The experience is minimal and knowledge is based on theory, and fairly on practice.

At the Foundation level, the IT architect is expected to have a good knowledge about the different EAFs, such as *Gartner* and *TOGAF*. They should also have a good understanding of the relationship that exists between the domains; which are business, information, application and technical architectures. At the Foundation level, an IT architect has the knowledge and skills that are required to design and document technical templates for processes, such as requirements specification. This level covers a range of EA basic terminologies, techniques and processes, and includes an understanding of roles and responsibilities of the architecture in an organisation. Also, it entails an understanding of systems, development, implementation and the deployment and maintenance guidelines.

Skill Capacity Assessment

EA is an approach through which governance and strategy are developed in supporting and enabling an organisation's profitability, competitiveness and sustainability. The organisations that plan for EA often have better advantages over others that do not, mainly because the concept helps to create global competition through governance, guidance and management of operations and services that are supported and enabled by IT solutions. It is therefore easier to achieve business success with EA, as the concept focuses on enabling and supporting the alignment of critical aspects between business and IT units, such as strategies and operations in an organisation. This makes it even more critical to have high skill set that can drive the development and implementation of EA in an organisation. To ensure sustainability, skill sets have to be evaluated for reasons that include the development of capacity and retention of personnel. The evaluation is an iterative process to ascertain the maturity levels of the skill sets and to detect gaps for improvement, continuity and stability.

As described in Table 12.1, there are four levels in the process of maturing the skill sets of EA. The main components that help to form the basics of the levels are depicted in Table 12.2. The components consist of common requirements and drivers from both business and IT units. The usefulness of the components is to assess and categorise skills into levels, towards maturity.

EA practice is based on capacity development and certification by which an enterprise formally recognises the skills of its practising IT architects, through the demonstration of their roles and responsibilities. Capacity building provides the necessary skills and experience among in-house employees and ensures the alignment of skills and experience with the IT architectural responsibilities (Shaanika & Iyamu, 2014).

Skill Set Maturity Model

As the EA discipline gains increasing attention and interest from various organisations, architecture skills are also in demand in achieving the goals and objectives. However, the skills are widely grouped and assigned to projects and teams. The skill sets are also vaguely used by recruitment agencies in their search and selection of candidates for IT architects' roles, which is often problematic for some employers. As shown in Figure 12.5, skill set can be professionally grouped and managed for the benefits of individuals and organisations. The value of the capacity model derives from the ability to provide a means of identification and categorisation of skill matches or gaps. The value of EA arises from the maturity of skill capacity, given the business and technical units that they support and enable. Levels of support can increase as the architect gains confidence in knowing what they do or do not know.

An IT architect should possess an extensive technical depth, which could be through training and experience in the industry. The depth of knowledge and

Table 12.2 Capacity Assessment

Component	Level 1	Level 2	Level 3	Level 4
Formal training and education	X	X	X	X
Understanding and documentation of organisation's rationale for EA	X	X	X	X
Organising EA effort: people, technologies and processes			X	X
Extracting business requirements for EA development	X	X	X	X
Defining EA domains in relation to business requirements			X	X
Assigning business requirements to the domains			X	X
Development of EA domains	X	X	X	X
Implementation of EA domains	X	X	X	X
Documentation of EA from initial to practice stages			X	X
Communication of the values and returns to stakeholders			X	X
Liaison with stakeholders at the different levels		X	X	X
Practice of EA at business units' level	X	X	X	X
Practice of EA at domain level	X	X	X	X
Management of EA iterative process			X	X
Practice of EA at the organisation's level			X	X
Evaluation and measurement of EA in the organisation				X
Institutionalisation of EA in the organisation				X

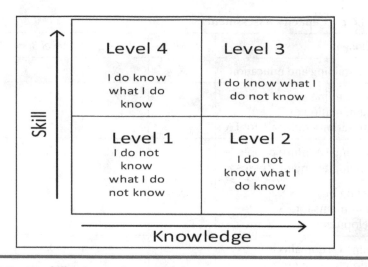

Figure 12.5   EA skill set maturity model.

experience should include application development and implementation, infrastructure deployment, networking administration and process engineering. Due to the heterogeneous nature of IT solutions, an IT architect should also be knowledgeable about the domains covering multiple platforms, distributed systems, enterprise servers and traditional mainframe environments. Thus, IT architects at this level should know what they do know as experts in the discipline.

Driven by competent skill, a well-defined and documented EA enables organisations to manage their technological infrastructure, plan for obsolescence and formulate business process change management. EA therefore depicts the components within an enterprise and describes how they relate and interact with one another. Each component serves a unique purpose and collaborates with other components within the enterprise.

Many organisations benefit from such a clear understanding, from current to future states about their products, services and technology, as this will assist in the planning and monitoring of innovations. The model can be applied through three main steps:

Step 1 – collate the current IT architects' skill sets in an organisation and put them into categories of levels as defined above and thereafter;

Step 2 – perform an assessment of the skill sets against the IT and business operations and activities to identify gaps and areas of improvement; and

Step 3 – perform regular reviews to assess and ensure the evolving maturity of available skill sets in the organisation.

The steps require institutionalisation in order to enforce them in the iterative approach that it deserves. Iyamu (2015) describes institutionalisation as a process where a practice is assimilated, sanctioned and legitimised into a norm which is not easily disassociated, dismantled or redesigned.

Summary

This chapter is intended to help managers and other stakeholders to gain a better understanding of the technical and non-technical factors that influence and impact the development, capacity and retention of EA skill sets in an organisation. The model can be used as a guide in reducing EA skill set gaps, from formally trained, experienced and senior personnel and from an organisational structure perspective.

The skill set capacity model is a contribution to best practices for managing and developing EA capacity in organisations. The model is intended to guide improvements in capacity building and retention strategy. This yields improved productivity, quality and continuity. Similar to other models, this model will establish a culture of excellence in the EA discipline. Most importantly, it helps both the employees (capacity) and the employers to examine and understand what employees think that they do know or do not know in the course of pursuing organisations' goals and objectives, over time and space of EA.

References

Aier, S., & Schelp, J. (2010). A reassessment of enterprise architecture implementation. *Service-oriented computing. ICSOC/ServiceWave workshops*, 35–47. Berlin/Heidelberg: Springer.

Brooks, P., El-Gayar, O., & Sarnikar, S. (2015). A framework for developing a domain specific business intelligence maturity model: Application to healthcare. *International Journal of Information Management, 35*(3), 337–345.

Crawford, J. K. (2006). The project management maturity model. *Information Systems Management, 23*(4), 50–58.

Curtis, B., Hefley, B., & Miller, S. (2009). *People Capability Maturity Model (P-CMM) Version 2.0* (No. CMU/SEI-2009-TR-003). Carnegie-Mellon University Pittsburgh Pa Software Engineering Institute. Url: ADA512354

Giddens, A. (1984). *The constitution of society: Outline of the theory of structuration*. Berkely, CA: University of California Press.

Gottschalk, P. (2009), Maturity levels for interoperability in digital government. *Government Information Quarterly, 26*(1), 75–81.

Hershey, P., & Blanchard, K. H. (1993). *Management of organisation behaviour: Utilizing human resources*. (3rd ed.). Englewood Cliffs, NJ: Prentice Hall, Inc.

Holland, C. P., & Light, B. (2001). A stage maturity model for enterprise resource planning systems use. *Database for Advances in Information Systems, 32*(2), 24–45.

Iyamu, T. (2015). *Enterprise architecture from concept to practice*. Victoria, Australia: Heidelberg Press.

Iyamu, T., Nehemia-Maletzky, M., & Shaanika, I. (2016). The overlapping nature of business analysis and business architecture: What we need to know. *The Electronic Journal Information Systems Evaluation, 19*(3), 169–179.

Khaiata, M., & Zualkernan, I. A. (2009). A simple instrument to measure IT business alignment maturity. *Information Systems Management, 26*(2), 138–152.

Lange, M., Mendling, J., & Recker, J. (2016). An empirical analysis of the factors and measures of enterprise architecture management success. *European Journal of Information Systems, 25*(5), 411–431.

Lapalme, J., Gerber, A., Van der Merwe, A., Zachman, J., De Vries, M., & Hinkelmann, K. (2016). Exploring the future of enterprise architecture: A Zachman perspective. *Computers in Industry, 79*, 103–113.

Lin, C., Wu, J. C., & Yen, D. C. (2012). Exploring barriers to knowledge flow at different knowledge management maturity stages. *Information & Management, 49*(1), 10–23.

Meyer, M., Helfert, M., & O'Brien, C. (2011). An Analysis of Enterprise Architecture Maturity Frameworks. In *International Conference on Business Informatics Research.* (pp. 167–177). Berlin Heidelberg: Springer.

Müller, R., & Turner, R. (2010). Leadership competency profiles of successful project managers. *International Journal of Project Management, 28*(5), 437–448.

Paulk, M. C., Curtis, B., Chrissis, M. B., & Weber, C. V. (1993). Capability maturity model, version 1.1. *Software, IEEE, 10*(4), 18–27.

Shaanika, I., & Iyamu, T. (2014). Developing Enterprise Architecture Skills: A Developing Country Perspective. In *IFIP Conference on Information Systems: Key Competencies in ICT and Informatics: Implications and Issues for Educational Professionals and Management.* 1-4 July, Potsdam, Germany.

Sluss, D. M., & Ashforth, B. E. (2007). Relational identity and identification: Defining ourselves through work relationships. *Academy of Management Review, 32*(1), 9–32.

Spillane, J. P., Halverson, R., & Diamond, J. B. (2004). Towards a theory of leadership practice: A distributed perspective. *Journal of Curriculum Studies, 36*(1), 3–34.

Tamm, T., Seddon, B., Shanks, G., & Reynolds, P. (2011). How does enterprise architecture add value to organisations? *Communications of the Association for Information Systems, 28*(10), 141–168.

Tiku, S., Azarian, M., & Pecht, M. (2007). Using a reliability capability maturity model to benchmark electronics companies. *International Journal of Quality & Reliability Management, 24*(5), 547–563.

Index

Note: Locators in *italics* represent figures and **bold** indicate tables in the text.

CPSIA information can be obtained
at www.ICGtesting.com
Printed in the USA
JSHW020221110522
25519JS00001BA/33

9 781032 145297